Debates in Sociology

For Anne Dix,
Administrative secretary of the BSA from 1950 to 1992,
and greatly admired by us all

Debates in Sociology

edited by
David Morgan *and* Liz Stanley

Manchester University Press
Manchester and New York

Distributed exclusively in the USA and Canada by St. Martin's Press

Published by Manchester University Press
Oxford Road, Manchester M13 9PL, UK
and Room 400, 175 Fifth Avenue,
New York, NY 10010, USA

Distributed exclusively in the USA and Canada
by St. Martin's Press, Inc.,
175 Fifth Avenue, New York, NY 10010, USA

British Library Cataloguing-in-Publication Data
A catalogue record for this book is available from the British Library

Library of Congress Cataloging-in-Publication Data applied for

ISBN 0 7190 3830 8 *hardback*
ISBN 0 7190 3831 6 *paperback*

Phototypeset in Linotron Ehrhardt
by Northern Phototypesetting Co. Ltd., Bolton

Printed in Great Britain
by Bell and Bain Ltd., Glasgow

Contents

Acknowledgements

We would like to thank Sarah Dimmelow and Lorna Tittle, the former and current editorial assistants to *Sociology*, for their hard work in making the publication of this book possible. We would also like to express our appreciation to all the contributors to the journal over the past twenty-five years, and particularly to those people whose work is represented in this collection.

The editors have made every effort to contact authors whose work has been extensively quoted from in this book. Our apologies to those we were unable to contact.

Contributors

Sara Arber is a Senior Lecturer in Sociology at the University of Surrey. She has served on various ESRC committees, including the Social Affairs Committee, and was Honorary Treasurer of the BSA, 1988–90. Her research, using secondary analysis of large datasets, focuses on gender and class inequalities in areas such as health, ageing and employment. She is currently working with Jay Ginn on a study of older women's working lives. She is co-author of *Gender and Later Life* (Sage, London, 1991) and *Doing Secondary Analysis* (Unwin Hyman, London, 1988), and co-editor of two 1990 BSA Conference volumes: *Women's Working Lives: Divisions and Change* (Macmillan, London, 1991), and *Families and Households: Divisions and Change* (Macmillan, London, 1992).

Rodney Barker is a political scientist who writes in the border territory between political ideas and political practice. His most recent book is *Political Legitimacy and the State* (Clarendon, 1990) and he is currently working on legitimacy in the United Kingdom, and on the history of political ideas in those countries since the beginning of the nineteenth century. He makes a passable cup of tea, and is happily married to a feminist.

Alan Bryman is Reader in Social Research in the Department of Social Sciences, Loughborough University. His chief areas of research interest lie in the areas of organisation theory and research methodology. He has a special interest in leadership and organisational change and has undertaken a number of projects in this area. His most recent books as author or co-author are: *Quantity and Quality in Social Research* (Unwin Hyman,

1988); *Research Methods and Organization Studies* (Unwin Hyman, 1989); *Quantitative Data Analysis for Social Scientists* (Routledge, 1990), and *Charisma and Leadership in Organizations* (Sage, 1992). He is editor of *Doing Research in Organizations* (Routledge, 1988).

Janet Finch is Professor of Social Relations at Lancaster University. She is a former editor of *Sociology* (1988–91) and a former Chair of the British Sociological Association. Her main academic work has been in the fields of family and gender, spanning the disciplines of sociology and social policy. She has also published on research methods and on educational policy. She is author of the following books: *Married to the Job* (Allen and Unwin, 1983), *Education and Social Policy* (Longmans, 1984), *Research and Policy* (Falmer, 1986), *Family Obligations and Social Change* (Polity, 1989) *Negotiating Family Responsibilities* (with Jennifer Mason, Routledge, 1992).

David Morgan is currently Joint Editor of *Sociology*; He is Senior Lecturer in Sociology at the University of Manchester, where he has been for a very long time. His main interests are the sociologies of family life and of gender, and books include *The Family Politics and Social Theory* (Routledge, 1985) and *Discovering Men* (Routledge, 1992). He has been an active member of the British Sociological Association in a variety of capacities.

Ray Pawson is a lecturer in Sociology at the University of Leeds. He is author of *A Measure for Measures: A Manifesto for Empirical Sociology* (Routledge, London, 1989). He is the secretary (and president-elect) of the Research Committee on Logic and Methodology (RC33) of the International Sociological Association. Recently he has spent much time in prison (for research purposes). He is a founding member of the International Forum for the Study of Education in Penal Systems. He is responsible for one of the eight hundred papers so far produced in *Sociology*.

Helen Roberts is a sociologist who has spent the last ten years working mainly on maternal and child health. Her latest books are the edited collections *Women's Health Counts* (Routledge, 1990) and *Women's Health Matters)* (Routledge, 1992). Her current work is on child accidents and child safety, looking in particular at the ways in which mothers keep their children safe. She is a happily married feminist and mother.

Michael Rustin has worked in the Polytechnic (now university) of East London and its predecessor colleges since 1964. He is now Professor of

Sociology and Dean of the Faculty of Social Sciences, and is also a Visiting Professor at the Tavistock Clinic in London. He is the author of *For a Pluralist Socialism* (1985), *The Good Society and the Inner World: Psychoanalysis, Politics, and Culture* (1991), and with Margaret Rustin, *Narratives of Love and Loss: Studies in Modern Children's Fiction* (1987), as well as of numerous articles. His main current research interest is the sociology of the transition in Czechoslovakia.

John Scott is Professor of Sociology at the University of Leicester, where he is head of department. He was editor of the BSA's 'Network' from 1985 to 1989 and is currently chairperson of the BSA Executive. His most recent books are *A Matter of Record* (Polity, 1990), *Who Rules Britain?* (Polity, 1991) and *Social Network Analysis* (Sage, 1991).

Liz Stanley is currently Joint Editor of *Sociology*. A senior lecturer in the Sociology Department at the University of Manchester, her main current research and writing interests are concerned with questions of epistemology, particularly in relation to feminist research and to historical sociology. Her main publications are: *Breaking Out: Feminist Consciousness and Feminist Research* (Routledge, 1983, with Sue Wise), *The Diaries of Hannah Cullwick* (Rutgers University Press, 1983), *Georgie Porgie: Sexual Harassment in Everyday Life* (Pandora Press, 1987; with Sue Wise), *The Life and Death of Emily Wilding Davision* (The Women's Press, 1988), *Feminist Praxis: Research, Theory and Epistemology in Feminist Sociology* (Routledge, 1990), *The Auto/Biographical I: Theory and Practice of Feminist Auto/Biography (Manchester University Press, 1992)*, and *Breaking Out Again: Ontology and Epistemology in Feminist Research* (Routledge, 1993; with Sue Wise).

Claire Wallace was educated at Kent University, where she also worked on an ESRC, project, 'Household Work Strategies in an Economic Recession', with Ray Pahl about the Isle of Sheppey. She is now a Lecturer in Applied Social Science at Lancaster University and has been seconded temporarily to Prague to develop a post-graduate training programme for Eastern European scholars. Her research covers the fields of sociology of youth, gender relations, social policy of the family, and comparative and rural sociology. Her recent books include *Youth, Family and Citizenship* with Gill Jones, and *The Family: Social Policy and the New Right in Britain and the USA* with Pamela Abbott.

Debates in sociology: contextual and procedural dynamics in the production of a discipline

The collection

In 1992, the year of the publication of this volume, Britain's main sociology journal, *Sociology*, celebrates twenty-five years of publishing. During that time some of the central debates which have occurred in sociology in Britain and elsewhere have appeared in its pages. The discipline of sociology has changed a good deal during this period, and such changes have included the crucial ideas and concerns that have at particular moments preoccupied its practitioners. Thus looking at changes and developments in the discipline around such debates is a particularly fruitful way of proceeding.

The main aim of this collection therefore is to present and reflect upon some of the main developments in British sociology that have occurred during this period, in particular the way these debates have been reflected within *Sociology*. Obviously this is not, and nor is it intended to be, a complete history of sociology in this period; no one journal can be the sole indicator of major trends in such a large and vibrant discipline. However, we should expect to find a close relationship between a large number of the developments within the discipline and the contents of its most central British journal.

Although this collection deals with the British form that these debates have taken, this does not mean its concerns are parochial; rather the reverse. There is an increasing awareness that national sociologies have their own organisational forms and develop their own agendas of research and theorising; these speak to and are analytically concerned with the historical and contextual specificities within which these sociologies are located. Thus it is important for sociology to recognise and to explore such cultural differences, and to include within this exploration an understanding of its own operations. We do not see such a recognition of difference as an inhibitor of theoretical generalisation, but rather as influencing the kind and scope of generalisations the discipline is concerned with, as we discuss in more detail in a later section of this introduction.

In addition, while there are these national/cultural/regional differences, there remain large commonalities in the concerns of sociologists. Beneath the specifics of the debates dealt with in this collection, some of the most fundamental questions that have concerned sociologists since the origins of the discipline can be discerned. In particular, there are two overlapping general preoccupations. One is the tension between voluntarism and determinism, sometimes expressed as a similar tension between structure and agency. The other is to do with the nature of social knowledge itself and the circumstances of its production.

In various respects the form of this collection is innovatory. Rather than simply producing a collection of extracts from some of the key papers that appeared in the journal, or producing a series of overview essays by new contributors, we have adopted a procedure which combines elements from both of these strategies. Our contributors, for the most part current or recent members of the editorial board, were asked to select extracts from clusters of papers representing particular debates – shared discussions rather than particular individual statements – and to produce a chapter which both included and commented upon these chosen extracts. They were also asked to comment on omissions from these debates as represented in the journal, to provide some overall assessment of each debate from the vantage point of the early 1990s, and to reflect upon possible future developments in these areas. The collection, therefore, is not simply a celebration of twenty-five years of achievement, but is a selective, although we hope not unrepresentative, set of critically appreciative discussions of some of the shared concerns of the sociological epistemic community over this period.

It is worth underlining at this point the fact that *Sociology* is the official journal of the British Sociological Association (BSA), the association of professional sociologists in this country, which has been actively in existence on behalf of the discipline for forty years. Later in this introduction we shall comment in more detail on the processes of academic production; however, we would like to acknowledge here the signal importance of the BSA for many people now active in research and teaching.

Looking back on this past twenty-five years, it is clear that some themes and issues proved particularly controversial or thought-provoking, such that one original article was followed by others dealing with the same topic from different perspectives, or by using different data, or through developing a different line of argument. Such debates are a reminder of the contested and uneven, rather than straightforwardly cumulative, development of sociology; we discern the same features as characteristics of all other disciplines. It is worth saying that the difference between sociology and other disciplines, including natural science disciplines, lies less in fundamentally different ways of conducting inquiry and more in the fact that most other disciplines have developed a public rhetoric of internal consistency and the cumulative development of knowledge. Thus sociology should be seen as better at acknowledging the internal tensions and differences of approach and emphasis that surely characterise all forms of human inquiry, rather than providing an example of a deviant or immature subject-area.

Implicit in both the title of this collection and the preceeding paragraph is a particular reading or interpretation of how we are to understand the nature of 'debates in sociology'. This is also a concern that runs through, if not all, then the large majority of the chapters. Consequently it makes good sense to confront these issues at the outset.

There are a number of linked questions that need to be considered here: What, precisely, is 'a debate'? How is it structured and conducted? And by whom? Who initiates a debate using what means and under what circumstances? Are its ideas centrally important regardless who proposes them? One response to the first of these questions (the others are considered elsewhere in this introduction) is that a debate is a means of moving forward an argument; that is, that it constitutes something which is demonstrably and measurably progress for the discipline. Another, not necessarily conflicting with the first, is that debates are indications of squabbles and unnecessary divisions within sociology which the discipline should eschew in the future. Our particular way of reading debates in sociology in general, and these debates in *Sociology* in particular, is that they most certainly mark change in particular sub-areas of the discipline, which members of such may well read, in that time and place, as indicative of progress. However, 'progress' is more properly – and sociologically – to be read as a knowledge-claim which may or may not be more widely accepted, and which other members of the discipline are free to accept, reject, challenge and debate in their own terms. There is no single discipline-wide criterion of evaluation as to what 'progress' consists of, nor which debates should be characterised in such terms. 'Challenge and change', then, indicates in a succinct and precise way how it is that we read these debates.

The character of debates

While the focus in this volume is on debates within *Sociology*, these do not
adhere to a common format. To some extent this may reflect editorial
practice; one example is that editors may deliberately commission responses to an original and particularly controversial contribution; another
example is that an important part of editorial practice may be to make
detailed suggestions for additions to and subtractions from submitted
papers. These practices will clearly vary between different editorial
regimes. Even allowing for this, however, the reader will find considerable
differences in the manner and sometimes the tone in which such debates
are conducted, and also in the responses of the present contributors. There
is now more awareness of and attention to the different choices that can be
made in adopting rhetorical structures and styles in sociological writing and
the very different impacts these make upon readers, not least in the varying
ways they construct or deconstruct the authority of the writer. Thus in the
extracted writings there are references to tennis matches as an appropriate
metaphor to characterise particular pieces of writing, while other debates
are more open for readers to take up varied positions in relation to their key
arguments and claims.

Sociology, in common with other scholarly journals, cannot be seen as
providing a merely passive reflection of debates within the discipline as a
whole nor indeed within the wider society. Cultures of expectation grow up
around all scholarly journals, even those such as *Sociology* where there is a
regular change of editorship, which influence not only what is submitted to
such journals but also the tone of submissions to them. In some cases these
expectations bear a somewhat distant relation to actual editorial policies;
nonetheless, here as elsewhere definitions of the situation are all important.
Therefore the wider debate that these discussions in *Sociology* are a part of
may have different emphases or even somewhat different defining concerns. One example is that the influence of Foucault is largely tangential to
the debate about power in the pages of *Sociology*, while elsewhere the
impact of Foucault's work has been of central importance. A second
example is that the preoccupation with theorising 'patriarchy' which
appeared in the pages of the journal is rather different from the more
general feminist concern with grounded theorising. In addition, it is also
the case that such cultures of expectation may lead to the situation where
important sociological debates do not appear in particular journals at all:
debate around the question of 'race'/racism, which we return to later, is
one example of this.

We have decided not to provide detailed summaries of the chapters in this collection, in part because we want to eschew providing an editorially-constructed preferred reading of them, in part because readers are best able to do this for themselves. Instead, in the rest of the introduction we have used our readings of the chapters as a point of departure for the exploration of some wider-ranging themes and issues. These are not necessarily overtly common to all the chapters, although they are dealt with at least implicitly throughout. In the first place we consider a seies of contextual features, those features of the intellectual and social environment which shape the production of sociological knowledge. And in the second place we discuss some procedural aspects of the conduct of social inquiry which underpin both research and theorising. In making these distinctions we are using them as convenient ordering devices for teasing out different, although related, aspects of the themes and issues dealt with; and, as we hope to demonstrate, there are complex movements between these two levels of activities.

Contextuals

Several of our contributors draw direct attention to the contexts within which the debates they are discussing took place, to consider reflexively the processes by which knowledge is constructed within the discipline. In part these processes serve to provide definitions as to what constitutes good or proper sociology, although these considerations were not routinely employed by the participants in the debates themselves. While most sociologists are clearly aware of issues in the sociology of knowledge, there are strong institutional and interpersonal pressures which serve to bracket these understandings, especially during the heat of sociological debate. But also of course, outside of such pressures, some sociologists willingly utilise stances which rebut or deny the validity of any kind of reflexivity in the discipline, and this is crucial to the explicit knowledge-claims, and implicit authority-claims, they engage in. Our contributors, on the other hand, writing at some distance from these debates, can perhaps not only take a somewhat more ironical view of these confrontations, but also engage with them by using understandings drawn implicitly or explicitly from the sociology of knowledge to analyse them as topics of investigation in their own right. We are arguing therefore that the debates outlined in the forthcoming chapters should be seen not simply in terms of different intellectual positions, but also in terms of socially located processes. This general observation has at least two facets.

In the first place any debate within sociology is clearly influenced by processes and developments outside or beyond the discipline itself. A good example here, and one cited by the majority of our contributors, has been the growth of feminist perspectives. Thus during this twenty-five year period we find feminism influencing the debates on women and social class, conceptualisation of the household, the concept of strategy, understandings of power, and, of course, the study of gender itself. Conversely, we may see the wider patterns of exclusion and marginalisation, patterns which gave rise to the development of at least some of these feminist understandings in the first place, as influencing what was *not* debated or incorporated into sociological discourse during this period. As Alan Bryman notes, the study of organisations can be discussed in such terms, while the different aspects of the 'class and mobility' debate looked at by Ray Pawson and by Helen Roberts provides a particularly fascinating example. A further example concerns marxism. Here again we have a movement which is wider than the discipline of sociology and one itself shaped by developments in the capitalist world and beyond. Marxism too is both a wider political movement which seeks directly to influence the pattern and course of social change, and also a set of intellectual and analytical concerns which have had a marked – and continuing – influence on the discipline of sociology as a whole. Debates within marxism and between marxists and non-marxists were clearly influential in the development of sociological thought generally during the period these debates are concerned with, even if the impact of this was perhaps less marked than that of feminism.

In the second place these debates were influenced by processes within the discipline, although one should underline the fact that these processes are not peculiar to sociology but are features common to all modes of intellectual inquiry and indeed to social organisation itself. Here we have in mind well-explored processes connected with the development of social networks, circles, communities, or invisible colleges, all terms used to describe the same basic social forms which are concerned with the social generation and distribution of 'knowledge' as seen from the viewpoint of such collectivites. We are here concerned with patterns of inclusion and exclusion, mechanisms of gatekeeping, the dynamics of both positive and negative evaluation and the accompanying assignment of appropriate rewards and sanctions, and their changing impact on the structure and organisation of the discipline. We can see these processes at work in familiar and routine aspects such as citation practices and the development of specialised sub-languages within the discipline. Hence most readers of any single issue of *Sociology* will experience a sense of distance from at least one article within it, and this feeling we are sure will be experienced in parts of the present volume as well. We need to take a temporal perspective here, for such appropriate sub-languages come into existence at particular points in time, and indeed the more advanced and highly specialised these are, the more likely they are to seem outdated to later generations of sociologists. The development of a newer sub-language which may well come to be used more widely is that surrounding postmodernist theory; and we discuss this in the last section of the introduction.

A striking illustration of the effects of these processes is provided by Alan Bryman's discussion of organisations. In the course of this analysis he draws our attention to the deployment of the term 'strategy' in relation to certain managerial practices, a term which is overtly used and defined. However, as Claire Wallace shows, explicit and focussed discussion of the concept of strategy more widely within sociology had to wait until the 1980s, for its origins lie in military discourse rather than any prior sociological work. What this suggests is that the term strategy did not enter into wider sociological debate initially largely because it originated in debates which were often cast as somewhat specialised and on the margins of what was seen to constitute 'the discipline'. Put another way, the 'career' of the term strategy can be understood in terms of the networks or social circles discussed earlier. Further, these networks are not of an equal weight or influence in terms of their ability to mark out what is centrally important and 'of' the discipline: there is not only the inclusion and exclusion of persons, but also of ideas.

While it is useful to isolate and scrutinise the wider influences on sociology and the organisational processes of the discipline itself, in practice the distinction between these two sets of influences is neither clear-cut nor easy to maintain when looking at concrete instances of the production and consumption of new ideas. For example, as Janet Finch points out, the discussion of gender in sociology has not been simply a question of research topics or theories, but is also to do with the structure of the profession and its response to innovations in teaching and writing. She also emphasises that it is not possible to consider the intellectual issues raised by feminism and by analysing gender without also understanding and analysing how gender affects the structure and workings of the discipline itself.

A related dimension of the interplay of structure and process within sociology is raised by considering, as Rodney Barker and Helen Roberts do, the intellectual history of sociological concepts, in their case the concept of 'power'. As they point out, these enter into the domain assumptions of sociologists, such that they structure not only *how* we see but *what* we see. However, this is not to suggest that this is a determined and unchanging sedimentation of ideas and assumptions within the discipline. Rather, it is to recognise both the existence of domain assumptions at the level of epistemology, and also the complex processes by which new ideas arise, are discussed and are responded to.

One important relatively recent example here concerns, as Mike Rustin's chapter discusses, the initial, often openly hostile, response to the stance and statements of ethnomethodology, and the gradual process over time of the assimilation of some of its fundamental precepts into general sociological understanding. The initial reaction seems to us to illustrate clearly the ways in which people often respond negatively to the 'strange', to ideas, practices or persons which appear foreign or alien to existing custom and practice, or which challenge existing sources of authority and power. In the case of ethnomethodology this was because many sociologists could not 'see', could not comprehend, its stance because the conceptual means of doing so had not yet become part of sociology's domain assumptions. However, some thirty years on now, the immensely complex processes by which erstwhile new ideas become assimilated have resulted in a situation in which ethnomethodology's insistence on the primacy of methodological considerations at all levels of sociological practice, and its crucial distinction between topic and resource, have indeed entered into the domain ideas of the discipline, even if this is not always openly acknowledged.

The processes which we have outlined can be seen as influencing claims and counter-claims as to what constitutes 'good sociology'. These appeals, examples of which may be found in some of the extracts included in the present volume, can be seen as part of the continuing struggle between establishments and outsider groups. While many claims to judge what constitutes good sociology make appeals to what are presented as relatively timeless criteria, these are arguably structurally located and mediated throughout the profession via social networks which are embedded in sub-organisational groups and practices. However, challenges to these dominant established ideas, at first marginalised or ignored, often gain ascendency through the establishment of alternative, although similarly constituted, social processes and networks. For instance, it has been the existence of the BSA, providing a loose organisational structure of committees, study groups and conferences, which has enabled many such new 'voices' to be articulated and heard. It has thus been a major dimension in the mechanisms of change within British sociology, acting as an overlapping set of countervailing networks to those of an erstwhile 'mainstream' located in other contexts, groups and organisations; over time it has thus helped to constitute groupings of persons, ideas and practices which themselves later have become emergent mainstreams.

The kinds of processes outlined above can be seen working at national and international levels as well. Differences between, for example, sociological concerns and practices in the United States and Great Britain (an issue addressed by Alan Bryman, among others) are part of our routine understandings of the discipline. While these differences are often understood in cultural terms, and are expressed in rather simple oppositions between the relative dominance of quantitative and qualitative modes of social inquiry, we would argue that greater explanatory power is found in the analyses of networks and strategies of inclusion and exclusion, as these respond to the intellectual currents that characterise different national settings.

It is important to note, however, that the story is not simply one of localised sociologies more or less enclosed within national or cultural boundaries; there are also numerous examples of networks and patterns of inclusion and exclusion which transcend these boundaries. Examples here may be found in the chapters on social mobility and women and class. Also, as Mike Rustin's paper demonstrates, the growth of ethnomethodology and conversational analysis cuts across national boundaries, in particular those between Europe and the United States. Research on such international networks and linkages is long overdue but needs to be incorporated into any general understanding of the process of academic life. It is also worth noting that current changes in Eastern Europe are happening in such a way that there is a mushrooming of such international links, here between particular groups of Western and particular groups of former Eastern bloc sociologists. This offers an interesting case study of the kinds of networking and accompanying processes of inclusion and exclusion we have discussed in operation. For instance, well-established links exist between feminist sociologists from Western and Eastern societies, and these seem hardly to overlap at all with the kinds of networks presently being established by male sociologists; perhaps what this illustrates is the construction of new academic elites and outsider groups in the former Eastern bloc countries.

Standing back a little from the details of the above discussion, we need to recognise that sociology is not apart from the historical processes it came into existence to study. Precisely the same kinds of conceptual and analytic stances that sociology uses to describe and theorise other social phenomena can and should be used in understanding the operations of all the academic disciplines, including the processes of change as well as of stasis within them. John Scott's discussion of the shift in sociological understanding represented by the change of theoretical emphasis from capitalism or industrialism, to modernity, and more recently to postmodernity, points up that sociology exists in what can be seen as a dialectical relationship to these historical and social processes. That is, rather than treating changes in societies as being the sole determiner of these changes in sociological conceptualisations of 'society', it is useful to turn our sociological attention to these conceptual changes as topics of investigation in their own right. Doing so tells us a good deal about the relationship between sociology and wider intellectual currents, and about networks in the discipline which create new agendas, ways of working and specialist languages which define as well as express these groupings. However, it remains a moot point, which should be subject to detailed empirical investigation rather than remaining solely within the debates of theoretical discourse, whether there have indeed been such widespread changes in social organisation as these different theoretical conceptualisations of society and social change suggest.

A point raised by Claire Wallace's discussion of strategies and Alan Bryman's chapter on organisations, but which could readily have appeared in any of the other contributions, reminds us that the influences between society and the discipline of sociology are not one-way. The terms and metaphors which we use, the topics we isolate for close investigation, as well as some of our major research findings, may well enter into wider social understanding and, although rarely doing so straightforwardly, themselves become part of the context within which sociology is operating. Thus the continuing use of the term 'strategy', as well as wider discourses around 'rational choice', may be seen as becoming part of the general intellectual climate, as Sara Arber's discussion of households suggests. Moreover, the choice of conceptual frameworks subtly shape and limit what may or may not be said, as Rodney Barker and Helen Roberts emphasise. One earlier illustration may be found in the broad set of assumptions and ideas associated with labelling theory, which became part of the commonsense routine understandings of police, social workers and others involved in the processing and administration of juvenile justice. An even earlier illustration is of course the sociological notion of 'suicide', which has so influenced commonsense understandings and theorisings that it dominates how people think of those who kill themselves. Clearly, these kinds of interplay between sociological ideas and social ideas are not merely of intellectual interest, but also point to the continuing responsibilities of sociologists in relation to the social consequences of their practices.

Procedurals

The issues and problematics dealt with above are concerned with the contextual underpinnings to the conduct of sociological inquiry and thus to the production of sociological knowledge. However, as we have argued, there are clear links between these contextual features and the ways in which fundamental procedural assumptions and ways of working come into existence. As we noted, new ideas become associated with particular groups and topics of inquiry, go through a process of sedimentation, and then either resist or assimilate or change as a response to challenges. That is, we cannot understand the process of sociological production at the level of ideas alone; rather we need to recognise the various dimensions of the material production and consumption of ideas already sketched out earlier in this introduction. We take this line of argument for granted in the discussion that follows, which centres upon some procedural aspects of sociological inquiry raised by various of the chapters in the collection.

Various debates in sociology generally as well as within the pages of *Sociology* appear to focus on technicalities. Many readers might feel lost in the details of relative versus absolute mobility, the classification of occupations, the identification and incidence of cross-class families, and so on. To some readers these disagreements may seem far removed from the key issues of the day or from central issues in sociological theory. Yet it is clear from the original articles themselves, as well as from the chapters dealing with these articles, that these debates are rarely just about technicalities, as Ray Pawson, for example, shows. To understand the debates, and sometimes the acrimonious tone of disagreements, it is important to go beyond the issues to hand. Very quickly it can be seen that we are dealing with different theoretical and often political stances, these positions being linked to the differential distribution of knowledge production within the discipline. This is not to commit the fallacy of reducing everything to ideology, nor uncritically to adopt metaphors of base and superstructure, nor indeed is to deny the power and importance of ideas themselves. It is not that we are talking about different levels of reality. Technical or methodological disagreements are *also* disagreements about theory and about overall orientations to the discipline; it is not a question of substituting one for the other.

Perhaps the clearest example here is the women and class debate. Helen Roberts takes us through some of the complex ins and outs of this debate whilst showing that more is at stake than, for example, whether households where the wife's class position is higher than that of her partner are sufficiently numerous to make a difference in terms of all kinds of social behaviour. Nor is it just a question of whether the social mobility of women can be analysed in the same way as the social mobility of men. Ultimately we are faced with questions of whether and in what ways gender is a key variable in all areas of sociological inquiry and, beyond these, whether it is meaningful or sensible to see gender as a 'variable' at all, indeed whether the language of variables is an appropriate one for sociological inquiry more generally.

It will also be observed that many of these controversies, rather than being concerned with narrow technicalities are in fact to do with fundamental units of sociological inquiry. Examples are numerous; Sara Arber considers whether couples or individuals are the appropriate basis for sociological generalisations, while Helen Roberts refers to the long-standing discussion as to whether the fundamental unit of the class structure is the individual or the family/household. Elsewhere Alan Brayman asks whether organisations can be taken as units of analysis, and similar questions are asked by John Scott in relation to societies.

Such questions reflect abiding debates within sociology. In other contexts they are described as the tension between holistic models and methodological individualism. How are we to deal with *social* processes by using methods or models which implicitly or explicitly take the individual as the unit of analysis? How are we to deal with social wholes – households, organisations, nations – without losing sight of the actors who comprise these entities? These questions and debates clearly reflect not just methodological positions but deeper epistemological, theoretical and political positions. One indication of this, as the chapters by Sara Arber, Rodney Barker and Helen Roberts, Alan Bryman and Mike Rustin discuss, is that it is not possible to solve 'consciousness issues' through methodological proceedures. Sara Arber, for instance, notes that understanding a set of social events requires a wider knowledge and understanding of the context these take place within; however, methodological proceedures direct us towards narrower technical solutions to what are in fact wider social as well as sociological problematics.

While there is no easy reconciliation of these different orientations to sociological inquiry, the grounds of a *rapprochement* can be discerned if we consider the ways in which sociologists routinely discuss such sociological debates in private and sometimes in public. Some will discuss or reduce these debates to individual personalities, to questions of personal agendas, political commitments or status considerations. Others may understand these debates in terms of broad categorisations: marxist, feminist, ethnomethodologist, positivist, and so on. In practice, however, we rarely make these stark oppositions but couch our explanations of sociological disagreements in terms of some combination of the individual and the collective. We can perhaps learn from our own routine practices something about the nature of social inquiry itself. It is not so much a question of whether we see the individual *or* the collective, but rather of *how* we see the individual *and* the collective.

This fundamental question is raised, or rather sublimated, in broad characterisations of sociology as a discipline. Sociology, for example, is often characterised not only as the 'study of society' but also as a discipline which by its very nature and constitution produces general statements about 'society' as a whole, something raised by Janet Finch's reference to what differentiates feminism inside from outside of sociology. This theme or assumption of generalisability is responded to very differently, both between the original debates and extracts which represent them, and between the approaches adopted in the various chapters in this collection. This points up a basic set of not so much divisions as unsettled epistemological debates about the intellectual defensibility or otherwise of producing generalisations based on different kinds of data generated by different kinds of modes of inquiry.

For example, a number of procedural questions and conventional answers come to mind here. One such question is whether general statements can be produced from small-scale qualitatively explored local contexts. The conventional or mainstream answer to this has been no, but, in contrast, such general statements can be produced from large-scale more representative samples producing quantitative studies, a viewpoint discussed in Sara Arber's chapter. However, such a response brackets a number of interesting and indeed fundamental problematics about the nature of generalisation that should exercise us all. Firstly, there are different kinds of 'general statements' that sociology is concerned with, one of which is statements referring to what is true or general for people of particular kinds in particular kinds of circumstances – patients in hospitals, for example, or employees in a particular workplace. Secondly, common social processes can be discerned within apparently very different or contrasting kinds of circumstances – between hospitals, submarines and convents, all examples of total institutions, for example. Thirdly, representative quantitive sample approaches produce general statements which, while being true for whole populations, do not necessarily hold true in particular circumstances or for particular sub-groups within the sample or outside the specific time the survey was conducted. And fourthly, it is as important sociologically to know and to conceptualise variants as it is general patterns. That is, to use another sub-language, that of the sociology of deviance, we cannot adequately understand conformity without knowing its relationship to deviance and thus also knowing the processes of labelling and thereby the distributions of both micro- and macro-power which produce both.

The problematics concerned with generalisation continue, implicitly more often than explicitly, to exercise sociological practice, or to be bracketed off from it. In addition, behind such assumptions and questions, and the debates which give rise to them, lies the relationship between foundationalism, as for example represented in the mobility studies discussed by Ray Pawson, and alternative epistemological positions, such as that characterising the Foucauldian notion of power discussed by Rodney Barker and Helen Roberts. However, matters are rarely so simple as an opposition between foundationalism and anti-foundationalism or varieties of relativism. For example, in the social mobility debate the contrast is between one form of foundationalism and two alternative foundationalisms. With hindsight, as Ray Pawson shows, neither of these has provided successful challenges to the mainstream in this domain of inquiry (although, as we have already recognised, feminism and ethnomethodology have been signally successful elsewhere in the discipline).

Similar issues surface in the relative invisibilities produced through conceptualising topic areas in particular ways. To continue with the same example, what would be the theoretical and other implications of recasting the sociological approach to social mobility in terms of racial/ethnic divisions and separations? Although Ray Pawson's argument lodges objections here, there are large numbers of people within the discipline who continue to think that 'race'/racism and ethnicity have signal importance for the question of social mobility. These issues also surface through investigating the 'same' topic area in methodologically different ways, in relations to mobility studies through using, for example, life history and other biographical approaches, or workplace ethnographies and case studies, or historical investigations of particular communities, and/or classes and genders and races of persons.

Another related fundamental procedural point concerns the question of the comparability of different events, times and places. At a societal level, this question is considered by John Scott in relation to revolutions and modernity, and by Janet Finch in relation to patriarchy. And at more local levels it is considered by Alan Bryman in relation to organisations, and by Sara Arber and by Claire Wallace in relation to households and their divisions of work and strategies for organising these. Such comparisons are achieved by, firstly, producing prior sociological definitions or sets of understandings or models which are taken to 'describe' the event, time, place; and, secondly, by treating specific examples as potential or actual instances of the phenomena as 'described' in such models. An example here is of defining what 'a revolution' comprises, and then looking at particular likely occurrences to establish whether they meet the criteria specified by the model or not. Succinctly, the perceived success of such comparisons hinges upon utilisation of a deductive way of working within the discipline.

It is interesting to ask whether and to what extent such an approach can be seen as intellectually defensible; that is, whether such comparisons tell us anything about social life, however much they may lead to more refined models. In the recent past even asking such a question about comparison in sociology would have been seen as committing sociological heresy. That it can both be asked, and moreover be seen as a sensible and indeed in some sense a necessary question to put, is one measure of how much sociology has changed over this twenty-five year period. However, it is worth noting that asking these and related questions is still considered a relative heresy in some sociological circles.

This is perhaps the point to consider explicitly the question of the nature of sociological knowledge in relation both to the means by which 'sociological topics' are marked out and investigated, and in the perceived relationship between such topics and the social actors who provide information about them. Thus, what problematics arise from proceeding from the investigation of sociological variables such as race, class, sex/gender, age and so on, and treating these as separable dimensions of social experience for the purposes of sociological inquiry? The pertinency of this question of course derives from the fact that in life these 'different' dimensions are not thus separable. Looking at this question the other way around, why has so much of sociology (perhaps less in Britain than in North America, but still the majority) turned its face away from investigating social life 'in the round', investigating all these and other 'variables' in particular settings?

The basic answer is that which we have already referred to: doing so, through for example ethnographic approaches, is not seen to be capable of yielding generalisations of sufficient power and plausibility. Behind this lies the assumption that generalisation of this kind is crucial for the production of 'good sociology' because it is this which is necessary for the production of 'good science'. And behind this lie more general foundationalist Cartesian assumptions, particularly those that assume that knowledge is generalisable because its production is not tied to specific producers or investigators – knowledge is seen to be independent of their interpretations if generated by using the 'right' or correct procedures; relatedly, basic social phenomena are seen as context-independent. The first of these assumptions has been challenged by the wider feminist intellectual presence only tangentially represented in the debates occurring in the pages of *Sociology*, which has argued that the researcher is an active presence who constructs and not merely represents the social world (and here it has much in common with later postmodernist arguments). And the second has been challenged by the ethnomethodological endeavour, in particular through its insistence on the indexicality of knowledge.

Just as it is important to consider issues of generalisation, so too sociologists need to consider whether and to what extent it is possible to make causal statements and conclusions from what kinds of data. Thus looked at from the viewpoint of foundationalist assumptions, there are problems with ethnographic research here also. The basic problem may be construed as to what extent one can tease out causal influences in the absence of the measurement of core variables. However, when looked at from the viewpoint of ethnography, 'the problem' is recast as rather the failure to recognise the irrevocable complexity of social situations, occurrences, persons and events within variable analysis, a complexity which good ethnography inscribes at its heart.

Many of the issues considered in the previous paragraphs raise some well-rehearsed issues in the sociology of knowledge. These issues are conventionally represented in the form of dilemmas or indeed paradoxes: does the recognition of the social context of knowledge production necessarily invalidate the knowledge thus produced? And if this is the case, does it simultaneously undermine the knowledge-claims of the sociology of knowledge itself? We are faced here of course with the familiar logical paradox, conjured up by the poignant image of the sociologist cheerfully sawing at the branch on which s/he is sitting.

Without pursuing these issues at any length, it is possible to identify two opposing dangers and the need for the sociologist to steer some path between them. The dangers of a facile relativism – 's/he would say that, wouldn't s/he' – are clear, as are the dangers which derive from an unswerving adherence to foundationalisms. In this latter case claims are clearly made in terms of right or wrong and the use of some absolute standards by which to make these claims. It is probably the case, as has been argued up to now, that sociology has leaned more to the latter danger than to that of relativism.

Our response is to call for some measure of what one might describe as 'sociological humility'. This is not so much a call for certain personal characteristics, but rather a recognition that the sociological perspective does not stop when the sociologist returns from the field. Put another way, this is to argue that the critical sociological imagination which characterises the best of all modes of social inquiry is not simply a question of us studying them, but also of us studying ourselves.

Sociological humility is perhaps most necessary in relation to the production of social theory. Social theory has often been seen as part of the 'commanding heights' of the discipline, a highly specialised area in which 'grand theory' accounts of different societies are produced either in comparison with each other and/or in comparison with themselves over time. This kind of social theory is thus concerned with modelling whole societies and the processes of social change. Two important questions are raised by John Scott's contribution in one way and by Alan Bryman's contribution at a different level of analysis. Firstly, in what ways and with what limits does it make intellectual sense to compare different social formations, either separated over time, or separated culturally and spatially? Relatedly, do modern versions of this avoid any of the difficulties of the earlier ones of Comte and Spencer, Hobhouse and Westermaark, Parsons and Eisenstadt? And secondly, does the isolation and analysis of particular dimensions of social structure and/or social process around which comparisons can be made (revolutions in John Scott's discussion and organisations in Alan Bryman's) avoid the problems of comparing like with unlike by proceeding in a Weberian manner through an ideal typology?

An awkward question to ask here is whether there is adequate empirical or indeed conceptual evidence successfully to argue that there has been social change (rather than sociological conceptual change) on such a scale and of such a type as to justify sociological claims that modernity has given way to postmodernity? An answer here, if not the only one, is to emphasise that different kinds of sociology implicitly adopt rather different definitions and measures of what constitutes 'social change'. To take another example arising out of John Scott's chapter, the notion of 'revolution' has been one means by which some sociologists have sought to look at a particular kind of social and political change. One way of responding to the sociological debate concerning the 1950s changes in Eastern bloc societies is to argue that 'revolution' was not used in an ideal type sense, but rather as a concrete description. Thus rather than changing and developing the model when particular rapid wide-scale social changes that had occurred could not be made to fit the notion 'revolution', the response was rather one which concluded that such changes were not *real* revolutions.

Although dealing with a very different level of analysis, Alan Bryman's discussion of sociological debates around the concept of organisation also point up various of these procedural issues. Thus the emphasis in this work has been on linking organisation to the generation of grand conceptual schema rather than empirical explorations of a grounded kind: the conceptual schema have been developed deductively and then 'tested', rather than these being developed inductively out of grounded detailed researches.

We are by no means denying the sociological importance of the comparative method here. Rather we are looking for a more grounded 'bottom-up' and sociologically reflexive approach to it. As well as the largely undiscussed procedural problematics we have referred to above, such a comparative approach results in strong claims-making about its products, claims-making which we would argue is not in the final result justified in relation to the kinds of generalisations and comparisons produced. In the terms already used, a greater degree of sociological humility is called for here; also, other sociologists working in different areas of the discipline need to develop more realistic appreciations of the limitations as well as the strengths of this kind of social theory.

There is a wider point which has already been touched upon, but given its emphasis in so many of the contributions in this collection it requires a more focussed discussion here. In various of the chapters it is argued that the use of sociological concepts and models constitutes in itself a truth-claim about the nature of the social world; that doing so not only defines but prescribes how the nature of 'reality' is understood; this limits the content of debates by virtue of the framework which constitutes how 'the debate' is defined and understood; and that accordingly it structures what we 'see' by virture of defining and structuring how we think. These are powerful claims indeed when brought together in this way. Even if this set of ideas is not accepted in its entirety, acceptance of even a limited part of these arguments should encourage sociologists to adopt the humility we have already referred to. However, equally importantly, it needs to be recognised that in order to think at all we necessarily think through what Alfred Schutz calls 'typifications'. Sociological humility consists not in seeking to abandon such typifications but rather in recognising both their limitations and their necessity. Further, the constitution and refinement of discourses and their attendant models and concepts – as Michel Foucault has emphasised – opens up new possibilities for thinking abouut the social world while also creating boundaries.

Omissions

From everything that has been said up to now, it will come as no surprise to note that some important debates have either taken place outside the pages of *Sociology*, or indeed outside the discipline altogether. We have said that no journal is a simple barometer, faithfully and passively recording changes in the wider social and intellectual climate; processes of selection take place. Here we provide examples of four such omissions. We should stress at the outset that these are simply examples; this editorial introduction cannot make claims to comprehensiveness any more than it is possible for a journal editor to make such claims.

The first example is a debate that took place, not in *Sociology*, but in the pages of the *Sociological Review*. This was a debate initiated by Jon Bernardes (1985–1987) around the definitions and understandings of the family and, relatedly, the extent and ways in which conventional sociological definitions not only distorted and simplified the complexities of the real world, but also provided definitions which were certainly limiting and potentially oppressive. A partial response to Bernardes was provided in a paper by Patricia Wilson and Ray Pahl (1988), which not only argued with Bernardes about the need to abandon the use of the word 'family' but also sought to rectify an earlier over-emphasis upon the household and to reassert the importance of family and kinship relationships across and between households. Other contributors to the debate included Bernardes himself (1988) and Jaber Gubrium (1988).

This debate had close affinities to debates taking place elsewhere, in feminist scholarship, in urban anthropology, and discussions about the desirability of family policy, for example. There was no logical reason why such a debate could not have originated in or have spread to *Sociology*, and the explanation why it did not is to be found in the social processes we have described. Given that the discipline of sociology is itself socially organised, there will always be examples of 'ones that got away'. Here too contextual elements have given rise to the raising, if not the solving, of procedural problematics, concerned largely with debating the definition and use of appropriate units of analysis.

The second example is rather different. Towards the end of the 1980s, an interesting debate was initiated by Mike Bury (1986) in the pages of the *Sociology of Health and Illness* around the limits of social constructionism in the analysis of illness, especially acute conditions. Clearly this is a matter of considerable importance experientially as well as intellectually. To what extent can sociologists provide a realist understanding of illness without undermining its own particular knowledge-claims in relation to anti-essentialism and anti-reductionism? In our terminology, this is a key procedural issue. What is also of interest here is the fact that the debate took place outside the pages of *Sociology* says something about the ambiguous status of medical sociology within British sociology as a whole (one important omission from the present volume, for example, is the debate in *Sociology* around women and depression and the work of George Brown (Brown *et al.* 1976, 1978; Hope 1977; Brown 1986; McKee *et al.* 1987)). While medical sociology represents the largest study group within the BSA, its membership goes beyond the conventional boundaries of the discipline to include a wide range of practitioners and researchers. Some members of this study group feel in a marginal position in relation to sociology and indeed may feel that the *Sociology of Health and Illness* is a more appropriate publishing outlet, while others see their primary allegiance to the medical rather than to the sociological establishment. Thus there are real and often sharp differences within the medical sociology study group. However, the overlaps are as important as the differences. Some important papers on medical sociology *have* appeared in *Sociology*, and a recent paper by Ted Benton (1991) may be seen as developing some of the deeper procedural points raised by Bury. Once again we see the interweaving of the contextual and the procedural by thus exploring omissions from the pages of *Sociology*.

Our third example is of a very different order. Our contributors have drawn attention both to the absence of papers focussing on 'race' and racism and the omission of considerations of 'race'/racism in papers discussing 'other' topics such as, for example, women and class, social mobility, the nature of the household and the family, power, and so on. There are obviously discussions of 'race' and racism taking place in British society, in British sociology, and in academic life more widely; indeed centres have been funded to investigate the dimensions, dynamics and consequences of this, and at least one journal has been founded. However, one would scarcely gain an understanding of the ensuing debates from the articles that have appeared in the three main British sociology journals.

At a contextual level, the assumption has tended to be made by white sociologists that 'race' should be studied and conceptualised by black sociologists, and that in some sense it would be out of order politically and also intellectually for white sociologists to do this. Relatedly, most black sociologists have experienced themselves as outsiders and have located themselves elsewhere in academic life, for example as marxists discussing race and class or as feminists concerned with race and gender.

But again contextual elements interweave with procedural ones. Underpinning the workings of sociological networks and the dynamics of inclusion and exclusion has been the constitution of a highly consequential set of assumptions and precepts that have conditioned white sociological response to questions of 'race'/racism. Coming together here have been two closely reinforcing domain assumptions. The first is that 'race' has been treated as a 'variable' which can be studied or excluded, thus relating back to our earlier discussion of domain assumptions about sociological units of analysis and the accompanying view that such 'variables' can be treated as discrete from each other. The second is that 'race' is treated as the personal characteristic of certain kinds of people but not others, and in particular of people 'of a different colour', implicitly taking whiteness as the norm. That is, 'white' assumptions have not only set the agenda, but also whiteness has been excluded from the category 'race'/ethnicity and has become a non-topic within sociology. This is interestingly contrasted with the contextual and procedural dynamics which surround the study of gender in the discipline. Increasingly gender is being seen in terms of gender *relations*, thus not as 'gender' as a characteristic which women alone possess, but rather as gender relationships as an interactional as well as structural feature of social reality. Here the domain assumption has developed that consequently male sociologists as well as female not only can, but in some sense should, be involved in the study of such relations. This is dramatically contrasted with the failure of most of white sociology to treat 'race' and ethnicity in terms of relations of super- and subordination between white and black people and thus in terms of the dynamics of power.

There are small signs of change. For example, the BSA has recently developed guidelines on non-racist language to parallel the ones already in existence dealing with non-sexist language, and has actively encouraged the formation of a black caucus within the Association. Also, some white sociologists are taking on board 'race'/racism as a set of relations in which whites as much as any other group are involved. But it remains difficult at this stage to discern in what directions these initiatives will take the discipline and what the wider impact will be in terms of sociological research and theory.

The fourth and final omission concerns postmodernism, including its overlaps with post-structuralism and deconstructionism. This omission is largely accounted for by the recent growth of specialist journals, and particularly here *Theory, Culture & Society*. However, also involved may be the perception that *Sociology* is predominantly, indeed almost exclusively, concerned with empirically-grounded discussions. But as some of the debates discussed in this collection – for instance, those concerned with patriarchy, with post-industrialism and revolutions, with ethno-methodology, with power – show we hope very clearly indeed, this view is a mistaken one. Nonetheless, the point remains that this new, lively challenging debate has been and is to date largely unreflected in the pages of *Sociology* apart from in book reviews.

Clearly the postmodernist debate raises crucial, indeed fundamental, contextual and procedural issues for the discipline. Claims concerning, for example, the end of grand narratives and instead the existence of a poly-phony of voices, the death of the author and the rise of the reader, the insistence that authoritative scientific texts are rather one partial account among many, the rejection of structural determinism and recognition of difference, and the fragmentation of experience, all raise serious issues for sociology and other social science disciplines.

Thus far we have focussed upon postmodernism as a set of theoretical ideas about the epistemological basis of social reality and thus of social science. For many commentators, postmodernism is irreducably linked to postmodernity as a change from modernity (linked to capitalism, bourgeois humanism and so forth) to a different order of society. We find the knowledge-claims of postmodernist theory interesting and challenging, although in large part with clear but unacknowledged origins within modernist intellectual and political formations such as marxism, feminism, psychoanalysis, humanism and, within sociology, the critique of positivism also. However, we remain unconvinced by claims concerning post-modernity as a new social order: in a sense the jury is still out concerning this particular aspect of the claims made by postmodernist theory.

The next twenty-five years

There are certain kinds of developments, already well under way at the present time in British sociology, which we see as coming more to the fore over the next twenty-five years. These developments have already been touched on in our discussion of contextual and procedural themes and issues, and here we draw together aspects of our thinking about the likely future directions of change in the discipline.

The production of sociological ideas will increasingly be seen as predi-cated upon the existence of networks, the concerted organisation of discourse, and the social production of mainstreams and hegemonies. Relatedly, this increased reflexivity will extend to a, perhaps largely impli-cit, critique about the 'objectivity' of knowledge production, instead recog-nising some of the fascinating, and sociologically highly challenging, prob-lematics engendered once we take on board the role of the social inquirer as an *agent of construction* and not just merely a passive *means of discovery*.

In addition to the indications of this shift which may be extrapolated from the contributions within the present volume, there are three further reasons which we provide for our expectation that such a development is likely to take place. Firstly, a concern with these kinds of issues has been a fairly constant presence within the discipline since discussion of them within German sociology and philosophy of the social sciences in the later nineteenth century, and periodically the perceived importance of such ideas has received wider recognition (and we see the current interest in postmodernism in this light). Secondly, since the 1960s the development of such thinking has provided a strong current within British sociology which has more recently been developed by a number of theoretical and epi-stemological perspectives. Thirdly, although such perspectives, including interactionism, phenomonology, ethnomethodology, hermeneutics, feminism and postmodernism, have contributed to these reformulations of the nature of social inquiry, such developments cannot be seen as the exclusive property of any one of these.

But as we have noted before, such change is always uneven and contested, and a variety of counterveiling tendencies also exist. There are strong political and other pressures for sociology to develop in the direction of a narrow professionalism and, accompanying this, an even more 'scientific' approach to questions of method or technique. There has been the growth of styles or genres of theorising – such as rational choice theory or the new household economics or, albeit in a different way, the revival of interest in the work of Parsons – which have a built in non- or even anti-reflexivity, for any acknowledge of the role of the researcher would undermine the epistemological stance they are taking. And there has also been the rapid development of ever more sophisticated techniques for the analysis of quantitative data, which have proved highly attrtactive to large and influential sections of the discipline. Perhaps paradoxically in view of what we have said about them thus far, these latter attractions have also appealed to many marxist and feminist sociologists; equally paradoxically, these techniques are also being increasingly applied to the analysis of qualitative data.

Earlier we commented upon the increased emphasis on the social production of knowledge. This is likely to result in a decreased willingness to treat ideas as solely the production of great minds, typically and indeed almost exclusively the production of great men. Instead of the continued development of sociological tribal totems – Marx–Weber–Durkheim–Parsons–Habermas–Garfinkel–Bourdieu–Foucault–Baudrillard – sociology's future approach to social theory will we think move, albeit hesitantly, in the direction of recognising the social, rather than individual, production and consumption of ideas. But perhaps this is to say no more than that the sociology of knowledge, what it has now become increasingly fashionable to call 'epistemology', will become more central in the discipline and be seen as less the preserve of an elite group, and, relatedly, be treated as the expression of the everyday working concerns of all sociologists.

Again, there are straws in the wind which support this argument, and each of these draws together both contextual and procedural elements. The first is the development of black and feminist groupings, largely operating outside of sociology conceived narrowly, which have rejected an individualist approach to the production of knowledge and instead seen this as located in group responses to and analyses of the experience of oppression. The second is the increasing recognition that 'theory' is not the preserve of a particular elite within a narrowly-defined professional group, but is a necessary part of the everyday lives and understandings of all people in society; this has been a stance promoted particularly with phenomenological, hermeneutic, feminist and ethnomethodological approaches. The third is the likelihood that the sociological community will include increasing proportions of teachers and researchers on short-term contracts, thereby inhibiting the model of the lone scholar developing theories over a sustained period of time. Of course all such developments are likely to contain their own ambiguities and paradoxes. In this case many of the tendencies which we have suggested – the disappearance of the lone scholar, increasing concentration on processes by which knowledge is produced, and a general sense of decentredness – have already been recognised and indeed applauded in various strands of postmodernist theorising. However, ironically, such theorising has relatively quickly produced its own totems, taboos and grand narratives and indeed its own lone scholars.

A future generation of sociologists will be able to compare this exercise in retrospective evaluation and speculative forecasting with the fruits of the next twenty-five years of sociological inquiry as represented in the pages of *Sociology*. While our particular impressions of future changes may well prove to be inaccurate in part or in whole, we are nevertheless confident that sociology will continue to be a challenging and intellectually rewarding discipline to belong to.

References

Benton, T. (1991), 'Biology and social sciences: why the return of the repressed should be given a (cautious) welcome', *Sociology*, 25, pp. 1–29

Bernardes, J. (1985), 'Family ideology': identification and exploration', *Sociological Review*, 33, pp. 275–97

Bernardes, J. (1987), ' "Doing things with words": sociology and "family policy" ' *Sociological Review*, 35, pp. 679–702

Bernardes, J. (1988), 'Founding the *new* "family sociology",' *Sociological Review*, 36, pp. 57–86

Brown, G., Bhrolchain, M., and Harris, T. (1975), 'Social class and psychiatric disturbance among women in an urban population', *Sociology*, 9, pp. 225–88

Brown, G., Bhrolchain, M., and Harris, T. (1977), 'A study of depression in women: a reply to Keith Hope's critical note', *Sociology*, 11, pp. 527–531

Brown, G. (1986), 'Statistical interaction and the role of social factors in the aetiology of clinical depression', *Sociology*, 20, pp. 600–06

Bury, M. (1986), 'Social constructionism and the development of medical sociology', *Journal of Sociology of Health and Illness*, 8, pp. 137–69

Gubrium, J. (1988), 'The family as project', *Sociological Review*, 36, pp. 273–96

Hope, K. (1976), 'Comments on a study of depression in women', *Sociology*, 10, pp. 321–3

McKee, D., and Vilhjalmssen, R. (1986), 'Life stress, vulnerability and depression: a methodological critique of Brown *et al.*', *Sociology*, 20, pp. 589–99

Wilson, P. and Pahl, R. (1988), 'The changing sociological construct of the family', *Sociological Review*, 36, pp. 233–272

Social mobility

The study of mobility remains the enigma of British sociology. In our embattled moments, the mobility studies are wheeled out as one of the major 'success stories', demonstrating the rigour, relevance, and rectitude of our discipline (Marshall, 1990; Westergaard, 1990). Yet, if one counts the actual number of studies, and perhaps more pertinently the number of participating researchers, one can readily gain the impression that such studies are the esoteric specialism of the few dozen British sociologists fortunate (or unfortunate) enough to be able to master log-linear analysis. If one considers the political reaction to mobility research, the sense of paradox deepens. The new right sees the mobility studies as part of the 'stifling collectivist-socialist orthodoxy' (Saunders, 1989), whilst the (old) left has long regarded the very concept of mobility as the *problématique bourgeois par excellence* (Poulantzas, 1974). Then there is the arena of greatest hostilities, the notorious potential for mobility studies for rendering half of the population invisible. Whilst the 'women and mobility' debate has probably limped to a rather tired end, it demonstrated, perhaps more than any other issue, the unfortunate, nay unforgivable, capacity of sociologists to 'talk past each others' positions' (Marshall *et al.*, 1988). This is only the beginning, of course, for mobility research has also spawned a range of much more closely-focussed debates on over-time analysis, measurement, cross-cultural comparison, unemployment and so forth, all of which have featured in the pages of *Sociology* over the past twenty-five years.

Readers will recognise such a prefatory paragraph as this author's way of ringing his hands at the enormity of the task of providing a complete review of the area. I aim to take on a more restricted task, which I can achieve first of all by reminding readers of a number of other significant reviews on the topic which have been published recently. On mobility in general there have been several masterful attempts at summary by Geoff Payne (most notably, 1980). Another useful recent source is the exchange between John Westergaard, Geoff Payne and John Goldthorpe, which does sterling work in relating mobility research to the competing traditions in British sociology (Clark *et al.*, 1990). On the women and mobility theme, there are, of course, volumes (Payne and Abbott, 1990; Clark *et al.*, 1990, section V etc.), while Helen Roberts' chapter in this collection faces the challenge of adding to this particular debate.

This work relieves me of the need to provide a 'general overview', to cover 'traditions', and to examine 'gender', and thus poses the question of what is left for me to tackle? First of all, by reporting what actually went on in the pages of *Sociology*, I find myself giving an account of Goldthorpe's work. I will refer to a whole series of articles, some of them co-authored by Catriona Llewellyn and Clive Payne, and I apologise to these two in advance for those occasions when, in order to help the ebb and flow of the story, I mention the senior author in the singular. Goldthorpe chose to publish as papers in *Sociology* what later became key chapters in both the first and second editions of *Social Mobility and Class Structure in Modern Britain*. Many of the key 'findings' on mobility were thus reported in the journal and it is an interesting exercise to look back at the subtle differences in interpretative gloss first placed upon the data, as compared to the later accounts.

What is also much in evidence over the years in the journal are critical accounts of Goldthorpe's work, which have invariably prompted replies and contributed to Goldthorpe's reputation for an intellectual style which one admirer has named 'the tennis player's' approach (Mayer, 1990). There is an old saw about sociology being a debate with the ghost of Marx. Whilst this rings less and less true, one can say with certainty that the topic of social mobility does consist of a tournament with Goldthorpe. In setting down examples of his various replies and rejoinders here, readers will be able to judge for themselves whether Goldthorpe's style owes more to Borg or McEnroe.

Finally, by way of preface I should introduce an axe of my own which I intend to grind. There is an age-old debate about the sense in which (if at all) sociology can be said to progress and its knowledge cumulate. Social mobility is a topic of such standing, and research into it longstanding enough to begin to make a decision about such issues. Crucial to such a judgement, in my view, is the blend of theory and empirical research attained in any research programme. A data-driven field of enquiry can soon get exhausted for lack of new things to say. Theory-driven modes of discovery can introduce endless new speculations without ever having the means of deciding which viewpoints take precedence. What do the pages of *Sociology* reveal on whether mobility research has achieved such a balance?

The 'Three Theses' paper

'Class Mobility in Britain: Three Theses examined' was first published in *Sociology* by Goldthorpe and Llewellyn in 1977 and remains the landmark study in the field. It owes its status to the fact that, at the time, it reported on the first new data on British mobility for over a couple of decades, data which, moreover, were not themselves superceded for many years. Rather less charitably, one might say that the reason why everyone knows this particular paper is that it is one of the few in the area of social mobility written at a level of technical complexity which the sociologist-in-the-street is able to follow. It is probably sensible to start with the data, for the 'inflow' and 'outflow' mobility tables reported therein are probably the most reproduced in the history of British social research. I follow custom by setting down only the former as Table 2.1.

Two immediate and relatively minor comments are relevant to begin. The first is simply to affirm the remarkable power that a few rows and columns of numbers can hold on the received wisdom of a discipline. It is quite possible, as we shall see later, to change considerably the picture of mobility regime presented here by changing the composition of the cells (class positions). Yet, it is exactly this version which has been reproduced endlessly in countless introductory texts. Moreover, it is this data which has become sociological folk knowledge, in the form of Goldthorpe's famous double-edged reading of it, namely that in the period examined there is upward mobility aplenty, but whose social impact may not be that considerable if we take into account the change in and relative size of the benchmark classes. Also in passing, it is worth a related aside on the curious, bracketed, two-in-one, presentation of the data, which was done in order to allow for potential ambiguities in the class position of those employed in agriculture. With the benefit of hindsight, it seems utterly perverse that the table was reconstructed because of doubts about class categorisation down on the farm, when it could equally have been so transformed in the light of furious debates which have taken place about the appropriate class location of almost every conceivable occupational group.

In terms of more substantial comments, I wish to pick up my sub-theme on the balance of theory and data as it appears in this particular paper. Firstly, and this is very much a case of all-credit-to-Goldthorpe, note

Table 2.1 *Class composition by class of father[a] at respondent's age 14*

Father's[a] class	Respondent's class (1972)							N	%
	I	II	III	IV	V	VI	VII		
	(percentage[b] by column)								
I	25·3 (24·2)	12·4 (12·0)	9·6 (9·1)	6·7 (6·0)	3·2 (3·0)	2·0 (1·8)	2·4 (2·0)	680 (688)	7·9 (7·3)
II	13·1 (12·5)	12·2 (11·8)	8·0 (7·6)	4·8 (4·4)	5·2 (4·9)	3·1 (2·9)	2·5 (2·2)	547 (554)	6·4 (5·9)
III	10·4 (10·0)	10·4 (10·0)	10·8 (10·2)	7·4 (6·1)	8·7 (8·2)	5·7 (5·4)	6·0 (5·3)	687 (694)	8·0 (7·3)
IV	10·1 (13·0)	12·2 (13·9)	9·8 (12·2)	27·2 (36·5)	8·6 (10·6)	7·1 (9·5)	7·7 (12·4)	886 (1,329)	10·3 (14·1)
V	12·5 (12·0)	14·0 (13·5)	13·2 (12·5)	12·1 (9·4)	16·6 (15·6)	12·2 (11·4)	9·6 (8·6)	1,072 (1,082)	12·5 (11·5)
VI	16·4 (15·7)	21·7 (21·0)	26·1 (24·8)	24·0 (19·2)	31·1 (29·2)	41·8 (39·1)	35·2 (30·5)	2,577 (2,594)	30·0 (27·5)
VII	12·1 (12·6)	17·1 (17·8)	22·6 (23·6)	17·8 (18·5)	26·7 (28·5)	28·0 (29·9)	36·6 (38·9)	2,126 (2,493)	24·8 (26·4)
N	1,230 (1,285)	1,050 (1,087)	827 (870)	687 (887)	1,026 (1,091)	1,883 (2,015)	1,872 (2,199)	8,575 (9,434)	
%	14·3 (13·6)	12·2 (11·5)	9·6 (9·2)	8·0 (9·4)	12·0 (11·6)	22·0 (21·3)	21·8 (23·3)		

Notes
(a) Or other 'head of household' (see text).
(b) Bracketed figures are those produced if farmers (category 11) and smallholders (category 24) are allocated to Class IV and agricultural workers (category 31) to Class VII.
Source: Goldthorpe and Llewellyn (1977), p. 262.

should be made of the explicit linkage to a 'structurational' view of
sociology:

> . . . to take over Giddens's terminology, the distribution of mobility
> chances which pertain within a given society has been seen as a basic
> source of class 'structuration', in that the greater the degree of
> 'closure' of mobility chances – both intergenerationally and within
> the career of the individual – the more this facilitates the formation of
> identifiable classes. For the effect of closure in terms of inter-
> generational movement is to provide for the reproduction of common
> life experiences over the generations. Secondly, the extent of
> mobility evident within a society has been recognized as a significant
> indicator of the prevailing balance of power and advantage in class
> relations and, further, of characteristic modes of class action. Parkin,
> for example, has argued that one important aspect of class conflict is
> expressed in the form of opposing 'strategies of closure': typically,
> those in higher-level class positions seek to preserve their superiority
> and to transmit it to their offspring by practising various techniques
> of exclusion against members of inferior classes, while the latter tend
> to exploit their solidarity and organizational strength in efforts to
> raise their levels of reward and opportunity – challenging where
> necessary the existing distributional system and the advantages of
> their superiors. Thus, mobility rates and patterns can serve to reveal,
> on the one hand, the effectiveness of strategies of exclusion and, on
> the other, at least the chances of success of counter-strategies of
> solidarism, which as Parkin points out, must be highly dependent on
> the participants being ready to commit themselves to collective
> interests and aspirations rather than to individual ones. (Goldthorpe,
> 1977, p. 258)

The ramifications of this statement are important. It amounted to the
announcement of a paradigm shift in the study of how placement into class
positions is to be understood. Previously such research had been subsumed
under the 'status attainment' research programme which, perhaps because
of its American pedigree, placed little emphasis on the structural constraints on people's ability to change class position, and concentrated
instead on an explanation by way of measuring the relative contribution of a
variety of background attributes and abilities to the individual's road to
success (Blau and Duncan, 1967). In the above quotation Goldthorpe can
be heard as stressing the need to understand mobility within a process in
which individuals are located within a class structure, but whose own
efforts and resources allow some of them to change class position, a state of
affairs which itself partly reproduces and partly transforms the class structure. Mobility, in common with all other social processes, should therefore

be understood in terms of individual choices and social formations being wrapped together in a process of constant social change.

Hand in hand with this ontologically-inspired shift to a process-centred explanation, came a methodological shift which saw a change in the basic task from one of searching out and measuring empirical regularities to one of seeking to discover the generative mechanisms which explain observed patterns of data. So, for instance, in Blau and Duncan's path analytic approach, the very process of calculating the various path coefficients between the factors related to occupational status is regarded as having explanatory force. In another, older approach in mobility research the basic task was viewed as arriving at some measure, some mobility coefficient, which would capture the essential picture of the social fluidity in a society. Goldthorpe surpassed these essentially descriptive approaches and sought to introduce what we now tend to call 'realist' explanatory forms in the study of mobility. In a nutshell, this means that we take a pattern of data such as in Table 2.1 and regard it, not as the end of the research process, but as a configuration to be explained. The explanation takes the form of postulating theories about the underlying causal mechanism which have produced the regularity. Those mechanisms which are considered to have explanatory potential in this case are outlined in the quotation above and concern the likes of class action, closure mechanisms, market changes, employment realignments, technical change and so forth.

This explanatory style has great advantages, indeed I have claimed elsewhere that the blend of theory and empirical research required to put it into practice is obligatory if sociology is to remain faithful to scientific explanatory standards (Pawson, 1989). However, such an approach does have costs in what is inevitably an 'open-system' mode of inquiry. To illustrate: consider again the pattern of data in Table 2.1. In order to explain the particular movement from, say, class 7 to class 1, one needs to call upon generative thinking about the changing work patterns which have led to an increase in professional and managerial positions, to consider the rising levels of working-class ambitions and the (limited) extent to which these were nurtured by the expansion of formal education in the period under observation. Other movements, say into the ranks of technical workers (class 5), may require understanding in terms of closure mechanisms through which certain occupational groups limit entry. These and scores of other market, occupational, and educational mechanisms act together to generate the snapshot captured as Table 2.1.

As well as these essentially class-based processes anticipated by Goldthorpe, a range of quite different mechanisms exert themselves on the overall pattern of data. Women do not appear in the data but gender-related processes make their presence felt. Consider as an example the rate of self-recruitment to class 3. This is the lowest of all the rates of self-recruitment, but the explanation lies (presumably) not with any mechanism accounting for the lack of class identity of this bunch of workers, but simply from the fact that women entered the designated occupations in droves leaving men to leap-frog elsewhere. Dozens of other, quite diverse, generative mechanisms also leave their mark on the data. One such process, not much contemplated in sociology circles, would be the genetic inheritance of intelligence and ability, which in so far as these qualities influence job attainment, could have a part to play in explaining the deeply rooted immobility always present in such tables. If one lets the imagination roam in this manner, it is not difficult to come to the view that the configuration of data assembled as Table 2.1 is the outcome of almost every conceivable individual and social mechanism. Realism (in all senses) has come to force us to that view. Sociologists can never aspire to control the underlying mechanisms they use in such explanations, they can only observe outcomes and this makes the business of choosing between potential generative processes an awfully difficult one.

Difficult, but not impossible! This is no place to set down the range of strategies available and here I want to mention just one, namely the significance of getting the correct measurement procedures in place in order to display (and test) the working of the mechanism hypothesised to be at work. For instance, if we are intent on testing a theory concerning high levels of self-recruitment of a propertied class, who are able to sustain their position by the mechanism of direct inheritance, we need to be sure that our measuring instruments pick up the factor of 'property' in identifying that particular class position. To turn to the different example of women's mobility and to reverse the moral methodologically, it has become obvious that a measurement scheme which differentiates clerical and sales and service workers, rather than lumping them all together, will display considerably different levels of female mobility and thus speak to entirely different labour-market theories.

I have engaged in this lengthy methodological interlude here, since this structurationist/realist explanatory format, which quite properly has become the dominant theoretical framework on mobility, places onerous demands on the process of empirical inquiry. In short, explanation works through a process of identifying the potential explanatory mechanism which generates an observed pattern of events. In explaining the 'pattern of events', generative thinking is thus also responsible for stipulating how the 'events' themselves can be conceived and measured. In the case of class mobility research, this means that actual mechanisms responsible for shifting individuals and groups around are the self-same processes which identify and constitute the base line classes. *This requires that theories have to be specified sufficiently clearly to distinguish their own from the explanatory mechanisms of potential rival theories, and this level of conceptual exactitude should be carried through to inform the instruments of data collection, thus assuring that the empirical test is a pertinent and accurate one.* This statement can be considered as an elemental requirement of quantitative social inquiry and I present it in this manner here since it encapsulates the point of dispute of much of the debate that has followed in the wake of Goldthorpe's original paper. Simple as it is, it will provide a useful yardstick in enabling us to follow (and even umpire) these debates.

One thesis reassessed

I have space here to re-examine Goldthorpe's treatment of only one of the 'three theses' and the obvious choice must be the most broadly based, namely the 'closure' thesis. This hypothesis is reconstructed by Goldthorpe as follows:

> Within the current literature of mobility research, a wide measure of agreement is apparent on what is taken to be the generic form assumed by occupational mobility patterns within modern industrial societies. The essentials of this agreement may be summed up in the following three interrelated propositions: (i) mobility is most likely to occur between groupings which are at a similar level within the occupational hierarchy, whether this is conceived of as one of desirability, prestige, or socio-economic status; (ii) mobility will tend thus to be greatest in the intermediate levels of the hierarchy and least towards its extremes – if only because at the intermediate levels the possibility will exist for mobility to occur within its most frequent range both upwards and downwards, whereas, as the extremes are approached, one or other of these possibilities will tend to be pre-cluded; (iii) the least mobility of all will be found towards the peak of the hierarchy, since those who hold the superior positions may be presumed to have not only a strong motivation to retain them, for themselves and for their children, but further the command over resources to enable them to do so, at least in terms of whatever aspects of social advantage it is that defines their position as superior in the first place. The consensus prevailing on these points, as will emerge, has been of very general influence on the writers whose work concerns us: in regard to the closure thesis specifically, the third proposition is of course that of most direct relevance (Goldthorpe, 1977, p. 260)

What is noticeable, indeed startling, on reading this statement some fifteen years on is how 'contentless' it is. By this, I refer to the lack of mention of any class grouping whatsoever, the interchangeable reference to the base-line measure of mobility ('desirability' or 'prestige' or 'socio-economic status'), and the rather loose formulations of the generative mechanism of mobility ('motivations' and 'resources'). I have argued that the derivation of a good empirical test is a function of the exactitude with which the theory is stated. The nearest thing to a measurement parameter suggested in the above are vague notions of 'peaks' and 'intermediate levels' in a 'hierarchy', and this gives Goldthorpe free rein to apply any measurement system he pleases. The stated choice was as follows:

> For purposes of applying our data to questions of class mobility, we have formed, as shown below, a sevenfold class schema or, more precisely, a schema of class positions, by aggregating categories from the collapsed (36-category) version of the Hope-Goldthorpe occupational scale. The degree of differentiation provided enables us to bring together within the classes we distinguish, occupations whose incumbents will typically share in broadly similar *market* and *work* situations – which, following Lockwood's well-known discussion, we take as the two major components of class position. (Goldthorpe, 1977, p. 259)

This brief statement is followed by a summary of some of the typical occupations and their characteristics which make up the seven occupational classes.

The empirical evidence in place, we now come to Goldthorpe's well-known passage which delivers the verdict on the closure thesis:

> For our present concern, what is immediately striking is that, directly contrary to any notion of closure at the higher levels of the class, Class I of our schema displays, on any reckoning, a very wide basis of recruitment and a very low degree of homogeneity in its composition. Although a quarter of the men it comprises are themselves the sons of Class I fathers, it can also be seen that the remainder of its member-ship is drawn from the other six classes of our schema in a remarkably even manner, with each contributing at least 10 per cent. It is true that if recruitment to Class I is judged against the standard of 'perfect mobility' – which would imply that the distribution shown in each internal column of Table I would reproduce the row marginal dis-tribution – then self-recruitment to Class I is over three times greater than the perfect mobility expectation and recruitment from Class II more than twice as great, while the inflow from Classes VI and VII is at only about half the expected level. However, if the focus of one's

interest is on class formation – rather than on questions of equality of opportunity – assessments of mobility in such relative terms would seem not altogether to the point: it is actual, *de facto* patterns which must surely be accorded greatest importance. In other words, what matters is not so much the degree of equality or inequality in chances of access to a class for persons of differing origin, but the *outcome* of these chances, whatever they may be, in terms of the composition of the class.

Continuing, therefore, from this point of view, a further aspect of recruitment to Class I which calls for comment is the extent to which, in absolute terms, it is in fact made up of men of working-class origins. Here, the relative size of classes is a crucial factor. In Table I, men allocated to Classes VI and VII together constitute well over 50 per cent of the respondents' distribution. Thus, although the sons of manual wage-workers are represented in Class I in much less than their due proportion, relative to the norm of perfect mobility, they still account for over a quarter of its membership . . . On the basis of these findings, therefore, the claim that access to the higher levels of the British class structure is tightly controlled, thus creating at these levels a marked homogeneity of social origins, would seem open to serious doubt. (Goldthorpe, 1977, p. 261)

Several comments are in order. It is, by any standards, a ringing denunciation of the 'closure' thesis and readers should note, contrary to Saunders's (1989) recent outburst about left-wingers cooking the books by only having eyes for *relative* mobility, that Goldthorpe could not be more clear in saying that *absolute* shifts are what people experience. Rather more significant for our purposes here is to consider the measurement basis of the particular test. Goldthorpe's change of heart on this matter is well known. It was at this point that the Goldthorpe and Hope scale was really ditched (the reference to it in the quotation above is, shall we say, disingenuous). Hence what is in use at this stage is fundamentally an *operational* definition, inspired loosely by Weberian notions of market position. Subsequent to this the scale gets a little *post-hoc* theoretical justification which provides a somewhat clearer rationale for the categories (Goldthorpe *et al.*, 1980: 39, 98–104). Finally, in the mid-eighties, came a further operational reworking justified, somewhat mysteriously, on the grounds of 'implementing the principles of the schema more precisely' (Goldthorpe *et al.*, 1986). I cannot give a clearer account of the evolution of the measure and one day perhaps we will get a confessional, doing-sociological-research type paper that will reveal all.

What can be said is that here, in 1977, the Marxist inspired closure arguments about the stranglehold of the capitalist/ruling classes are transformed into opaque propositions about positions in hierarchies before being put to test by Weberian measures. Goldthorpe, of course, was hardly unaware of this lack of precision, particularly in respect to the large size of his class I grouping. He chose at the time, however, to pass the blame for the ambiguity onto the original proponents of the thesis in what now reads as a classic two-wrongs-make-a-right argument.

> The writers in question show a good deal of imprecision or uncertainty in their conceptualizations, and not least when they come to relate them to empirical material. In particular, confusion arises from a failure to make, or to make consistently, the distinction between what could be termed élite occupations, on the one hand, and, on the other, élites *within* these occupations (Goldthorpe, 1977, p. 263)

A proper test of the closure thesis, in other words, requires distinctions to be made within class I, or, to be more precise, explicit statements are needed about the mechanisms by which closure is supposedly achieved, allied to concrete statements of the nature of the groups constituted by such practices. The Nuffield data could furnish the requisite information, of course, but it was left to Heath (1981) to deliver the goods in what has turned out to be a remarkably 'unreproduced' piece of data (see Table 2.2). Here, class I is subdivided into five distinct constituencies with considerably different levels of closure which are explained by the different mobility mechanisms or 'channels of recruitment' available in each. I list

Table 2.2   *Social origins of men in elite occupations*

Father's class	Respondent's class %				
	Self-employed professionals	Salaried professionals	Senior administrators	Industrial managers	Large proprietors
I	40·2	24·3	20·0	18·7	44·2
II, III, IV	35·8	37·2	37·4	27·4	29·4
V, VI, VII	24·0	38·5	42·6	53·9	26·4
Total	100·0	100·0	100·0	100·0	100·0
N	92	432	446	193	34

Source: Heath (1981), p. 66.

these in a drastic, but I hope self-evident, shorthand as follows: large proprietor = inheritance of property; industrial manager = promotion from the shop floor; salaried professionals = education; self-employed professionals = cultural capital; senior administrators = promotion from the office. These routes clearly offer quite different potential for the preservation of position through the generations, and lay the ground for a more sophisticated understanding of class formation within the service class. On this note, I can conclude narrowly by pointing out that it was thus the fate of the 'closure thesis' to become the 'closure theses', and more generally to note that the struggle reported here of getting theory to match data is the one that underlies the remainder of the mobility story.

Crompton versus Goldthorpe

By the turn of the eighties, the Nuffield Mobility Project had been substantially published and critics lined up to see if they could take a set or two from the top seed. Two of the most significant of these encounters took place in *Sociology* and they reveal a good deal about the substance and style of the mobility debate in a way which is wondrous to behold.

Rosemary Crompton (1980) attacks on two fronts. Firstly on the grounds of inconsistencies between the 'Goldthorpe-Hope' and the 'Class Mobility Scale' (these days referred to more economically as the 'Goldthorpe Schema'). She argues that, whilst the former unequivocally assumes a hierarchy of positions, the characterisation of upward and downward mobility tends towards the arbitrary in the latter.

> For example, a move, say, from machine setter or printer (H-G category 22, Class 6 on the sevenfold scale) to a caretaker, doorman (H-G category class 34, Class 3 on the sevenfold scale), would be characterized as 'upward' class mobility. I would suggest that, in terms of 'market' and 'work' situations, the description of such moves as 'upward' is doubtful. (Crompton, 1980, p. 117)

Goldthorpe replies with incredulity, the academic equivalent of McEnroe's 'you cannot be serious!' outbursts:

> To this, I must reply simply that the claim is without any warrant, and note that Crompton fails to provide either a quotation or a page reference in support of it. In fact in our paper, as in all others reporting on our research, we speak of upward mobility *only* in cases of movement into Class I or II from other origins in other classes, and of downward mobility *only* in cases of movement from Class I or II origins to other class destinations. Thus Crompton is quite wrong

> when she states that a move . . . from machine setter or printer . . . to
> caretaker, doorman would be characterized as 'upward' class
> mobility. I can only suggest to her that she reads our paper again, and
> rather more carefully than before. (Goldthorpe, 1980, p. 121)

I would be inclined to be a bit more charitable than this. Although
Goldthorpe is, of course, correct on the detail of his labelling of these
specific occupation to occupation moves, the dividing line between
'Goldthorpe-Hope'-based occupational attainment studies and the
'Goldthorpe'-based mobility research is not as clear as he is apt to declare.
For instance, I have already referred to the lack of candour in describing
the latter as a 'collapsed' and 'aggregated' version of the former ('sown' and
'scattered' might be a more pertinent phrase). Furthermore, I have already
quoted and referenced the passage in which an explicitly *hierarchical*
version of the closure thesis is prepared for test against the *nominal*
Nuffield categories.

This was merely the warm-up, however. A more substantial rally
resulted from Crompton's next serve:

> If . . . the sociologist wishes to claim that changes in the occupational
> structure more or less directly reflect changes in the *class* structure
> . . . some fairly important assumptions must be made. In particular, it
> must be assumed that the *class* position of particular occupations
> remains more or less constant over time. More specifically, if we use
> the concepts employed by Goldthorpe and Llewellyn, then the 'mar-
> ket' and 'work' situations of occupations within each of the seven
> categories must be assumed to be roughly the same in 1972 as they
> were in 1921 – the earliest date at which the occupation of a
> respondent's father could have been identified. However, given the
> rapidity of technical and social change, can this assumption be made
> with any confidence? Rather, it may be suggested that the last few
> decades have not only seen changes in the occupational structure, but
> also considerable changes in occupational *content* – even though the
> 'label' may remain the same.' (Crompton, 1980, p. 118)

To support the point, Crompton mentions material from a series of case
studies in the Braverman tradition which lay claim to observe the pro-
letarianisation and mechanisation of the nature of many clerical, professional and managerial occupations. Under a bit more pressure here,
Goldthorpe replied with a series of points doubting whether such case
studies lend systematic and comprehensive support to the thesis of the
wholesale deterioration in such market positions. I leave readers to make
their own judgement on this. Aware that he is not playing on his best
surface, he brings the whole issue back to the court of mobility:

Furthermore, the findings on class differentials from our mobility inquiry itself can also serve to throw serious doubt on Crompton's position . . . If she is correct in arguing that the class situation of men in professional, administrative and managerial groupings is now less advantaged than four or five decades ago . . ., one would expect the mobility chances of both men in these groupings and of their sons to show some decline relative to those of other groupings. But in fact the results of our inquiry give no indication whatsoever of such a decline. Men entering work in occupations covered by our Classes I and II have the same high chances of lifetime continuity in such occupations . . . whether they made their entry in the inter-war or post-war years; and successive birth cohorts of sons of Class I and II fathers have entirely preserved their very favourable relative chances of themselves acceding in turn to Class I and II occupations. (Goldthorpe, 1980, p. 122)

This is, by Goldthorpe's standards, a relatively defensive reply, but I believe it to be a case of modesty being the best policy. There is no reason why any single class schema should have the capacity to investigate both theories of the changing nature of work in post-industrial society and detailed changes in mobility regimes. Following the movement of incumbents across class positions and the relative changes in the sizes of those class positions is difficult enough, but dealing with changes in the relative position of these class positions on top would blow too many mental and computational fuses. Thus, I read this reply as a declaration that the Goldthorpe scale and its usage is deeply embedded in and receives its justification from the explanation of mobility rates. Although some of his followers seem to have quite forgotten this and declared the scale the most 'robust' for all types of class analysis (Marshall *et al.*, 1988, Ch. 2 and 3), I take the ability of a specific measure to deliver in the support of specific theories to be a sign of its strength.

Penn versus Goldthorpe

The most sustained attack on the 'Nuffield Class Categorization' appeared in *Sociology* in 1981. Roger Penn challenges the coherence of the categories as follows:

It is a central assumption of all class analyses that classes encapsulate or embody significant social relationships and that it is the task of any class categorization, however derived, to discriminate significant social distinctions within a societal matrix. It is also normally the case that each class that is identified should be relatively homogeneous *qua* its 'classness' or, in other words, classes should encompass typical bundles of market and work situations. (Penn, 1981, p. 265)

The Goldthorpe scale does not meet these objectives since:

   (i) The Nuffield class categories cross-cut significant social relationships.
  (ii) Their class categories are not always relatively homogeneous.
 (iii) On occasions their class categories are not as described.
 (iv) Their categories are poorly labelled and serve to confuse class
discourse, particularly at the conceptual interface between
sociology and Marxism. (Penn, 1981, p. 265)

In what follows I will rework highlights of the exchange on a point-by-point basis. Readers will not fail to miss the tone of contest. This was a showdown – a case of the Poisoned Penn versus being Goldfingered.

Penn   Social Class I. Clearly most of the capitalist class is ignored
since the model only includes working proprietors. The team's
justification for including *some* capitalists within a predominantly
non-capitalist class is that they constitute but a small proportion of
the whole. This is quite irrelevant. One might ask why their
sampling frame was not designed to include more capitalists but
given that the sample turned up some, albeit of a particular kind, it
is not adequate to label them part of the service class of advanced
capitalism. (Penn, 1981, p. 266)
Goldthorpe Penn airily remarks: 'One might ask why their sampling
frame was not designed to include more capitalists'. But to ask this
is in fact either to be disingenuous or to display an unfortunate
ignorance of the practicalities of survey research. Would Penn like
to tell us what sampling frame *could* be obtained which would
enable one to stratify a national sample so that members of his
'capitalist class' could be represented in sufficient numbers to
permit reliable analysis? (Goldthorpe, 1981, p. 273)
Penn   Social Class 2. This is described by the Nuffield team as
'lower-grade professionals, administrators and managers, supervisors and higher-grade technicians'. However, upon closer
inspection it becomes clear that it also includes some other rather
odd groups. It encompasses self-employed professionals like
clergymen, authors, opera singers and television actors. Again it is
hard to see from a class point of view, rather than in terms of
relative status, why such occupations are not located in social class
4 along with the bulk of the self-employed. Even stranger is the
inclusion of laboratory technicians and draughtsmen within what
Goldthorpe refers to as the 'subaltern or cadet levels of the service
class. (Penn, 1981, p. 267)

Goldthorpe These (self-employed professionals – clergymen, authors, etc.) are often highly borderline cases ... since any classificatory scheme must have borderline cases, it should be a matter for satisfaction where these prove to be quantitatively rather insignificant. (Goldthorpe, 1981, p. 274)

Penn Social Class 5. The *'Labour Aristocracy'*. This is an extremely strange class category. It is supposed to contain lower-grade technicians and supervisors but when the Hope-Goldthorpe scale is examined in greater detail it becomes evident that it also includes a range of other kinds of occupations, such as garage mechanics, Post Office engineers and electronic fitters. It is hard to know why such occupations are not placed within the skilled manual category especially given the four-year formal apprenticeship for garage mechanics and the 'quasi-apprenticeship' constituted by the grade structure of Post Office engineering. The 'aristocracy of labour' also includes footballers and cricketers and when we discover that football coaches, presumably like Malcolm Allison, are also to be regarded as 'labour aristocrats', it becomes difficult not to believe that normative bias has intruded into the Oxford team's approach. (Penn, 1981, p. 268)

Goldthorpe Penn's objections here are again in some part merely terminological – i.e. directed against the idea that this class might be described as 'a latter-day aristocracy of labour'. But this phrase is actually used, so far as I can see, only twice in *SMCS* and then, clearly enough, *only as a label* and without any commitment, explicit or implicit, to any of the theories of the aristocracy of labour to which Penn refers. Again, if Penn does not like the label, he is welcome to change it. In fact, I myself more often use the alternative suggestion, 'blue-collar élite'. (Goldthorpe, 1981, p. 275)

Penn At the end of the day, the Nuffield team are forced to rely on the OPCS schemes and ... this also weakens the plausibility of their own class model. (Penn, 1981, p. 266)

Goldthorpe Penn asks why we did not develop a class schema independently of the OPCS ... system. The answer is obvious – only the OPCS system is linked to a detailed occupational index ... I look forward to seeing the (reliability checks) reported by Penn in connection with his own research – especially if he relies on 'category' coding methods. (Goldthorpe, 1981, p. 273)

The substance of Goldthorpe's reply, in short, is that:

Penn's criticism is flawed throughout by his failure to recognize that the development and application of any kind of classificatory device is not only a conceptual, but also an intensely *practical task* ... little is gained by having a conceptually immaculate schema if this does not allow acceptably reliable coding procedures to be followed. (Goldthorpe, 1981, p. 273)

My preference would be to play this down as a contest between the armchair-theorist and the horny-handed technician. *The* ultimate test of any classificatory scheme is not its conceptual coherence nor its practical applicability but its *explanatory power*, and to have explanatory power such as a scheme needs to be embedded in some kind of *propositional theory*. Penn's real mistake, in this piece, is that such a theory is only mentioned as an afterthought. Having 'demolished' the Goldthorpe scheme, he seeks to replace it with his own 5 class model, the explanatory potential of which ends up being expressed as a speculative, single-line mobility hypothesis: 'My own view is that far more rigidity would be discerned' (Goldthorpe, 1981, p. 270).

This is the feeblest lob one would imagine and Goldthorpe smashes it away by taking the trouble to put it to the test, by way of constructing a new mobility table based on the Penn schema (reproduced here as Table 2.3). This is then compared back to (a slightly simplified version of) Table 1. Several measures of overall mobility are extracted from each and compared, which enables Goldthorpe to declare:

> In sum, then, whatever conceivable meaning is given to the idea of 'rigidity', the foregoing results are disastrous for Penn's position. A class schema incorporating a large part of the changes Penn would favour not only fails to reveal a greater degree of rigidity but obscures much of the structuring of mobility, and immobility, that the original schema displays. (Goldthorpe, 1981, p. 274)

Apart from it being the liveliest debate, I have chosen to spend more time on this particular debate for an even more compelling reason. In some ways it can be regarded as a symbol of the *great lost opportunity* in mobility research. Goldthorpe went to the trouble of using the Penn classification for one central reason, namely to crush the thesis about greater overall rigidity. However, if one compares Table 2.1 and Table 2.3 at a cell-by-cell level, one cannot fail to note a multitude of particular differences. Starting with an elementary comparison between the levels of self-recruitment in class 1 of the respective schemes, we see the significantly greater holding power of Penn's bourgeoisie in inflow terms. This follows, of course, from its composition, which resembles the 'large proprietor' and 'self-employed professions' categories employed by Heath in Table 2.2. A similar tale could be told about several other cells and the fact that all the differences

Table 2.3 *Intergenerational mobility rates (men aged 20–64, England and Wales 1972) based on 'alternative' class schema; outflow % upper-right entry, inflow % lower-left entry*

		Respondent's class, 1972					% of total
		I	II	III	IV	V	
	I	Bourgeoisie	26·6 / 38·0	29·2 / 16·1	10·8 / 12·0	13·3 / 9·9	20·1 / 12·9	15·8
	II	Service class	10·4 / 19·3	45·4 / 32·5	16·2 / 23·5	14·2 / 13·8	13·8 / 11·4	20·6
Father's class (at respondent's age 14)	III	Routine white-collar workers	9·9 / 7·3	35·4 / 10·0	23·6 / 13·5	15·0 / 5·8	16·1 / 5·3	8·1
	IV	Skilled manual workers	7·2 / 17·9	22·1 / 21·2	13·1 / 25·5	30·4 / 39·4	27·1 / 30·0	27·5
	V	Nonskilled manual workers	7·0 / 17·6	20·7 / 20·1	12·9 / 25·4	23·6 / 31·2	35·8 / 40·4	28·0
		% of total	11·1	28·7	14·2	21·2	24·8	N=9434

Source: Goldthorpe (1981), p. 277.

even out in the round to give a relatively fluid picture is by far from the most important feature of the data.

The lesson from Tables 2.2 and 2.3 and the moral of the story in general is that *measurement categories do make a difference* and that systematic work needs to be done in comparing conceputally different occupational and class unit groups in order to tease out the real underlying mechanisms that actually generate mobility. British research has preferred to steamroll on keeping faith with the Goldthorpe scheme (Marshall *et al.*, 1988). To my knowledge only Geoff Payne has constantly supported the usage of an alternative *occupationally*-based scheme for mobility research, but this, so far, has resulted in little systematic adjudication of the kind that I have called for here.

The reason? I crank out the tennis-player metaphor for the last time and hint at the reluctance of any other individual to face the blistering volleys of the kind we have seen here. But personally, I am more persuaded by a 'cultural' interpretation. The precision of hypothesis making and the level of detail of analysis in introducing alternative measurement parameters into the reckoning would simply be beyond the taste and the training of the typical British sociologist. We prefer a discipline with controversy raging between perspectives and paradigms and to argue at the level of what-it-all-means-in-the-first-place. It is no accident that what tends to be remembered about the 'mobility debate' are not the shades of grey covered here but glorious, bruising, black-and-white, 'class and gender' battles.

Mobility trends

No record of the work on mobility in *Sociology* would be complete without mention of the two most substantial pieces on the topic of over-time trends (Goldthorpe *et al.* 1980; Goldthorpe and Payne, 1986). The former paper covered the period from 1908–72 and the latter can be considered as an update to 1983. For a précis of the earlier paper, I can do no better than to quote the 1986 summary:

> (i) From at least the inter-war years through to the time of the 1972 inquiry, men of *all* class origins had become progressively more likely to move into professional, administrative and managerial positions – or into what we termed the 'service class' of modern British society; at the same time they had become less likely to be found in the manual wage-earning positions of the working class.
> (ii) These trends could be attributed more or less entirely to changes in the shape of the class structure – that is, to the growth of the service class and the contraction of the working class; they were, in other

words, the result of changes in objective mobility opportunities, and did not reflect any changes in *relative* mobility rates or changes in the direction of greater equality of opportunity or 'openness'.

(iii) Thus, while upward mobility into the service class from other class origins steadily increased across successive birth cohorts, downward mobility from service-class origins to other class positions steadily decreased; and correspondingly, while the working class became somewhat less stable intergenerationally the stability of the service class was enhanced. (Goldthorpe and Payne, 1986, p. 1–2)

These thoughts proved far less controversial than those related to the closure thesis. What reaction there was may be thought of as 'political'. From the right came the continuing refrain about the concentration on 'relative' mobility and its effect of masking the progressive upgrading of people's working lives. Here I can only join Goldthorpe on his high horse and point out that if such critics had actually read passages such as the above more carefully, then the even-handedness between usage of relative and absolute viewpoints is plain to see.

From the left came the opposite charge that the long march of upward mobility suggested (in part) above could be an over-rosy picture brought about by the timing of the Nuffield inquiry, which stopped in 1972. It thus missed a massive period of slump and depression of the kind which capitalism is prone to generate. What would be the effect of the 'double digit' unemployment of the late 1970s and early 1980s on mobility trends? Whilst the critics pondered on this potential oversight, the Nuffield computers churned out the answers which are summarised here in Table 2.4. These record what Goldthorpe sees as a 'polarisation' of chances. Unemployment, it comes as no surprise, hits hardest at, and generates a considerable amount of 'downward mobility' from, the working class. However, the chances of upward mobility from the working class had *not* fallen since the 1972 inquiry and had, by any measure, continued to improve. The main effect of mass unemployment on mobility is thus to 'raise the stakes' for the working class, in that it renders very little room between falling and flying.

Such a conclusion, together with Goldthorpe's other findings on trends in mobility, has passed into the conventional wisdom of the discipline without much contention, mainly, I suspect, because the generative mechanisms accounting for the 'long waves' of mobility concern economic, industrial and post-industrial transformation. Whilst these, of course, are matters of great controversy, there are simply not too many toes to tread on in terms of alternative theories of the relationship between economic change and social mobility rates. In many ways we have progressed little

Table 2.4   *Class distribution of respondents by class of father, 1983 inquiry, according to old and new versions of the class schema and with the unemployed treated separately*

Father's class	Schema	Respondent's class					
		I & II	*III–V*	*VI & VIII*	$U^{(a)}$	$UL^{(a)}$	*N*
		percentage by row					
I & II	old	63·1	23·2	9·3	4·4	(2·5)	204
	new	60·1	21·2	14·3	4·3	(2·4)	210
III–IV	old	32·7	36·2	22·8	8·2	(5·2)	373
	new	31·9	32·9	26·2	9·0	(6·0)	350
VI & VII	old	20·5	29·5	39·5	10·5	(5·9)	599
	new	22·6	23·1	44·0	10·2	(5·5)	616

Note:
(a)   U = all unemployed at time of inquiry
       UL = unemployed at time of inquiry for more than one year
Source: Goldthorpe and Payne (1986), p. 17.

beyond the half-baked Lipset-Zetterberg thesis in this respect, and this is another of those remarkably 'contentless' theories which names no classes, identifies no explanatory mechanisms and thus only affords arbitrary empirical testing (Pawson, 1989, pp. 160–2; Goldthorpe, 1985). We await the complete publication of the comparative analysis of social mobility in industrial nations (CASMIN) project to see if this situation is remedied but, as of summer 1991, it is appropriate to say that work on trends and international comparisons has continued to be data-driven, responding to its own set of Goldthorpian questions with Goldthorpian evidence.

Conclusion

It is appropriate to end with a thought or two on my own question, about whether mobility research can be said to be successful and progressical. Such a discussion can be usefully combined with the overall aims of this volume in trying to obtain a sense of the direction(s) in which the discipline as a whole is travelling. In particular, I will pick up the contrast drawn in Liz Stanley and David Morgan's introduction about the opposing goals of Cartesian, variable-fixated foundationalism versus the constructivist, discourse-oriented, sociology-as-the-sociology-of-knowledge approach.

Let me first attempt a down-to-earth answer about the success of the mobility studies unburdened by the discourse-wise refrain about 'ah but what precisely does success mean'. There is no need to be mealy-mouthed about this issue at all. The work reported on here, together with the monographs which followed in its wake, constitute one of the finest achievements of British sociology. The entire framework for analysis, from the basic mobility matrix, to the meticulous dissections of absolute and relative rates, to the microscopic interpretation of period and cohort effects, has been borrowed the research world over. On another plane, the findings about the continuing expansion of upward mobility, if not equal opportunity, have contributed to debate in the public domain in a way which is not typical of some of the more esoteric concerns of sociology in the period under review in this book.

I am inclined to observe that such an assessment speaks for itself, but since we all know a thing or two about the theory-ladenness of observations these days, I will not reach for the citation counts as 'proof', but confront instead the rival, sociology-of-knowledge view of why this has all come to pass. This would explain the pre-eminence of the Goldthorpian tradition and the stranglehold of the mobility matrix as *the* way of portraying movement between social classes as all a matter of, shall we say, academic power play. Arguably there are other potential approaches to the 'same topic' which have been relatively overlooked on the pages of *Sociology* and perhaps in the discipline as a whole. The editors pass a remark along these lines in the introductory chapter. They are thinking of workplace ethnographies, life histories, case studies and historical investigations, which tell the tale of experience and change in work and family locations (e.g. Cavendish, 1990; Westwood, 1984; Davidoff and Hall, 1987).

So have we been over-impressed by all this stuff from the chaps at Oxford? There is little doubt that editors and publishers will have jumped to include the Nuffield Studies in their listings. Beyond that, however, I am little persuaded by contextual explanations of the might of ideas. There is always a chicken and egg aspect to such a project in that eminence of location can indeed explain the priority given to certain ideas, but then again, the power of certain ideas can also explain their rise to institutional prominence. In general, given the staggering rate of change of intellectual fashion in sociology, I am not persuaded that thought control is our most pressing problem. Indeed I perceive quite the reverse difficulty, in that the flourishing of so many ideas has led to the situation in which there is a failure to understand the appropriate nature of the relationships between the babel of discourses in sociology.

The sociology of knowledge forever falls over its feet in confusing the 'power to influence' and 'the power to explain' of any particular set of ideas. In the last analysis we must be prepared to give credit for sociological work at the level of ideas alone. A minimal step in this regard, but one which would amount to a huge leap away from the present internecine squabbles, would be to appreciate the limited scope that any sociological explanation carries. Goldthorpe's mobility research, all research for that matter, is limited in what it says in terms of place, time, context, substance etc. Accordingly there is very little to be gained from a criticism which says, 'something has been left out', 'here's another viewpoint' and so on. Hence, my reaction to the point that there are rival ways of studying what might loosely be called 'social mobility', by looking at case studies, autobiography, historical approaches and so forth, is basically to say – so what? A study of the first-hand experience of the degradations of assembly-line work is unlikely to be much improved if it were informed by knowledge of cross-class, cross-cohort disparity ratios. Why should we begin to assume the reverse is true?

I have much the same reaction to the editorial call to the providers of each chapter to pay heed to the attention or lack of attention paid to 'race' and racism within each topic area. Arguably we are all structurationists now and we understand that actions are both the *outcome* of the totality of social processes which precede them as well as the *medium* which constrains future possibilities. A mobility matrix, in fact, captures such an idea rather better than many static, stock-in-trade sociological concepts. As pointed out earlier, it is quite literally true that the movement from one social class to another in these matrices is influenced by every social process under the sun. The chances of moving from class X to class Y are undoubtedly different for blacks and for whites. Racism undoubtedly lurks in the rows and columns of mobility tables.

Mobility rates are also influenced by gender, by region, by religion, by age, by culture and so on, and as well, perhaps, by processes captured by phrases which do not trip so easily from the sociological tongue like – by ability, by genetic background, by intelligence etc. If you think of the intricate tale of how *you* got where you are today and picture the moblity matrix as the sum total of all such adventures and misadventures, then you get a feel of the limitless scope of what *could* be included in 'mobility analysis'. Whilst I utter some deep ontological truth here, I am clearly talking nonsense in terms of a real research agenda. There has to be a division of labour; there has to be a decision to focus in on some set of mobility processes and I take it to be Goldthorpe's privilege to home in on middle-range theories about the interface between class formation and mobility. If researchers are forever looking over their shoulders in fear of not having given due weight to, say, 'race' in their particular inquiries, then just as reasonably they can be called to account for ignoring the impact of any other potentially ubiquitous social force.

It puzzles me greatly that, in studying a world in which we acknowledge that everything influences everything else, sociological debate is far more likely to descend to the matter of the correctness of standpoints and perspectives thann to promote methods to assess the actual products of inquiry. In terms of a vision of how the discipline might change in the next twenty-five years, I can do no better than to quote Dorothy Smith's suggestion that there is an obvious converse to the sociology of knowledge approach: 'If it is a power play to claim the veracity of one version . . . is it not also essential to the most modest possibilities of knowing how things work that a social scientific account can be called into question? And therefore that another version can be on some grounds preferred? (Smith, 1987, p. 122). This latter objective resonates with what the editors would regard as foundationalist aims. My hope (quite possibly, against hope) is that the next twenty-five volumes of *Sociology* will see the rise of studies which exemplify Smith's objective of adjudicating between rival explanations. There are, of course, a range of scientific realist (and thus non-positivist) strategies which have been developed to such ends. A penultimate paragraph is no place to lay out a manifesto on how this might be achieved, though it is appropriate perhaps to mention a previous effort of my own in this regard in *Sociology* (Pawson, 1990). The key point is that middle-range theories *can* be evaluated empirically against each other to the extent that they agree on some common ideas and concepts which then can act as mutual vantage points against which disagreements can be tested.

Turning my gaze backwards again, we began to see the start of such a research strategy in Penn's debate with Goldthorpe, which got down to the real details of how the mechanisms of class action facilitated or prevented mobility. That particular debate brought us to the brink of making real progress since there was some common theoretical ground between combatants which enabled their disagreements to be cast in empirical terms. In general, however, there has been little progress at this level in terms of what one might call the fine tuning of class mobility theories. Goldthorpe has perhaps been responsible for stifling some of this invaluable debate with hard words on the hard practicalities of research. To say this, however, is to blame the messenger for lack of other messages. The real spur to debate and progress would involve the production of rival *theories* of mobility, and by this I mean specific propositions explaining the level of movement from well-circumscribed origin classes to well-circumscribed destination classes. Goldthorpe's thinking in this respect has been summarised in a tightly packed six pages of propositions in *Social Mobility and Class Structure in Modern Britain* (pp. 98–104). It remains a bit of a mystery why the rest of us have not been able to add a page or two of alternatives.

References

Blau, P. and Duncan, O. D. (1967), *The American Occupational Structure*, New York, Wiley.

Cavendish, R. (1990), *Women on the Line*, London, Routledge.

Clark, J. *et al.* (1990), *John H Goldthorpe: Consensus and Controversy*, London, Falmer Press.

Crompton, R. (1980), 'Class mobility in modern Britain', *Sociology*, 14, pp. 117–19.

Davidoff, L. and Hall, C. (1987), *Family Fortunes, 1780–1850*, London, Hutchinson.

Goldthorpe, J. H. (1980), 'Reply to Crompton', *Sociology*, 14, pp. 121–3.

Goldthorpe, J. H. (1981), 'The class schema of *Social Mobility and Class Structure in Modern Britain*: A reply to Penn', *Sociology*, 15, pp. 272–80.

Goldthorpe, J. H. (1985), 'On economic development and social mobility', *British Journal of Sociology*, 36, pp. 549–73.

Goldthorpe, J. H. (1990), 'A response' in Clark *et al.*

Goldthorpe, J. H., Llewelyn, C. and Payne, C. (1980), *Social Mobility and Class Structure in Modern Britain*, Oxford, Clarendon.

Goldthorpe, J. H. and Llewelyn, C. (1977), 'Class mobility in modern Britain: Three theses examined', *Sociology*, 11, pp. 257–87.

Goldthorpe, J. H., Llewelyn, C. and Payne, C. (1978), 'Trends in class mobility', *Sociology*, 12, pp. 441–68.

Goldthorpe, J. H. and Payne, C. (1986), 'Trends in intergenerational class mobility in England and Wales, 1972–83', *Sociology*, 20, pp. 1–24.

Heath, A. (1981), *Social Mobility*, London, Fontana.

Marshall, G. (1990), *In Praise of Sociology*, London, Unwin Hyman.

Marshall, G., Rose, O., Newby, H., Rogler, C., (1988), *Social Class in Modern Britain*, London, Hutchinson.

Pawson, R. (1989), *A Measure for Measures: A Manifesto for Empirical Sociology*, London, Routledge.

Pawson, R. (1990), 'Half truths about bias', *Sociology*, 24, pp. 229–40.

Payne, G. (1980), 'Social mobility', *British Journal of Sociology*, 40, pp. 000.

Payne, G. and Abbott, P. (eds), (1990), *The Social Mobility of Women*, London, Falmer Press.

Penn, R. (1981), 'The Nuffield class categorization', *Sociology*, 15, pp. 265–7.

Poulantzas, N. (1974), *Les Classes Sociales Dans Le Capitalisme Aujourd'hui*, Paris, Seuil.

Saunders, P. (1989), 'Left Write', *Network*, 44.

Smith, D. (1987), *The Everyday World As Problematic*, Milton Keynes, Open University Press.

Westergaard, J. (1990), 'Social mobility in Britain', in Clark *et al.*

Westwood, S. (1984), *All Day and Every Day*, London, Pluto.

Further reading

Clark, J., Modgil, C. and Modgil, S. (1990), *John Goldthorpe*, London, Falmer Press.

Erikson, R. and Goldthorpe, J. (1992), *The Constant Flux: A Study of Class Mobility in Industrial Societies*, Oxford, Clarendon Press.

Payne, G. (1992), 'Competing views of contemporary social mobility and social divisions', in Burrows, R. and Marsh, C., *Consumption and Class*, London, Macmillan.

The first of these, like this volume, is a stock-taking exercise, so the reader will find more details on mobility as well as further observations on how 'friendly-hostile cooperation' makes for good sociology! The second volume is the long-awaited produce of the CASMIN project. The third is the latest piece from the 'other voice' of British social mobility study, Geoff Payne, in which, amongst other things, he engages in a 'hostile-friendly' examination of a 'genetic' model of mobility.

For a contrasting view, which will please those seeking to 'breach the hegemony of a method', consult:

Bertaux, D. (1991), 'From methodological monopoly to pluralism in the sociology of social mobility' in Dex, S., *Life and Work History Analyses*, London, Routledge.

The women and class debate

The aim of this chapter is not to address the entire body of work on class which has been published in the journal over the last quarter of a century, nor even to discuss all of those articles which refer to women and class or women and social mobility, but rather to address some aspects of a sub-set of that literature, a debate which took place on women and class between 1983 and 1988. What follows does not comprise a full summary of this debate. Those wishing to familiarise themselves with this literature can see the complete account in the relatively compact, and surprisingly readable, articles from *Sociology* over the relevant period in the bibliography below. In this discussion, I simply pick up some aspects of this debate and ask what, as sociologists, we might make of its content and progress.

The precursor to the debate was perhaps a review article in *Sociology* (Newman, 1980) covering a number of books on class including *Social Mobility and Class Structure In Modern Britain* (Goldthorpe in collaboration with Llewellyn and Payne, 1980). Although in general favourable to John Goldthorpe's work, Otto Newman wrote: 'Most remarkable . . . is the fact of the missing millions. Both texts [the review also covered Halsey's (1978) work] are exclusively male-centred, and accord to females, if at all, only a very subsidiary role. Goldthorpe gives no grounds for this oversight. . . . To mislay the female majority once may be pardonable, but to do so through-out . . .' (Newman, 1980:633). This, and a number of reviews elsewhere making similar points, may well have provided the impetus for the 1983 article by Goldthorpe which opened the debate on women and class in *Sociology* by defending what had become known as the 'conventional' view.

CRITIQUES which have alleged 'intellectual sexism' in stratification theory and research appear generally to be directed against a

'conventional' view which maintains the following: (i) it is the family rather than the individual which forms the basic unit of social stratification; (ii) particular families are articulated with the system of stratification essentially via the position of their male 'heads' – which, in modern societies, can be most adequately indexed by reference to their occupational category or grade. This view is then typically attacked on two rather different levels. First, it is argued that such a view entails a disregard of certain increasingly important features of contemporary social reality: most obviously, the proportion of families which do not have a male 'head'; and the proportion of even 'normal' families in which the wife as well as husband is found in gainful employment – and perhaps in a different occupational category or grade to that of her husband. Secondly, though, and more fundamentally, it is held that the conventional view effectively pre-cludes examination of what should be recognized as one major feature of the stratification system as a whole; that is, sexual stratification, which, of course, cuts directly through the conjugal family. It follows, then, that not only are women rendered largely 'invisible' within the study of stratification, but furthermore that the existence of sexual inequalities becomes more or less disregarded. (Goldthorpe, 1983:465)

By the time this article appeared, there had already been a very consider-able body of work, largely although not exclusively from feminist sociologists, in Britain, Europe and the United States (Watson and Barth, 1964; Acker, 1973, 1980; Haug, 1973; Oakley, 1974; Garnsey, 1978; Roberts, 1979; Land, 1980; Llewellyn, 1981; Delphy, 1981) criticising both the theoretical and the empirical basis of work on stratification which appeared so much at odds with the world in which most of us live. A view of the world from which social class issues could be adequately addressed through the male 'head of household' may not have appeared quite so odd to the class theorists of Oxford and Cambridge. They could barely bring themselves to cite each others' work (Delamont, 1989), let alone address the problems raised for the conventional view by the growing number of households with no male 'head'. Out of the frame altogether was a recogni-tion that a male 'head of household' is itself a social and cultural construct. Mirza's (1985) work, investigating the ways in which gender and 'race' affect educational outcomes for young black women, draws attention to the inappropriateness of classifying West Indian children by the father's occu-pation in families which are headed by females. As Mirza points out, this convention is based on an ethnocentric assumption concerning the nature of family structure and the distribution of resources with the family.

As well as a general disinclination by some of the class theorists to cite

one another's work so well described by Sara Delamont, we might note an
interesting omission from Goldthorpe's (1983) references to work on
women and class. Catriona Llewellyn, who worked with Goldthorpe on the
Oxford mobility study (Goldthorpe and Llewellyn, 1977a, 1977b;
Goldthorpe, Payne and Llewellyn, 1978; Goldthorpe in collaboration with
Llewellyn and Payne, 1980) had in 1975 undertaken with Sara Graham a
pilot project with the aim of investigating the occupational experience of
both men and women in one occupational setting. This work, by no means
irrelevant to this debate, was reported in 1981 in an edited collection
(Llewellyn, 1981). Although Goldthorpe refers to the important work of a
French sociologist published in the same collection (Delphy, 1981), he
does not refer to his colleague closer to home. Citation moves in mysterious
ways.

While Goldthorpe's engagement with the issue of women and class came
relatively late in the day, such is his stature within British sociology that, as
Delamont points out: '. . . the emergence of Goldthorpe into public debate
on the topic of women and the class structure *in itself* gives greater credence
to the criticisms of stratification theory as sexist . . .' (Delamont, 1989:335)

Given the gentlemanly terms on which the debate on, for instance,
power had been conducted in the pages of *Sociology*, Goldthorpe's entry
into the debate on women and class was distinctly hawkish. Having introduced some of the criticisms of conventional studies of class, he writes:

> Taken at face value, such critiques may be thought cogent. However,
> they appear somewhat less impressive once more attention is given to
> their alleged target. For, on closer examination of the matter, it
> becomes clear that the conventional view which they seek to oppose
> occurs in more than one version. While it is true that most
> stratification theorists *have* treated the family as the unit of
> stratification and have seen the position of its members as being
> crucially dependent on the location of the family head within the
> occupational division of labour, what needs also to be recognized is
> that this view has been arrived at through different and, in the two
> most important instances, sharply contrasting theoretical routes.
> (Goldthorpe, 1983: 465–6)

It is unclear why the fact that the conventional view appears in more than
one version, and that this view has been arrived at through different, or
even contrasting, theoretical routes, should render the critique less
impressive. As sociologists, we might expect conventional views to appear
in more than one version. We might be surprised if different theoretical
routes were not sometimes followed to reach similar destinations.

Goldthorpe devotes the next part of his article to an examination of some of the empirical data on women in the workforce, concluding:

> Changes in the extent and nature of the employment of married women over recent decades are far less damaging to the idea of the family as the basic unit of class stratification than it has of late become fashionable to suppose. While the proportion of married women who have at some time or other been engaged in paid employment has substantially increased, the adoption of a work-life perspective fully reveals the intermittent and limited nature of this employment – even discounting the considerable extent to which it is undertaken on less than a full-time basis. There can be little doubt that within the conjugal family it is still overwhelmingly the husband who has the major commitment to labour market participation, and there are, furthermore, various indications that the pattern of employment of married women is itself conditioned by their husband's class position, or class mobility, as achieved in the course of working life. Finally, evidence has been brought forward to suggest that differences in the type of employment engaged in by husbands and their wives are far less than would appear from the official statistics that have been widely cited, at all events if attention is focussed on the kinds of market and work relations that are involved. And 'cross-class' families may thus in turn be regarded far more as artefacts of an inappropriate mode of categorization than as a quantitively significant feature of present-day society. (Golthorpe, 1983:481–2)

Finally:

> For those who believe that conventional ideas on the articulation of the conjugal family with the system of social stratification are now outmoded by the frequency with which married women are found in paid employment, the general direction of the conceptual and methodological shift that is needed in response to this change would appear clear enough. Instead of the position of the family as a unit being seen to follow from the location within the occupational division of labour of its (usually male) 'head', it should rather be understood as being determined in some more complex way in which the work-force participation of wives may appropriately figure.
>
> In attempting to establish the case that joint classifications are necessary and valid, their proponents have typically presented evidence to show that the employment situation of married women 'makes a difference': that is, that when a joint classification is utilized, more of the variance in some set of attributes of the conjugal family (or of its individual members) can be accounted for than if the position of the family were to be indexed by the nature of the husband's employment alone. Such exercises may be open to criticism on technical grounds, in particular for containing biases in

favour of the effect that they wish to demonstrate. Thus, for example, the analyses offered by Britten and Heath may be biased in this way through their reliance on inadequate categorizations of husbands' occupations as well as of wives', and again because they make no attempt to check on the extent to which the 'differences' produced by the inclusion of wife's employment status may be merely spurious ones. However, a more basic issue that may be raised is that of why it is supposed that this approach to the validation of joint classifications is appropriate at all. The answer that would be given, it appears, would be on the lines that what is being sought is an indicator of the 'social background' of families which can then be applied in an attempt 'to map the basic structure of socio-cultural differences' within the population at large; thus, the degree to which a classification can account for – or at least display – variance in family members' social characteristics and life-styles must be the key criterion in its evaluation. But, if this *is* the position taken up, two further things may be said.

On the one hand, it may be remarked if it really is an indicator of 'social background' that is wanted, it is unclear why a specifically *class* schema, even if a 'joint' one, should be proposed. It would seem far better to seek to construct some measure of the general 'socio-economic status' of families, in which could be represented not only husbands' and wives' occupations and employment status, but further such other relevant factors as their levels of education and qualifications, family income, housing type etc. Judged by the criterion of socio-cultural variance explained, one could safely predict that such a measure would give a superior performance to that of any kind of class categorization. On the other hand, though, it must also be observed that to account as fully as possible for the range of socio-cultural variation existing in the population at large is *not* in fact the objective of class analysis as this would be understood by writers such as those earlier referred to in this paper. As was noted, the first empirical concern of class analysis must be that of establishing how far classes have formed as relatively stable collectivities through their continuity with which individuals and families have been associated with particular class positions over time. It is then only to the extent that classes prove to be in this way indentifiable that the further question can be raised of how far they are also differentiated in socio-cultural terms. By pursuing this question, it may be found meaningful to speak of the differences existing between, say, working-class life-styles and those of the petty bourgeoisie, or of other classes; but this would still of course be only in terms of central tendencies. It has never been supposed by class analysts that the variable of class membership itself – or even if supplemented by that of class mobility – can provide the basis for any complete mapping of socio-cultural patterns. Indeed, one of their preoccupations has been with the way in which the effects of class in this respect are cut across both by the effects of stratification within classes as, for example, by income, and by those of other affiliations – religious, ethnic, regional etc. The grounds on which some confusion of purpose may be alleged can thus be summed up as follows: joint classifications of the kind proposed are unlikely to perform as well as other measures of 'social background' the task that is apparently intended for them by their proponents, but this is not in any event a task towards which class analysis is primarily oriented. (Goldthorpe, 1983:482–3)

The basis of this first contribution is well described by Michelle Stanworth (1984), responding to Goldthorpe two issues subsequently:

First, by elaborating the positions of class analysis and of structural functionalism on the relation between the stratification system and the family, Goldthorpe seeks to make clear that the treatment of women in class analysis is not based upon assertions about the inevitability of sexual inequality. Second, his discussion of wives' employment histories challenges the claim that there are substantial numbers of contemporary marriages in which the wife's class position is superior to that of her husband, and, thus, the claim that women's class position must be taken into account. (Stanworth, 1984:159)

Stanworth's response focusses on Goldthorpe's elaboration and defence of the grounds for the common practice of making general claims about class from research focused mainly or exclusively on men. This defence ignores the way gender is implicated in the production and reproduction of the class system. She suggests that his account closes off some of the most interesting questions about class analysis; but even within the terms of reference established by Goldthorpe, his views about the incorporation of women are open to doubt (Stanworth, 1984:159):

The difficulty emerges with Goldthorpe's attempt to move from empirical observations about women's employment experience to the practice of disregarding it altogether. That wives' employment experience is often inferior to that of their husbands might constitute an argument for choosing husbands over wives only *if* it could be shown that a single 'representative' had to be found for the 'unitary family'. It does not in itself indicate that the family must be treated as a unit, nor does it establish that married women's position in the class structure can be adequately merged with that of their husbands. Throughout Goldthorpe's article, the issue of whether the family is a unit, and the relation of that issue to women's employment, is inadequately, even circularly, argued: on the one hand, it is only because the unitary family must have a single representative that women's limited employment is deemed irrelevant; on the other, it is only to the extent that the employment of family members other than the head is irrelevant that the family can be deemed a unit. In sum, in Goldthorpe's paper, an unargued insistence on the unitary nature of the family is used to transform an 'inferior' work-force history into one that is, for purposes of class analysis, discounted.

Moreover, Goldthorpe's argument implies that to take account of the direct class positions of employed married women would add nothing to our understanding of class formation, class inequality and class action. This flies in the face of accumulated information about the ways in which married women's and men's class 'fates' are mediated through the family.

The second claim in Goldthorpe's conclusion is that wives' employment is 'conditioned' by its class context, i.e. that the contours of married women's employment can be largely explained by the class position of their husbands. This claim is buttressed by evidence from the 1974 inquiry to the effect that the timing of wives' withdrawal from, and re-entry to, the labour force varies between subsamples where husbands have differing class mobility experience. Goldthorpe interprets this as support for his view that wives, unlike husbands, do not have a direct relation to class structure: it is husbands' jobs which determine wives' employment profiles.

But the data allow for another, equally compelling interpretation which Goldthorpe fails to consider. Since the occupational class of wives also varies between these subsamples, it may be the wives' own class location that determines women's employment decisions. For example, Goldthorpe proposes that the early withdrawal from employment of the wives of working-class men reflects stable sub-cultures, based on husbands' class, which generate a high number of early pregnancies; one could as easily suggest that the (largely working-class) occupations held by the women themselves provide little incentive to postpone withdrawal from employment. Or again, Goldthorpe argues that the privileged economic position of service-class men enables them to facilitate their wives' early return to the labour force; given that individual mothers shoulder the major financial and organizational burden of providing 'substitute' domestic and childcare services when they are employed, it is more likely that the relatively well-paid and flexible jobs of many wives of service-class men are the most important factor enabling an early return to employment (Moss 1980). Thus, on Goldthorpe's own evidence, it is reasonable to suppose that the 'class context' which shapes women's work-force involvement reflects to a far greater extent than Goldthorpe acknowledges the direct class location of the women themselves.

Goldthorpe's argument that women's employment histories are unique in that they are 'conditioned' is further called into question by his own evidence. He observes that the wives who remain in employment for the longest period after marriage are those whose husbands experience class mobility; extended employment is most marked for women whose husbands achieved upward mobility in the course of their careers. One interpretation of this, which Goldthorpe surprisingly seems to endorse, is that in some way wives' employment assisted or 'conditioned' men's advancement – by enabling them to take a job with low pay but good prospects, perhaps or by helping to finance relocation or the setting up of independent practice. On Goldthorpe's own account, then, 'conditioning of employment experience' can occur from wife to husband as well as from husband to wife. 'Conditioning' is in no way unique to wives' employment experience, and can not justify denying women's direct relation to the class structure.

Nor does the claim that wives' employment represents 'part of a family plan ... aimed at social advancement or social survival' (Goldthorpe 1983: 479) rescue Goldthorpe's argument; one has only to refer to the sociological literature on work and on intra-generational mobility to find overwhelming evidence of men who shape their employment decisions and career aspirations to current and future family needs (e.g. Benyon 1973; Goldthorpe *et al.* 1968; Goldthorpe 1980: 240). Participation in a 'joint economic strategy' does not mark a qualitiative distinction between married men and employed married women; still less does it justify the practice of assigning women to the class position of their husbands. Indeed, Goldthorpe's conventional view has the effect of obscuring the more crucial distinction between the employment experience of husbands and wives: that, far from creating for spouses an identical class position, such 'family projects' tend to have the effect of enhancing men's direct class position, while more often diminishing women's. (Stanworth, 1984: 161–163)

Finally she suggests:

If Goldthorpe took fully seriously his own account of the conventional position – if he selected heads of families for study according to their commitment to the labour force, rather than simply studying males – the methodological difficulties would be every bit as awkward as those he attributes to cross-class analysis. The most substantial group of women in his sample would presumably be those whose 'headship' came about through the dissolution of marriages due to widowhood, separation or divorce. It is sobering to consider the problems thrown up for Goldthorpe's work by the single fact that a third of current marriages will end in divorce. First, the rate of mobility of family units would be considerably increased by substantial movement in and out of the working class as women assumed an independent class position on divorce, and subsequently 'relinquished' that position through re-marriage. Second, the structure of positions – that is, the very starting-point of Goldthorpe's analysis – would itself alter constantly. On re-marriage, divorced women in employment would generally become 'non-heads', and their positions in the occupational division of labour would suddenly cease to be potential bases of social classes. In effect, the conceptual status of a position would change with the marital circumstances of its occupant. Third, families with heads in routine non-manual occupations would be assigned different class locations according to the sex of the head. This is of course just one dimension of the more wide-ranging problem of incorporating women in occupational classifications designed, as Goldthorpe admits, to accommodate male occupational experience. These difficulties imply that class analysis cannot escape a confrontation with the methodological issues raised by the consideration of women's direct class positions: it is not enough simply to re-affirm the conventional view. (Stanworth, 1984:165)

She concludes:

In short, women's restricted employment opportunities – their subordinate class positions – are an expression of the dominance of men over women through processes of class formation and class action, and not simply, as Goldthrope would have it, of the familial dominance of husbands over wives. Goldthorpe's account ignores the way gender is implicated in the production and reproduction of the class system, and the extent to which the subordinate class positions of women, married or otherwise, are shaped by the dynamics of class itself. (Stanworth, 1984:167)

Two issues later there was a bumper crop of articles within, or alongside, the debate. Robert Erikson's (1984) contribution, neatly sidestepping the issue of whether the family is the appropriate unit of stratification, adopts a refreshingly pragmatic approach. He tackles head-on the combined issues of the labour force participation of women and social classification, suggesting a way of ascribing a class position to families, and therefore family members. Using the work positions of both spouses and based on an order of dominance, occupations high in the order are presumed to influence the market situation of the family more than occupations of lower levels. His key observation that 'the two basic questions in the study of social structure are how production is organised and how the results of production are distributed' (p. 512) provides a succinct summary of why the issue of women and social class is important. This is followed almost immediately by the suggestion that: 'Sex seems irrelevant to the classification of work positions. Each individual incumbent of an occupation is classified on the basis of his occupation. This of course does not imply that the distribution of work positions will be independent of sex.' What is apparently absent here is an understanding that the classification of work positions, as well as their distribution, is not in fact independent of sex (for a discussion of what people are doing when they grade women's work, see Roberts and Barker, 1989).

Anthony Heath and Nicky Britten, writing in the same issue, present further data to confirm and extend their (1983) findings, which had been criticised by Goldthorpe in his 1984 article. Opening the batting with appropriate courtesy, they write: 'John Goldthorpe's paper raises, and eloquently defends, some important issues in class theory'. Like Erikson, they concentrate on the empirical, suggesting that: . . . more progress is likely to be made if we focus clearly on the relation between theory and evidence' (p. 475). They look at career paths for women across three distinct labour markets, demonstrating very different conditions of employment for women. They conclude:

> We have shown that there are real differences in the market and work situations of women in office and sales jobs, such that both the Registrar General's class schema and the Goldthorpe classes need to be revised for use with women's occupations. We have also demonstrated that our classification holds good over time: that is, our classification is not an artefact of cross-sectional analysis as there is little movement between categories over the course of women's working lives . . .
>
> Thus the intermittent character of women's jobs is not a serious problem for class analysis as Goldthorpe suggests. Given the attachment of women to particular occupational profiles, it is therefore not surprising that women's work should have explanatory power for class and family behaviour over and above that attributable to their husbands' class positions. Women's jobs do make a difference. (Heath and Britten, 1984:489)

In the same issue, Goldthorpe replies to the replies, beginning by saying how congenial he finds it to see his critics at odds amongst themselves. Aggrieved by his perception that the protagonists had 'failed to engage with the central thrust of my original argument' (p. 491), he helpfully summarises his original points:

(i) Class analysis aims first to establish how far classes have formed as relatively stable collectivities.

(ii) To the extent that classes are in this way identifiable, the question then arises of the degree of socio-cultural differentiation of these collectivities – together with that of how such differentiation is affected by mobility between classes – and further of the degree to which classes form the basis of socio-political mobilization and conflict.

(iii) From the standpoint of class analysis, how far variation in any particular aspect of social behaviour or relationships, within the population at large, can actually be accounted for in terms of class membership is entirely a matter for investigation. As I wrote (Goldthorpe, 1983: 483): 'It has never been supposed by class analysts that the variable of class membership itself – or even if supplemented by that of class mobility – can provide the basis for any complete mapping of socio-cultural patterns. Indeed, one of their preoccupations has been with the way in which the effects of class in this respect are cut across both by the effects of stratification within classes as, for example, by income, and by those of other affiliations – religious, ethnic, regional etc.' (Goldthorpe, 1984: 491)

He vigorously responds to the critics of the conventional view, disagreeing sharply with Stanworth, to some extent with Britten and Heath, but demonstrating a degree of sympathy with Erikson, with whom he emerges as a joint author later in the debate. He writes:

> I remain an entirely unrepentant supporter of the conventional view of the class position of the conjugal family, as I earlier construed it. I would, however, in conclusion want to make it clear that I would regard both the 'dominance' and the 'worktime' methods of family class assignment that are suggested by Erikson as being among the possible ways in which this view can be operationalized for research purposes. Both of these methods reflect what is essential to the conventional view: namely, that the class position of the conjugal family should be seen as unitary and as determined by the position of that family member who has, in some sense, the highest level of labour-market participation. I would myself prefer the sense that is captured by the 'worktime' approach, which Erikson also regards as theoretically if not practically the best choice. (Goldthorpe, 1984;497)

That Goldthorpe was riled by the arguments he was opposing may be indicated by the fact that his tone, hardly collegial at the start of the debate, becomes frankly bad-tempered as time goes on. The irritation evident in 'Does one sociologist really have to point out to another . . .?' (1984:499, n.2) is matched by his assertion that: 'Stanworth's 're-analysis' is largely a waste of time and space' (1984:493). Whether the referees of Stanworth's article had in fact let the editors down by letting through a piece which was 'largely a waste of time and space' is a matter for readers of the debate to judge. I do not believe that they did (and I was not one of the referees). But in my view there is no doubt that the editors did a disservice to the scholarly community by allowing the debate to be conducted in these terms.

A different kind of approach was introduced in Angela Dale, Nigel Gilbert and Sara Arber's (1985) contribution. They argue that while all individuals in paid employment may be allocated a class position on the basis of their relationship to the labour market, this represents only one dimension of class, and that a second dimension, relating to consumption, should also be considered. They go some way towards constructing guidelines for an occupational classification based on relationships to the labour market and appropriate to women.

Also essentially practical in orientation is John Goldthorpe and Clive Payne's (1986) discussion of the class mobility of women, analysing British data following the 'conventional', 'individual' and 'dominance' approaches to the problem of determining women's class location. The attractions of the conventional approach are reiterated, together with a new emphasis on mobility through marriage:

> Exponents of the conventional approach would argue that, to date at least, studies of class mobility that concentrate on men are unlikely to have produced any very misleading conclusions. Despite the general tendency in modern societies for the participation of married women in the labour market to increase, their employment still tends to be more intermittent than that of men, is less often full-time, and is only rarely such as to place them in what could be regarded as dominant class positions relative to those held by their husbands. Thus, it can be maintained, whatever the future may hold, so far as the experience captured in present-day studies is concerned 'it has been through the role of their male members within the social division of labour that families have been crucially articulated with the class structure and their class "fates" crucially determined. Or conversely, one could say, the way in which women have been located in the class structure has reflected their general situation of dependence.' (Goldthorpe, Llewellyn and Payne, 1980:288).
>
> From this standpoint, there is one deficiency of class mobility research that is restricted to men that must clearly be acknowledged: namely, the omission of those cases where women live unattached or are themselves family 'heads' as defined above. But, it can then be maintained, this problem is a sufficiently minor one not to create any serious distortion in the general pattern of results obtained. How-

ever, there is another and a larger objection to the neglect of women that can in fact be made without departing from the conventional approach, and indeed by simply following through its logic. If women do mostly derive their class positions from those of the male heads of the families to which they belong, then a full account of class mobility would seem to require that attention be paid to the mobility that occurs as a result of women marrying: that is to say, as a result of their moving from their family of origin (or perhaps from an unattached state) to enter into a conjugal family. Moreover, the importance of considering such 'marital' mobility is underlined by the suggestions that are rather frequently encountered in sociological – and also in various kinds of lay – literature to the effect that in modern society marriage does afford particularly wide opportunities for mobility. (Goldthorpe and Payne, 1986:535)

Here Goldthorpe and Payne criticise their critics for not having made more effort to work on data to support the non-conventional view and throw out a challenge:

. . . those who have argued for the individual approach have thus far failed to meet the responsibility which must fall on them to bring forward systematic evidence in support of the assumption that married women's own employment *can* be reliably taken as a major determinant of their class identity – or, say, of their participation in class-linked life-styles, patterns of association or modes of collective action. (Goldthorpe and Payne, 1986:550)

Two articles published in *Sociology* the following year did just that. Pamela Abbott's (1987) paper looked at the social class and class images of 342 working married women drawn from a national survey conducted between 1981 and 1984. She found no evidence to sustain the view that the occupation of the 'head of household' is the best single indicator of a woman's social imagery. She concludes:

We can no longer naively assume that a woman's class position is given by that of her (male) head of household. As previous research has indicated, it is by identifying individuals' class images that we can begin to explain how the objective features of the class structure are sustained. Ideas are of course influenced by the material environment, but at the same time they can help to shape, sustain and change that environment. Consequently, by situating an individual's orientation towards action in the context of his or her social imagery we can help to explain how systems of inequality are both sustained and changed. Women are doubly constrained by gender and by class relations; it seems likely, therefore, that their social images will be different from those of men . . .

Research is needed that attempts to provide an understanding of women's experiences in the private and public spheres, and how in making sense of these a woman's class orientation is formed and translated into action. We need to explore how women actually perceive the social world and their position in it. However, women's perceptions must not be analysed as a special case or a form of deviation from some underlying male standard; they must be seen as having a validity of their own. What is required is descriptive, exploratory and analytical work on women's social imagery that enables us to see the world through the female prism; only then will it be possible to incorporate women into social class analysis. (Abbott, 1987;101–2)

Two isues later, Håkon Leiulfsrud and Alison Woodward brought forward some evidence from their own study. The title they gave their contribution, 'Women at class crossroads: repudiating conventional theories of family class', perhaps offered an unwise hostage to fortune. The upholders of the conventional view responded by suggesting that in Leiulfsrud and Woodward's work '[a] large gap . . . exists between these authors' ambitions and their achievements . . .' (Erikson and Goldthorpe, 1988:545). Leiulfsrud and Woodward contended that, contrary to the arguments of both Goldthorpe (1983,1984) and Erikson (1984),

female workers are directly influenced by the class structure in many matters, rather than receiving indirect messages mediated by their husband's position. Women's participation in the labour market has implications for all families, whether class homogeneous or class heterogeneous. Further, families with partners in different class positions, cross-class families, are not merely 'an artefact of an appropriate mode of categorisation', but *a significant element within the class structure'*. (Leiulfsrud and Woodward, 1987:394)

Their study of what happens in practice in a number of situations in 'cross-class' families indicates an erosion of dominant class and gender roles in certain family constellations. They make the point that 'Life would be simpler if one could classify all families as units based on the major breadwinner's class position, but the most elegant solution is not necessarily the correct one' (p.408).

In responding, Goldthorpe and Erikson joined forces. They correctly suggest that the nub of the women and class debate is one of research practice:

Should the class position of married women be 'derived' from that of their husbands or the position of both partners be given by that of whichever is 'dominant' in the labour market (the conventional or what LW call the 'revitalised' conventional approach); or should the positions of husbands and wives be individually determined by their own – past or present – employment; or should the class position of marriage partners be in some way determined jointly? From this standpoint, then, the key questions that arise are essentially empirical ones concerning which approach can, on the one hand, most fully reveal class effects while, on the other, not generating spurious or artefactual effects – e.g. regarding class mobility – or confounding class effects with those of other factors – e.g. household composition or life-cycle effects. (Erikson and Goldthorpe, 1988:545)

Leiulfsrud and Woodward are accused of not having taken up these questions in any serious way; their qualitative ('one could as well say "impressionistic" ', p.546) findings are ridiculed.

To have provoked such an unkind note from two of Western Europe's most senior sociologists cannot have been a pleasant experience. Leiulfrsud and Woodward's spirited response in the same issue reiterated their confidence in their data and their arguments:

In our questioning of the conventional approach, we hope to demon-strate first that women's wage labour influences both their own, their spouse's and their family's life situation. Further we note that with higher female employment frequency and continuing gender segmentation of the labour market, one obtains a number of families with cross-class experience. Our second major point is that these partnerships differ in many crucial ways from class homogeneous families. Thus, the spouse's class is germane to any analysis of families in the class system. Analyses which ignore one partner are based on assumptions which are difficult to defend either theoreti-cally or empirically.

Erikson and Goldthorpe accuse us of not clearly supporting either model (b) or (c) nor suggesting some new model. We look for a class analysis where individuals occupy positions in mediating instances such as the family, unions, interest organisations and political parties (1987a:395). Such institutions provide at least a potential base for class action. Thus for us the conflict is not about the use of *individuals versus families*. We consider individuals as people stamped by their expeience *in* families, as well as in other situations. We have approached our analysis by attempting to present individuals in the appropriate context for the problem under consideration, meaning that at times we consider individuals, and at times look at individuals as members of *specific sorts of family or other constellations such as unions*. We do not accept the criticism that we have misunderstood what the whole *Sociology* debate has been about because that criticism is based on a distortion of our position. (Leiulfsrud and Woodward, 1988:555–6)

They conclude

... our ... material makes us wonder whether pure number games really help us understand political consciousness within the family ... Discussions centring on methodology will most probably not offer the solution to the questions ultimately under discussion, especially given that our knowledge about the relations between gender, family and working life is still so incomplete (p.560).

This was the last word in the debate thus far. But the problem remains, and I imagine that when analyses of 1991 census data are published, together with the discussions of class which will ensue, particularly in relation to longitudinal studies, the problem will be raised yet again and the issue will re-emerge in the pages of *Sociology* and other journals.

It remains to those re-reading the debate in twenty years' time to judge where good sociology lay in this exchange. Meanwhile, we might note that this was not simply a debate about women and class. It was at the same time a dispute about academic power, with all the associated grooming behaviour (through citation and lack of it), and patterns of deference and bonding. The language and tactics of the protagonists defending the conventional view should remind us that they have a great deal to lose.

But it does seem that the upholders of the conventional view may have seen the writing on the wall. While apparently unconvinced by the arguments of those opposing their own perspective:

... we do not wish to take up any strong position on what future developments in regard to family class are to be expected. More important than prophecy, in our view, is that sociologists should as far as possible ensure they have available the concepts and methods that will be needed in research aimed at tracing and analysing whatever changes do come about. It is clearly conceivable that the proportion of conjugal families in which the wife has the greater involvement in, and commitment to, the labour market will increase – in which case, we would note, the dominance method would be capable of revealing the effects of this trend. It may also be that the class position of married women as defined in terms of their own employment will in general become a more powerful determinant of their class awareness, social imagery, political partisanship etc.; and further, perhaps, that cross-class effects, both within families and on the socio-political characteristics of their members, will take on greater significance than they would presently appear to possess. But if such charges are anticipated, we need to understand in what ways we should analyse what kinds of data in order to establish whether or not they do materialise. The issues raised by family class are of evident substantive importance, but they are also complex; in their resolution, technique will be of far greater use than value-commitment. (Erikson and Goldthorpe, 1988:550)

Acknowledgements

I am grateful to the editors, to Rodney Barker and to Sara Delamont for their comments on this chapter.

References

Abbott, P. (1987), 'Women's social class identification: does husband's occupation make a difference?, *Sociology*, 21, pp. 91–103.

Acker, J. (1973), 'Women and stratification: A case of intellectual sexism', *American Journal of Sociology*, 78, pp. 936–45.

Acker, J. (1980), 'Women and stratification: a review of the literature', *Contemporary Sociology*, 9 (January), pp. 25–39.

Benyon, H. (1973), *Working for Ford*, London, Allen Lane.

Britten, N. and Heath, A. (1983), 'Women, men and social class', in E. Garmarnikow, D. Morgan, J. Purvis and D. Taylorson (eds.), *Gender, Class and Work*, London, Heinemann.

Dale, A. Gilbert, G. N. and Arber, S. (1985), 'Integrating women into class theory', *Sociology* 19, pp. 384–409.

Delamont, S. (1989), 'Citation and social mobility research: self defeating behaviour?', *Sociological Review*, 37, 332–37.

Delphy, C. (1981), 'Women in stratification studies', (trans. Helen Roberts) in Roberts, H. (ed.), *Doing Feminist Research*, London, Routledge and Kegan Paul.

Erikson, R. (1984), 'Social class of men, women and families', *Sociology*, 18, pp. 500–14.

Erikson, R. and Goldthorpe, J. H. (1988), ' "Women at class crossroads": a critical note', *Sociology*, 22, pp. 545–53.

Garnsey, E. (1978), 'Women's work and theories of class stratification', *Sociology*, 12, pp. 224–43.

Goldthorpe, J. (in collaboration with Catriona Llewellyn and Clive Payne) (1980), *Social Mobility and Class Structure in Modern Britain*, Oxford, Clarendon Press.

Goldthorpe, J. (1983), 'Women and Class Analysis', *Sociology*, 17, pp. 465–58.

Goldthorpe, J. (1984), 'Women and class analysis: A reply to the replies', *Sociology*, 18, pp. 491–99.

Goldthorpe, J. H., Lockwood, D., Bechhofer, F., and Platt, J. (1968), *The Affluent Worker: Industrial Attitudes and Behaviour*, Cambridge, Cambridge University Press.

Goldthorpe, J. and Llewellyn, C. (1977a), 'Class mobility in modern Britain: three theses examined', *Sociology*, 11, pp. 257–87.

Goldthorpe, J. and Llewellyn, C. (1977b), 'Class mobility: inter-generational and worklife patterns', *British Journal of Sociology*, 28, pp. 269–302.

Goldthorpe, J., Payne, C. and Llewellyn, C. (1978), 'Trends in class mobility', *Sociology*, 12, pp. 441–68.

Goldthorpe, J. and Payne, C. (1986), 'On the class mobility of women: results from different approaches to the analysis of recent British data', *Sociology*, 20, pp. 531–55.

Halsey, A. H., Heath, A. F., and Ridge, J. M. (1980), *Origins and Destinations: Family Class and Education in Modern Britain*, Oxford, Clarendon Press.

Heath, A. and Britten, N. (1984), 'Women's jobs do make a difference: a reply to Goldthorpe', *Sociology*, 18, pp. 475–88.

Haug, M. (1973), 'Social class measurement and women's occupational roles', *Social Forces*, 52, pp. 86–98.

Land, H. (1980), 'The family wage', *Feminist Review*, 6, pp. 55–77.

Leiulfsrud, H. and Woodward, A. E. (1987), 'Women at class crossroads: repudiating conventional theories of family class', *Sociology*, 21, pp. 393–412.

Leiulfsrud, H. and Woodward, A. E. (1988), 'Women at class crossroads: a critical reply to Erikson and Goldthorpe's note', *Sociology*, 22, pp. 554–62.

Llewellyn, C. (1981), Occupational mobility and the use of the comparative method in Roberts, H. (ed.), *Doing Feminist Research*, London, Routledge and Kegan Paul.

Mirza H. (1985), 'Distortions of social reality: a case for reappraising social class schema definitions', (Paper presented to the postgraduate women's seminar, University of London, Goldsmith's College).

Moss, P. (1980), 'Parents at work', in P. Moss and N. Fonda (eds.), *Work and the Family*, London, Temple Smith.

Newman, O. (1980), 'Class matters', *Sociology*, 14, pp. 631–36.

Oakley, A. (1974), *The Sociology of Housework*, Oxford, Martin Robertson.

Roberts, H. (1979), 'Women, social class and IUD use' *Women's Studies International Quarterly*, 2, pp. 49–56.

Roberts, H. and Barker, R. (1989), 'What are people doing when they grade women's work?', *British Journal of Sociology*, 40, pp. 130–46.

Stanworth, M. (1984), 'Women and class analysis: A reply to Goldthorpe', *Sociology*, 18, pp. 159–70.

Watson, W. B. and Barth, E. A. (1964), 'Questionable assumptions in the theory of social stratification', *Pacific Sociological Review*, 7, pp. 10–16.

Further reading

Crompton, R. and Mann, M. (1986), *Gender and Stratification*, Cambridge, Polity Press.

Dex, S. (1985), *The Sexual Division of Work*, Brighton, Wheatsheaf Books.

Dex, S. (1987), *Women's Occupational Mobility: A Lifetime Perspective*, Basingstoke, Macmillan.

Newton, J. L., Ryan, M., and Walkowitz, J. (eds.) (1983), *Sex, Class and History*, London, Routledge and Kegan Paul.
Walby, S. (1986), *Patriarchy at Work*, Cambridge, Polity Press.

The nature of organisation structure: Constraint and choice

The chief focus for this chapter is a debate inaugurated by John Child in an influential article published in 1972. The article did not generate a lengthy debate within the pages of *Sociology*; there was only a short critical note by William Tyler (1973) and an equally brief response by Child (1973). The debate that Child's article generated took place outside the pages of *Sociology* as the ideas were taken up by writers concerned largely with the implications for organisation theory. Sociologists were involved in the elaboration of the issues that Child presented, but as with so many contributions by sociologists to the study of organisations, the ideas were rapidly incorporated into organisation theory, an area that is increasingly located in business schools in North America and the UK.

Child offered a critique of 'contingency theory' (although he did not use this term), which at the time was the dominant perspective in organisation theory. However, it was not simply his critique of a fairly established orthodoxy which generated a great deal of interest, but his proposal for a highly contrasting way of examining organisations. Briefly, contingency theory proposes that an organisation's performance is profoundly influenced by the extent to which its structure fits with the particular situational exigencies with which it is confronted.

Tom Burns and G. M. Stalker's (1961) contrast between mechanistic and organic organisations exemplifies contingency theory fairly well. On the basis of their research findings, Burns and Stalker argued that mechanistic structures, which closely resembled Weber's characterisation of bureaucracy, were most appropriate when environmental conditions were stable and simple. However, when environments were in flux, as was the case with some of the Scottish Electronics companies they encountered, a more open and flexible structure was superior, which they dubbed organic. When environments are changing very rapidly by virtue of such factors as greatly increased competition or rapid transformations in technical developments, a mechanistic structure is unlikely to be sufficiently flexible to adjust to the new conditions. In other words, these findings were seen as suggesting that organisational performance was conditional upon the 'fit' between structure and context. Contingency theory was seen as implying a rejection of the universal prescriptions that were a feature of classical management theory. While contingency theory's heyday was probably during the 1960s and early 1970s, it has not been killed off by the critiques offered by Child and others (e.g. Clegg and Dunkerley, 1980). Years after it had lost its position as a major framework for organisational enquiry, contingency theory still had its advocates (especially Donaldson, 1985; 1988) and research broadly within a contingency framework was still being published in major journals (e.g. Gresov, 1989; Hull, 1988).

Child's article began with a summary of the chief tenets of contingency theory, as well as some major findings concerning the impact of such situational factors as organisational size, technology and the environment. He gradually moved towards a critique by introducing the idea of 'strategic choice', which implied that organisational structure and performance were influenced by the actions of senior executives, who have much more choice in the design of organisations and more influence over the contexts within which organisations find themselves than contingency theory allows for. This orientation was very much in line with David Silverman's (1968) critique in *Sociology* of much of the study of 'formal organisations'. He called for an action approach which would entail, *inter alia*, the examination of the goals of organisational actors, the impact of organisational context on those goals, the means for their attainment, and so on. This article also generated a debate in *Sociology*, but its significance in the present context is that Child's proposal for an emphasis on strategic choice had a number of points of affinity with Silverman's article. Child recognised this when he drew attention to Silverman's (1970) later work in the course of the article:

> Systematic comparative investigation of the relationships between organizational structure and situational variables has been the guiding principle for major research programmes both in the United States, under Blau, Hage and Aiken, Hall, Lawrence and Lorsch, and in Britain under Pugh and Woodward. . . . these researchers have attempted to discover the degree of empirical variation in organizational structures and to establish the conditions of such variation. Their findings, together with those from other less extensive studies, provided the material from which models of structural

determination have been constructed. . . .

However, research designed to establish statistically the presence of associations between organizational characteristics usually leaves underlying processes to be inferred . . . The difficulty here is that adequate explanation derives from an understanding of the process, and in this regard the 'fact' of a statistically established relationship does not 'speak for itself'. At the very least, it may mask a more complex set of direct and indirect relationships . . . In addition, little understanding is afforded as to how the relationship was established and whether it is a necessary condition for the presence of other, perhaps less desirable, phenomena. For these reasons, not only is research into organization of a processual and change-oriented type still required but so equally is an attempt to offer more adequate theoretical schemes in step with the advance of empirical research. At the present time, some of the most influential models of organization explicate little more than positively established associations between dimensions of organizational structure and 'contextual' (i.e. situational) factors such as environment, technology or scale of operation. These models proceed to the simplest theoretical solution which is that the contextual factors determine structural variables because of certain, primarily economic, constraints the former are assumed to impose.

It is the purpose of this paper to argue that this simple theory is inadequate, primarily because it fails to give due attention to the agency of choice by whoever have the power to direct the organization . . .

Available Theoretical Models
There are three particularly influential arguments relevant to an explanation of variation in organizational structure. Each postulates the effects of a major contextual factor. The first argument is from environment, in which environmental conditions are posited as critical constraints upon the choice of effective structural forms. The second and third arguments single out the influence on structure of two physical organizational attributes: technology and size. These three arguments highlight constraints upon structural design because contextual factors are regarded as important determinants of structural patterns. The need to secure a certain level of organizational performance is seen to lend contextual factors an exigent character . . .

The three preceding arguments attempt to explain observable patterns of organizational structure by reference to constraints imposed by contextual factors. These constraints are assumed to have force because work organizations must achieve certain levels of performance in order to survive . . .

Organization and Environment
... [T]he analysis of organization and environment must recognize the exercise of choice by organizational decision makers. They may have some power to 'enact' their organization's environment, as Weick has put it (1969: 63ff). Thus to an important extent, their decisions as to where the organization's operations shall be located, the clientele it shall serve, or the types of employees it shall recruit determine the limits of its environment ... [E]nvironmental conditions cannot be regarded as a direct source of variation in organizational structure, as open systems theorists often imply. The critical link lies in the decision-makers' evaluation of the organization's position in the environmental areas they regard as important, and in the action they may consequently take about its internal structure.

Organization and Performance
The available theoretical models ... assume at least implicitly that the sanctions that would be invoked against organizational decision-makers in the event of not achieving a certain level of organizational performance act as a severe limitation on the degree of indeterminateness that exists in the relationships between contextual factors and organizational structure.

A theory of organizational structure has, therefore, to take account of performance dimensions. [In] most research on organizational performance within the social sciences ... structural and other variables have normally been treated as independent, with some measure of effectiveness constituting the dependent variable. Performance has been treated as an outcome. In contrast, a theory of organizational structure would posit structural variables as depending upon decisions which were made with reference to some standard of required performance as well as to some prediction of the effects of structural alternatives upon the performance achieved. Performance is treated as an input to this model, as well as an outcome. Thus two questions which are of some moment for a theory of organizational structure are, first, how performance standards and their degree of achievement may act as a stimulus to structural variation, and, secondly, how far structural variation is likely to effect performance levels. ...

There is little research evidence on the effect that performance standards and their degree of achievement will have upon structural variation. A primary condition here would seem to be that the operation of any particular structural arrangement depends upon a sufficient supply of resources. A declining level of performance, or even a level that fails to meet expectations, may therefore lead to decisions aimed at effecting administrative economies, probably in the direction of simplified procedural and paperwork systems together with a proportionately lower administrative staff component. Allowing for the possibility that alternative structural designs are available and that they represent rather similar overhead costs, then a further condition for performance considerations to influence structural choice must be that those making the choice believe that structural arrangements do have some influence on the level of organizational effectiveness achieved. . . .

[I]t is likely that in most cases organizational decision-makers do believe that structural design has some consequences for performance. In this event, the level of performance actually achieved will probably influence decisions on structural design, subject to an important proviso. This is that the performance attained does not exceed any target which the decision-makers may have decided is adequate. If performance exceeds this 'satisficing' level . . ., then the decision-making group may take the view that the margin of surplus permits them to adopt structural arrangements which accord the better with their own preferences, even at some extra administrative cost to the organization . . . The conclusion reached once again is therefore that organizational decision-makers may well perceive that they have a substantial element of choice in the planning of organizational structure. . . .

The second question concerns the extent to which structural variation is likely to affect the levels of organizational performance actually achieved. Is there any reason to believe that other strategic choices, such as the choice of environment, of market strategies or of operating scale and technology, could significantly influence performance outcomes quite apart from the structural design which is adopted. The results of economic research into business organizations suggest that other strategic considerations may have considerable influence. For instance, the choice of markets to be served can considerably affect the performance of an enterprise because the return available from different markets and industries varies considerably and because some markets are expanding while others are not – a poor choice here leads to 'market efficiency'. . . . However, it is sufficient to demonstrate that structural design is likely to have only a limited effect upon the level of organizational perform-ance achieved, even though the type of structure utilized may affect the quality of other strategic decisions because of the way it influences the communication of necessary information and so on.

The conclusion that the design of organizational structure may have restricted influence upon performance levels, and that perform-ance standards may themselves allow for some 'slack' weakens the general proposition that contextual factors will exert a high degree of constraint upon the choice of structural design. In practice, there does appear to be some variation in the structures of otherwise comparable organizations, a variation which is sustained over periods of time without much apparent effect on success or failure. This is frequently remarked upon by the senior personnel within such organizations, and is not refuted by the fact that multi-variate predictions of particular structural dimensions still leave large proportions (40 per cent upwards) of the structural variance unaccounted for (cf. Pugh *et al.*, 1969a). . . .

Strategic Choice and Organization Theory

The considerations so far raised direct our attention towards those who possess the power to decide upon an organization's structural rationale, towards the limits upon that power imposed by the operational context, and towards the process of assessing constraints and opportunities against values in deciding organizational strategies. Up to this point, there has been implicit in our analysis an assumption that in work organisations the actions of all members are not usually of equal weight in identifying the source of variation in major organization-wide features such as the formal structure of work roles, procedures and communications. The term 'decision-makers' has been employed to refer to the power-holding group on the basis that it is normally possible within work organizations to identify inequalities of power which are reflected in a differential access to decision-making on structural design, and even in a differential ability to raise questions on the subject in the first place. While it has often been suggested that the advancing level of technical expertise required to operate large, sophisticated organizations is in effect taking many decisions out of the hands of senior administrators or officials, there is little evidence to show that the latter do not retain control over policy initiation and implementation (Burns, 1966). This conclusion speaks for the relevance of the 'dominant coalition' concept which was formulated by Cyert and March (1963) . . . The dominant coalition concept opens up a view of organizational structures in relation to the distribution of power and the process of strategic decision-making which these reflect. If, as we have argued, there is some freedom of manoeuvre with respect to contextual factors, standards of performance and structural design, then some choice is implied as to how organization as an on-going system will be maintained. The dominant coalition concept draws attention to the question of who is making the choice. . . . In shifting attention towards the role of choice, we are led to account for organizational variation directly through reference to its sources rather than indirectly through reference to its supposed consequences. This shift of emphasis meets one of the major criticisms that Silverman (1970) has raised against much contemporary organization theory.

In the course of his historical study of American industrial enterprise, Chandler (1962) developed the concept of strategy in referring to the exercise of choice by a dominant coalition as the major source of organizational variation. Chandler's insight lies at the heart of the argument being developed in this paper . . .

In Chandler's view, the modification of organizational goals is . . . a major source of changes in size, technology and location. In regard to structure, his general thesis (which he supports with comparative historical data) is that 'a new strategy required a new or at least refashioned structure if the enlarged enterprise was to be operated efficiently'. (1962, p. 15).

Chandler's analysis, and that presented in this paper, leads to the conclusion that strategic choice is the critical variable in a theory of organizations. Other variables which have often been regarded as independent determinants of organizational structures are, within this perspective, seen to be linked together as multiple points of reference for the process of strategic decision-making . . .

Conclusion

Our contention in this paper has been that many contributions to a theory of organizational structure do not incorporate the direct source of variation in formal structural arrangements, namely the strategic decisions of those who have the power of structural initiation – the dominant coalition. In this respect, the theoretical models we reviewed . . . draw attention to possible constraints upon the choice of effective structures, but fail to consider the process of choice itself in which economic and administrative exigencies are weighed by the actors concerned against the opportunities to operate a structure of their own and/or other organizational members' preferences. A theoretical incorporation of the structural decision-making process has suggested that constraints upon structural choice are weakened in their effect to the extent that:

1. The design of organizational structures only has a limited effect on performance levels achieved, and this is perceived to be the case by a dominant coalition.
2. Because of this, contextual variables only represent limited exigencies bearing upon structural design, and this is perceived to be the case.
3. Even though they perceive structural design to have some effect upon performance levels because of contextual pressures, organization decision-makers may be in a position to institute modifications to the context (though, for instance, a revised environmental strategy) in order to retain a preferred structure without serious detriment to performance.
4. If they perceive structure as possessing performance implications,

organizational decision-makers may prefer to satisfice: to 'trade off' some potential gain in performance for a congenially structured mode of operation. In other words, they may be able and willing to exercise some choice over performance standards.

5. Organizational decision-makers perceive that the nature of contextual constraints pose conflicting implications for structural design – this could, for example, be the case with a combination of large size and location within a variable environment. Conflicting implications derived from contextual combinations of this kind themselves impose some degree of structural choice.

The type of theoretical development suggested by these considerations centres upon the concept of strategic choice exercised by an organization's 'dominant coalition'.

[In order to express some of these ideas, Child presents a 'theoretical model'] . . . in which the exercise of strategic choice by the dominant coalition refers to a process the first stage of which is the coalition members' evaluation of their organization's position – what expectations are presented by resource providers such as business shareholders, what is the trend of events in the environment, what has been the organization's recent performance, the congeniality of its present internal configuration, and so on. Their prior ideology is assumed to colour this evaluation in some degree. The choice of goals or objectives for the organization is seen to follow on from this evaluation, and to be reflected in the strategic action which is decided upon. With respect to external variables, strategic action may include a move into or out of given markets or areas of activity in order to try and secure a favourable demand or response that will be expressed by a high valuation of the organization's products or services. (Child, 1972: 1–3, 8, 10–17)

At the time that this article was published, Child was associated with the Aston Group, a group of researchers under the leadership of Derek Pugh, who had developed a scheme for the conceptualisation and measurement of organisation structure and contextual variables. Child refers to a number of articles deriving from the original Aston study of forty-six West Midlands firms. Child worked on a replication of this research, known as the National study, based on eighty-two firms. The following very brief selection from an article published in *Sociology* is not part of the debate that Child initiated, but provides a flavour of the kind of research that he had criticised. The following passages are concerned with extent to which organisational size or technology are the chief determinants of structure. At the end of the article, Child and his co-author introduce some speculations that relate to the idea of strategic choice. These passages also provide a flavour of the multivarite analysis that was a feature of much research in the contingency tradition:

> . . . [F]or the sample as a whole workflow integration is related to the structural variables of functional specialization, role specialization, standardization and role performance recording. The strength and direction of the correlations are very similar in both the Aston and National studies. However, the relationship of size to these structural variables is much stronger, and the variance explained by technology independently of size is less than 10 per cent in all but two cases: functional specialization and centralization . . .

The results of both the Aston and National studies taken together would appear to refute any argument that technology is the single major correlate of organization structure . . . Many of the standard deviations around industry mean scores on technology are fairly small, suggesting relatively restricted degrees of intra-industry variance in technology. This is particularly the case with the production continuity measure. At the same time it may be noted that organizations in the pharmaceutical and chocolate and sweet industries tend to be similar to each other in terms of the technological variables while differing considerably in structure.

If technology is clearly associated with industry and some structural measures themselves vary significantly between industries, then this suggests certain problems. Either the measurements of technology employed or the framework of analysis, or both, are at least in some respects inadequate. If the differences between industries on structural variables in fact largely reflect technological differences between those industries, then it follows that the measures of technology used are not strong enough.

If, however, the differences between industries are due to non-technological variables, then the close relationship between industry and technology is likely to confound the relationships between technological and structural variables. In particular, environmental variables and managerial ideologies have not been systematically related to technology and structure in any large scale study, but may reasonably be expected to vary by industry. As the theory of open systems suggests that there will be interaction effects between the variables in question, for example between environment and technology . . . , and since ideology and perceived interests are likely to influence the attempts of organizational decision-makers to manipulate these interactions (cf. Child, 1972), the problems remaining to be solved are complex indeed. Clearly, substantial advances in knowledge of these areas require improvement of the measures of structure and technology currently being used and further research relating these variables to measures of organizational environments

and managerial ideology within an adequate theoretical framework.
(Child and Mansfield, 1972: 388–391)

In the next issue, Tyler's critique appeared. The following passages
address especially central issues:

The core of Child's critique, however, appears to be not alleged or
empirical failings of statistical analysis, but the substantial irrelevance
of objective constraints, of any kind, to the prediction of administrative behaviour. This is expressed in the conclusion that 'strategic
choice is the critical variable in a theory of organisations'. One may
enquire as to the place that such constraints hold if they are relegated
to the status of 'simple points of reference' to the decision maker. If
the major independent variable is the caprice of a 'dominant coalition' such a theory can be little better than random chance in
predicting structural variance among organisations. At the level of
explanation, the five propositions offered in the conclusion of Child's
article provide little more than a vocabulary for describing a particular course of action, after the fact (e.g., '4. If they perceive
structure as possessing performance implications, organisational
decision makers may prefer to satisfice: to "trade off" some potential
gain in performance for a congenially structured mode of operation.'). Such a theory, therefore, runs the risks of being either empty
or tautological.
   An obvious way to reconcile the 'iron law of constraints' with the
'caprice of coalition' would be found in a more formal status for
rational choice in decision making. On the one hand, this would open
the way for theoretical predictions of administrative behaviour from a
knowledge of the effect of various strategies on the attainment of
quantifiable pay-off values; on the other, it would subsume contextual variables by estimating the limitations they impose on the
formulation of strategies. This is not to imply that decision makers
will prefer to either 'optimise' or 'satisfice' in a given situation but that
their behaviour will be amenable to theoretical (and perhaps more
general) interpretation. The distinction between predicted and
actual behaviour underlying this is similar to that made in gaming
between normative and descriptive theory. The danger with a theory
which lacks such a general point of reference is that its predictions
will become trivial and its explanations anecdotal. (Tyler, 1973: 126)

Tyler was clearly uneasy about the apparent randomness implied by the
notion of strategic choice. Child's response was set out on a single page,
from which the following passage is especially salient in the light to Tyler's
critique:

Having in his comments set out his two polar extremes of the 'iron

law of constraints' and the 'caprice of coalition', Tyler then concludes with a reconciliation between them. A way forward, he argues,
would be found in a more formal status for rational choice in decision
making within organizations . . . Apart from adding the qualification
that rationality may be 'bounded' for various reasons, I would accept
this as a description of an important framework for future research
into the sociology of organizations. It is, however, hardly at variance
with the view expressed in my article in regard to the more specific
question of organizational structure; namely, that we should 'consider the process of choice itself in which economic and administrative exigencies are weighed by the actors concerned against the
opportunities to operate a structure of their own and/or other
organizational members' preferences' (p. 16). Child, 1973: 447)

Commentary

There is a sense in which Child's article represented the beginning of the
end for contingency theory, because by implication he raised the issue of
how much further its central ideas could be taken. One implication of the
article was that the rather static relationships between variables that were a
feature of findings associated with contingency theory were bound to be
limited until a sense of process and agency could be injected into the field.
Tyler clearly felt uneasy about the 'caprice of coalition', but it is difficult to
imagine that the central ideas of contingency theory had much further to
run unless the factors underpinning the observed relationships could be
unpacked, although not all writers would agree with this view (cf.
Donaldson, 1985). Moreover, from the mid-1970s onwards, other
critiques of contingency theory surfaced (e.g. Burrell and Morgan, 1979;
Clegg and Dunkerley, 1980), while the emergence of new theoretical
perspectives, such as those discussed below, dented its position. Of particular theoretical significance during this period was the rise of theoretical
approaches that were not wedded to the notion of rationality which was the
backcloth to contingency theory (Bryman, 1984). For example, the 'garbage can' model proposed, *contra* contingency theory, that:

an organization is a collection of choices looking for problems, issues
and feelings looking for decision situations in which they might be
aired, solutions looking for issues to which they might be the answer,
and decision-makers looking for work (Cohen *et al.*, 1972: 2)

When such a perspective is taken, the image that underpins much contingency theory, of organisation structures as rational responses to the
exigencies of the environment or technology in order to maximise organi-

sational performance, seems faintly naive. On the other hand, there are strong undertones of rationality in the concept of strategic choice, to which Tyler and Child allude but without delving very deeply into the issue.

Some effects of Child's article

Child's article had a number of longer term effects in addition to its impact on contingency theory. It was almost certainly a contributory factor to the surge of interest from the late 1970s in strategic management, which has become a major field in business schools with its own journals, like *Strategic Management Journal* and *Journal of Business Strategy*. Undoubtedly the innovative work of writers like Alfred Chandler (1962) and Richard Rumelt (1974) was of great importance as well, but Child's article almost certainly played a part.

A second effect of Child's article was that it formed a major component of a debate about the relative importance of determinism as against voluntarism or agency in organisation theory, and where different perspectives on organisations should be placed in terms of this contrast. This dichotomy parallels the 'two sociologies' that Alan Dawe (1970) distinguished. Contingency theory is conventionally depicted, along with the 'population ecology' approach (see below), as indicative of a deterministic approach. In the case of contingency theory, this determinism is manifested in the tendency to conceive of the environment as carrying clusters of imperatives to which the organisation must respond, so that the range of possible variation in organisational structures available to decision-makers is characterised as substantially constrained. By contrast, strategic choice opens up the prospect of much greater managerial control over the environment and over the structuring of organisations than contingency theorists and others recognise. The strategic choice viewpoint is much more consistent with theories and research that project an image of senior managers as capable of exerting considerable influence over the direction and affairs of their organisations (Bryman, 1992).

Thus, the determinism-voluntarism contrast became a major dimension for conceptualising the nature of different organisation theories (e.g. Astley and Van de Ven, 1983) and organisational adaptation (or its absence). Some writers have expressed reservations about considering determinism and voluntarism as opposite ends of a continuum. Lawrence Hrebiniak and William Joyce (1985) propose treating strategic choice and environmental determinism as separate dimensions, with high and low levels on each dimension yielding a 2 × 2 typology. High strategic choice plus low environmental determinism and low strategic choice and low levels of determinism represent the 'pure types' that were the focus of Child and contingency theory respectively. Hrebiniak and Joyce show that the other two combinations are feasible. For example, they point to research which demonstrates the coexistence of high levels of both environmental determinism and strategic choice, citing research on large companies in one industry which 'despite government regulation, controls, and mandatory warnings to consumers about the detrimental effects of their products', were able to pursue clear strategies and to 'affect their markets through extensive advertising, marketing, and lobbying' (p. 341). R. Whittington (1988) proffers 'environmental structure' and 'human agency' as separate dimensions and also generates a 2 × 2 typology.

The critique of strategic choice

Child's article generated fewer critiques than might have been expected, especially since it sounded the death-knell of an established orthodoxy. It has been accused of being somewhat ambiguous in its overall intent. Michael Reed (1985), for example, has remarked that it is not clear whether Child was seeking to present a radical alternative to contingency theory or whether strategic choice was supposed to complement it. Certainly, contingency theory is capable of accommodating strategic choice and members of the Aston Group sought to do just that when they wrote:

> Yet these results [of the Aston Group], . . . did not mean a working world immovably fixed by a few major elements. Not only did all of these elements change all the time . . . but all these and the other elements studied were open to *strategic choice*. Indeed, they had all in some sense been chosen, and were continually being chosen. Managers and administrators choose whether or not an organization is to grow or to enter into contracts that make it dependent on others. They choose the means of management and control which structure its activities and concentrate its authority. But *one choice constrains another* – each choice (e.g. of size) the options open for the next (e.g. of the degree of structuring to be adopted). (Pugh *et al.*, 1983: 40 – emphases in original)

This passage represents an interesting attempt by major contributors to contingency theory to embrace strategic choice. It also represents an imaginative solution to the constraint-versus-agency issue, though Child's original formulation seemed to place greater emphasis upon choice over constraint. Howard Aldrich (1979), echoing the assumptions of the population ecology model, argued that the capacity of leaders to manipulate

their organisations' environments is probably restricted to larger organisations and that habit and inertia restrict the frequency of strategic choice.

However, probably the chief critique of Child's article can be found in
Lex Donaldson's (1985) defence of organisation theory, which in large part
is treated as synonymous with the contingency approach. Child's strategic
choice critique is one of a number of criticisms of contingency theory that
Donaldson seeks to rebut. Donaldson argues that Child's aim was to
account for variation in organisational structure, but this is unlikely to
provide the kinds of practical findings produced by researchers like Paul
Lawrence and Tony Lorsch (1967) and Joan Woodward (1965), who
sought to establish how the goodness of fit between context and structure
affects organisational performance. He also argues that Child recognises
the importance of power in considerations of the impact of strategic choice
on organisational structure, but that he neglects the fact that power is
affected by structure, so that the room for manoeuvre for leaders is more
structurally constrained than is implied in the article. Donaldson makes a
similar point about ideology, which has an important role in determining
the nature of strategic choice in Child's work. Ideology too is influenced by
structure. As a result, Donaldson proposes that Child's thesis 'is determinism at one remove' (1985: 145). It could be argued that Donaldson's
observation about power does not allow sufficiently for its shifting and fluid
nature, which has been a major area of interest for many organisational
researchers (Pfeffer, 1981). The point about ideology is slightly strange, in
that while it is clearly the case that structural location in part affects
ideology, it is another thing to say that it determines it. If structural position
does determine ideology, and the latter feeds into strategic choice, then
organisations would presumably exhibit much less variability than is
apparently the case according to contingency theory.

In spite of Donaldson's critique, the concept of strategic choice has
retained its cutting edge for many organisation theorists and researchers,
and its influence can be discerned in recent attempts to examine the effects
of the environment on organisations.

Environment and organisation: recent theoretical perspectives

One of the legacies of the contingency approach for organisation theorists
is a continuing concern with the relationship between the organisation and
its environment. In the immediate aftermath of the contingency approach,
the 'resource dependence' perspective attracted a great deal of attention.
As its name implies, this perspective views the organisation as dependent
upon resources from its environment in order to survive. The approach

directs attention to the way in which organisational activities and internal arrangements are substantially affected by the dependence that arises on other organisations and groups which are the source of resources (such as components, financial support, or information). This concern can be detected in the interest in inter-organisational relationships and the power differences that arise in the context of interaction between organisations (e.g. Benson, 1975). Resource dependence theory's version of the impact of environments on organisations appears to correspond closely to the determinism that Child rallied against.

However, the organisation is not perceived in resource dependency theory as passively responding to environmental constraint; instead, the main focus of interest is the variety of strategies that are pursued in order to mitigate the extent of dependency, such as cartels, co-operation, joint ventures, and lobbying government agencies (see, for example, Pfeffer and Salancik, 1978). It has been suggested that the resource dependence approach really only applies to large organisations, since they are more likely than smaller organisations to possess both the resources and muscle to have a major impact on their environments (e.g. Aldrich, 1979). In response, one of the chief proponents of the approach has observed that many of the main ways in which organisations 'enact' their environments is to pursue joint activities with other organisations, and that this possibility is not restricted to the largest firms (Pfeffer, 1982).

The resource dependency approach is congruent with the general drift of Child's article, in that it recognises the role of environmental constraint but it also gives a substantial role to the capacity of organisational actors to carve out areas of self-determination, although one might reasonably argue that Child gave greater emphasis to the latter element. However, two other theoretical perspectives concerned with the relationship between organisations and environments emerged in the late 1970s and these seem to have been of increasing interest among organisational researchers, with the resource dependence approach fading into the background slightly. The interesting feature of these two approaches – known as the population ecology and institutional perspectives – is that they signal a revival of environmental determinism in a form that, if anything, is more extreme than that associated with contingency theory. It is also interesting that these two theories have prospered at the same time that strategic management and a focus on executive leadership, both of which attribute considerable influence to the actions of senior managers in the determination of organisational survival and success, have been major areas of interest among researchers (Bryman, 1992).

Unlike most approaches in organisation theory, population ecology theory does not focus on individual organisations; rather its primary emphasis is on populations of organisations (Hannan and Freeman, 1977). Each population of organisations is depicted as occupying an ecological niche, but each niche has a limited carrying capacity. Once this capacity is breached, some members of the population will be unable to survive and will therefore be eliminated. New entrants to the population will also find it difficult to survive once the carrying capacity has been arrived at. Of special interest to the kinds of issues with which Child was concerned is the suggestion that organisations will move towards a common organisational form. Organisations will seek to adopt the organisational form that appears most successful in adapting to the requirements of survival in the relevant environmental niche. Thus, particular management and organisational structures that are viewed as successful become exemplars, which spread through the population and become models for new entrants. Members of the population come to exhibit 'structural inertia' by virtue of the reputation for reliability that certain organisational forms acquire (Hannan and Freeman, 1984). Major structural change requires great risks which are unlikely to be acceptable, especially to longer-standing organisations, and is most likely to occur through the introduction of novel organisational forms by new entrants, who are able to demonstrate the superior adaptive capability of alternative organisational arrangements.

The most striking feature of this theoretical perspective is the way in which actors and agency are written out of the story by the imperatives of environmental constraint and determinism. Indeed, there is an implication that it would be naive to believe that senior leaders can do any more than make a marginal difference to the course of an organisation's performance in the face of these environmental pressures. It is no wonder that Hrebiniak and Joyce (1985) describe the population ecology approach as exemplifying the combination of high environmental determinism and low strategic choice. The second major perspective on organisation-environment rela-tionships – the institutional approach – can likewise be characterised as concerned with the overwhelming impact of the environment and with the pressure toward uniformity of organisational form.

Institutional theory depicts organisations as impelled by normative pressures deriving from the environment (e.g. Meyer and Rowan, 1977; Zucker, 1987). Organisations are viewed as adopting structures and pro-cedures that are valued by the wider society. Thus, an organisation may introduce practices or forms, not because they are believed to be imperative to the efficient accomplishment of its primary task, but in order to achieve legitimacy in the eyes of significant environmental agencies and therefore to enhance the prospect of survival. Because there is some commonality of view in society regarding appropriate or ideal procedures and forms, organisations tend towards broadly similar structures. The term 'institutional isomorphism' is employed by some proponents of the approach (e.g. DiMaggio and Powell, 1983) to express the tendency for organisations to reflect the normative pressures of their environments.

A number of writers have criticised this approach for its tendency to view the organisation as a passive reactor to the environment and for its consequent inclination to eliminate from consideration the possibility of deflecting or disregarding institutional pressures (e.g. Covaleski and Dirsmith, 1988). Christine Oliver (1991) has sought to effect a *rapprochement* of the institutional and resource dependence approaches, through which she has identified a number of strategic responses to institutional pressures: acquiesce; compromise; avoid; defy; and manipulate. Such considerations generate a way of thinking about organisational processes and the creation of structures that is closer to the programme that Child envisaged, in that it comprises elements of both constraint and agency. However, a convergence of population ecology theory and aspects of the strategic choice notion seems more difficult to envision, because the former implies a much stronger role than in the institutional approach for the environment in the genesis of organisational forms. Raymond Zammuto (1988) has made a start in generating a reconciliation by showing, for example, that the success of different strategies is dependent on the stage of development of an industry and its level of density at the time. However, this kind of reconciliation still seems to convey a sense of the influence of strategic choice as being fairly marginal.

Interestingly, some writers have conducted studies which allow the relative potential of some of the different theories that have been examined in this chapter to be tested. This 'testing of competing theories' approach to the empirical examination of core themes in organisation theory is an interesting methodological development which is occurring with increasing frequency within the field. Neil Fligstein (1985) has employed data on the spread of the multidivisional organisational structure among large US firms between 1919 and 1979 in order to test five relevant theories. These theories include the population ecology and institutional approaches, as well as an emphasis on strategy, which, while following Chandler (1962), has clear points of affinity with Child's central arguments. The data were most consistent with three of the five theories: strategic choice, institutional theory, and an emphasis upon power bases in organisations. Oliver (1988) reports a test of the relative importance of population ecology, institutional, and strategic choice perspectives in explaining the organisational characteristics of inter-organisational relationships among voluntary social service

D

organisations in the USA. An emphasis upon strategic choice proved to be the most effective in accounting for the observed patterns. These findings are important in that they imply that environments are less deterministic than population ecology and institutional theories suggest and that environments can accommodate more variability of structure than these same theories imply. In the case of both tests, a strategic choice perspective emerged as a powerful factor in the determination of organisation forms, thus providing support for Child's argument that senior decision-makers are often the real source of variation in organisation structures.

British sociology and organisation theory

It is very striking that British sociologists were highly influential in the development of contingency theory and many key articles were published in *Sociology*; indeed, the first issue contained an early report of a selection of the Aston Group's findings (Hinings *et al.*, 1967). Bob Hinings (1988) has also observed that British sociologists were heavily involved in the critique of contingency theory, albeit from a variety of perspectives and stances. Yet British sociologists have not made substantial contributions (if any) to the population ecology and institutional approaches to the environment-organisation relationships. Three recent textbooks written by British sociologists concerned with organisations do make substantial reference to the two approaches (Clegg, 1990; Morgan, 1990; Thompson and McHugh, 1990), but it would be difficult to find significant contributions by British sociologists to theory and research relating to these two per-spectives. Instead, in the years since the gradual erosion of contingency theory's ascendancy, British sociologists have made major contributions to organisational analysis through such areas as organisational culture and symbolism (for example Turner, 1988; 1992), power in organisations (for example Clegg, 1989), and the working through of implications of labour process theory for the analysis of organisations (for example, the con-tributors to Knights and Wilmott, 1990). Moreover, ethnographic studies of such milieux as the police (for example Fielding, 1988) and clinics and hospitals (for example Silverman, 1984) have added greatly to the under-standing of organisational processes, although it could be argued that their links with organisation theory require more explicit treatment. British sociologists have also contributed greatly to the understanding of the significance of gender for organisational processes, often through the medium of detailed ethnographies of the workplace (for example, Hearn *et al.*, 1989; Pollert, 1981). Interestingly, issues of 'race' and ethnicity share with gender considerable potential for introducing new insights into organisation theory. However, writers on gender issues are currently achieving a greater impact on organisational analysis (for example, Calás and Smircich, 1992).

The relative lack of interest among British sociologists in the population ecology and institutional approaches is surprising in view of the fact that, in North America, sociologists have been the chief contributors to research relating to the two perspectives. Also, the impact of the environment and other contextual factors on the organisation was an area which was of considerable interest to British sociologists during the heyday of contingency theory. In the USA, by contrast, sociology journals have been among the main outlets for articles associated with the two perspectives.

British sociologists have sometimes been uneasy about organisation studies, because of its connection with business schools and the associated taint of managerialism. In fact, the population ecology and institutional approaches tend to be given scant attention in books on organisational behaviour or organisation theory written for a predominantly business school audience. In a way this is not surprising, since the message that emanates from the two perspectives is that there is very little open to the organisational leader other than to submit to environmental imperatives (population ecology) or to act as a 'cultural dope' and to absorb the organisational arrangements of the day (institutional approach). Instead, it tends to be textbooks written at least in part for sociologists, such as the three previously cited, that pay greater attention to these two perspectives. One factor behind the relative non-interest among British sociologists may be a methodological one, in that the bulk of published research deriving from the two approaches depends on highly complex statistical models, which represent a style of investigation that has rarely appealed to British writers.

A major issue for the future, however, is the degree to which human agency can be introduced into the stark environmental determinism that the two approaches represent, and Child's notion of strategic choice may be helpful in this connection. It is hard to believe that organisation studies could accommodate for long a situation in which perspectives which give scant consideration to human agency could coexist with theory and research on strategic management and leadership. Wherein agency occupies a prominent role. It could be argued that sociology has existed perfectly well with such a split personality (Dawe, 1970), but the 'applied' focus of much organisational research may limit the extent to which the two sets of themes can coexist without some form of resolution.

A further area likely to be of considerable interest is the working through of postmodern analysis for the study of organisations. A number of British writers have already made inroads here (e.g. Clegg, 1990; Cooper and Burrell, 1988), while in the USA Kenneth Gergen (1992) has produced an important statement on the significance of postmodern themes. Thus the exploration of emergent organisational forms and of the implications of postmodern approaches for organisational analysis has already begun. These concerns are likely to intensify in the light of growing interest in such areas as 'new organisation' (Scase, 1991), 'new leadership' (Bryman, 1992) and 'post-Fordism', which share certain themes that postmodernist writers have identified as constitutive of a new social order. The themes of trust, empowerment, use of symbols, de-differentiation, cultural artifacts, and flexibility, along with a dilution of the traditional emphases on direct control and rationality, provide recurring motifs in some recent writing on developments in modern organisations. These or similar themes can be discerned in some writings on postmodernity. The examination of such issues is likely to prove a burgeoning area, if only because it represents a point of potential overlap between current social theory and the pre-occupation with 'efficient organisation' among many writers within organi-sation studies. However, a major consideration will probably be the extent to which postmodernist writings can legitimately be employed in this way and for such ends. Nonetheless, in view of the interest in postmodernism among British sociologists and the predilection among British writers on organisations for European streams of thought, this area is likely to provide a fruitful focus of future theoretical enquiry.

References

Aldrich, H. E. (1979), *Organization and Environments*, Englewood Cliffs, NJ, Pre-ntice-Hall.

Astley, W. G. and Van de Ven, A. H. (1983), 'Central perspectives and debates in organization theory', *Administrative Science Quarterly*, 28, pp. 245–73.

Benson, J. K. (1975), 'The interorganizational network as a political economy', *Administrative Science Quarterly*, 20, pp. 229–49.

Bryman, A. (1984), 'Organization studies and the concept of rationality', *Journal of Management Studies*, 21, pp. 391–408.

Bryman, A. (1992), *Charisma and Leadership of Organizations*, London, Sage.

Burns, T. (1966), Preface to second edition of Burns and Stalker (1961).

Burns, T. and Stalker, G. M. (1961), *The Management of Innovation*, London, Tavistock.

Burrell, G. and Morgan, G. (1979), *Sociological Paradigms and Organizational Analysis*, London, Heinemann.

Calas, M.B. and Smircich, L. (1992), 'Re-writing gender into organizational theorizing', in M. Reed and M. Hughes (eds.), *Rethinking Organization: New Directions in Organization Theory and Analysis*, London, Sage.

Chandler, A. (1962), *Strategy and Structure: Chapters in the History of the Industrial Enterprise*, Cambridge, Mass., MIT Press.

Child, J. (1972), 'Organizational structure, environment and performance: the role of strategic choice', *Sociology*, 6, pp. 1–22.

Clegg, S. R. (1989), *Frameworks of Power*, London, Sage.

Clegg, S. R. (1990), *Modern Organizations: Organization Studies in the Postmodern World*, London, Sage.

Clegg, S. R. and Dunkerley, D. (1980), *Organization, Class and Control*, London, Routledge and Kegan Paul.

Cohen, M. D., March, J. G. and Olsen, J. P. (1972), 'A garbage can model of organizational choice', *Administrative Science Quarterly*, 17, pp. 1–25.

Cooper, R. and Burrell, G. (1988), 'Modernism, postmodernism, and organizational analysis', *Organization Studies*, 9, pp. 91–112.

Covaleski, M. A. and Dirsmith, M. W. (1988), 'An institutional perspective on the rise, social transformation, and fall of a university budget category', *Administrative Science Quarterly*, 33, pp. 562–87.

Cyert, R. M. and March, J. G. (1963), *A Behavioural Theory of the Firm*, Englewood Cliffs, NJ, Prentice-Hall.

Dawe, A. (1970), 'The two sociologies', *British Journal of Sociology*, 21, pp. 207–18.

DiMaggio, P. J. and Powell, W. W. (1983), 'The iron cage revisited: institutional isomorphism and collective rationality in organizational fields', *American Sociological Review*, 35, pp. 147–60.

Donaldson, L. (1985), *In Defence of Organization Theory: A Reply to the Critics*, Cambridge, Cambridge University Press.

Donaldson, L. (1988), 'In successful defence of organization theory: a routing of the critics', *Organization Studies*, 9, pp. 28–32.

Fielding, N. (1988), 'Competence and culture in the police', *Sociology*, 22, pp. 45–64.

Fligstein, N. (1985), 'The spread of the multidivisional form among large firms, 1919–1979', *American Sociological Review*, 50, pp. 377–91.

Gergen, K. J. (1992), 'Organization theory in the postmodern era' in M. Reed and M. Hughes (eds.), *Rethinking Organization: New Directions in Organization Theory and Analysis*, London, Sage.

Gresov, C. (1989), 'Exploring fit and misfit with multiple contingencies', *Administrative Science Quarterly*, 34, pp. 431–53.

Hannan, M. T. and Freeman, J. H. (1977), 'The population ecology of organizations', *American Journal of Sociology*, 82, pp. 929–64.

Hannan, M. T. and Freeman, J. H. (1984), 'Structural inertia and organizational change', *American Sociological Review*, 49, pp. 149–64.

Hearn, J., Sheppard, D. L., Tancred-Sheriff, P. and Burrell, G. (1989), (eds.), *The Sexuality of Organization*, London, Sage.

Hinings, B. (1988), 'Defending organization theory: a British view from North America', *Organization Studies*, 9, pp. 2–6.

Hinings, C. R. Pugh, D. S., Hickson, D. J., and Turner, C. (1977), 'An approach to the study of bureaucracy', *Sociology*, 1, pp. 61–72.

Hrebiniak, L. G. and Joyce, W. F. (1985), 'Organizational adaptation: strategic choice and environmental determinism', *Administrative Science Quarterly*, 30, pp. 336–49.

Hull, F. (1988), 'Inventions from R & D: organzational designs for efficient research performance', *Sociology*, 22, pp. 393–415.

Knights, D. and Wilmott, H. (1990) (eds.), *Labour Process and Theory*, Basingstoke, Macmillan.

Lawrence, P. R. and Lorsch, J. (1967), *Organization and Environment*, Cambridge, Mass., Harvard University Press.

Meyer, J. W. and Rowan, B. (1977), 'Institutionalized organizations: formal structure as myth and ceremony', *American Journal of Sociology*, 83, pp. 340–63.

Morgan, G. (1990), *Organizations in Society*, Basingstoke, Macmillan.

Oliver, C. (1988), 'The collective strategy framework: an application to competing predictions of isomorphism', *Administrative Science Quarterly*, 33, pp. 534–61.

Oliver, C. (1991), 'Strategic responses to institutional processes', *Academy of Management Review*, 16, pp. 145–79.

Pfeffer, J. (1981), *Power in Organizations*, Boston, Pitman.

Pfeffer, J. (1982), *Organizations and Organization Theory*, Boston, Pitman.

Pfeffer, J. and Salancik, G. R. (1978), *The External Control of Organizations: A Resource Dependence Perspective*, New York, Harper & Rowe.

Pollert, A. (1981), *Girls, Wives, Factory Lives*, Basingstoke, Macmillan.

Pugh, D. S., Hickson, D. J., Hinings, C. R. and Turner, C. (1969a), 'The context of organization structures', *Administrative Science Quarterly*, 14, pp. 91–114.

Pugh, D. S. Hickson, D. J., Hinings, C. R. and Turner, C. (1969b) 'An empirical taxonomy of structures of work organization', *Administrative Science Quarterly*, 14, pp. 115–26.

Pugh, D. S., Hickson, D. J., and Hinings, C. R. (1983, 3rd edn.), *Writers on Organizations*, Harmondsworth, Penguin.

Reed, M. (1985), *Redirections in Organizational Analysis*, London Tavistock.

Rumelt, R. P. (1974), *Strategy, Structure and Economics Performance*, Boston, Division of Research, Harvard Business School.

Scase, R. (1990), 'Is Britain ready for the "new organisation" ', *Social Sciences News from the ESRC*, 12 (November), p. 8.

Silverman, D. (1968), 'Formal organizations or industrial sociology: towards a social action analysis of organizations, *Sociology*, 2, pp. 221–38.

Silverman, D. (1970), *The Theory of Organizations*, London, Heinemann.

Silverman, D. (1984), 'Going private: ceremonial forms in a private oncology clinic', *Sociology*, 18, pp. 191–204.

Thompson, P. and McHugh, D. (1990), *Work Organisations: A Critical Introduction*, Basingstoke, Macmillan.

Turner, B. A. (1988), 'Connoisseurship in the study of organizational cultures' in A. Bryman (ed.), *Doing Research in Organizations*, London, Routledge.q

Turner, B. A. (1992), 'The symbolic understanding of organizations' in M. Reed and M. Hughes (eds.), *Rethinking Organization: New Directions in Organization Theory and Analysis*, London, Sage.

Weick, K. E. (1969), *The Social Psychology of Organizing*, Reading, Mass., Addison-Wesley.

Whittington, R. (1988), 'Environmental structure and theories of strategic choice' *Journal of Management Studies*, 25, pp. 521–36.

Woodward, J. (1965), *Industrial Organisation: Theory and Practice*, London, Oxford University Press.

Zammuto, R. F. (1988), 'Organizational adaptation: some implications of ecological theory for strategic choice', *Journal of Management Studies*, 25, pp. 105–20.

Zucker, L. G. (1987), 'Institutional theories of organization', *Annual Review of Sociology*, 13, pp. 443–64.

Further reading

For a general overview of organisation theory and a limited attempt to undertake a postmodern analysis, see Clegg (1990). For useful summaries of the main ingredients of the institutional approach, see Oliver (1991), which also examines the resource dependence perspective, and Zucker (1987).

Interesting critical summaries of both the institutional and population ecology approaches can be found in:

C. Perrow, (1986, 3rd. ed.), *Complex Organizations: A Critical Essay*, New York, Random House.

Critical assessments of the population ecology and institutional approaches respectively can be found in:

R. C. Young (1988), 'Is population ecology a useful paradigm for the study of organizations?' *American Journal of Sociology*, 94, pp. 1–24, and in W. R. Scott (1987), 'The adolescence of institutional theory', *Administrative Science Quarterly*, 32, pp. 439–511.

Reflections on the concept of 'strategy'

The concept of 'strategy' has recently entered the sociological vocabulary and has a variety of different meanings; Graham Crow (1989), for example, describes at least seventeen different ways in which it is used. However, the debate which has developed in the pages of *Sociology* stems from its particular application to families and households. How did it become possible to speak of household activities in terms of 'strategies'?

The concept of strategy has been used for some time in rural sociology to refer to the ways in which farming families organise their labour and resources. Here the family is a source of labour and is often mobilised to help expand or survive. Since the household is also a business unit, strategic thinking is imposed to some extent through financial necessity – those who do not survive go bankrupt – and also through the intervention of institutions such as banks on which many farmers depend (Redclift, 1986). The concept did not, however, originate in rural sociology. According to Michael Redclift (1986), it was imported from studies of urban poor in the Third World, particularly Latin America. In this context, the idea of 'survival strategies' could be used to show how poor people's struggles to survive poverty could be both logical and resourceful. From the 1970s it was associated with analysis of the role of the 'informal sector' and was used to illustrate how the activities of poor people were important for the kind of capitalist development which took place, and how such activities were not simply the product of dependent economies (Roberts, 1978). In Britain the activities of marginal groups such as ethnic minorities or the poor have also been characterised as 'survival' or 'coping' strategies. The connection between urban development in the Third World and agricultural develop-ment in industrialised countries is made because in both contexts households have to manage in a risky environment:

> In the discussion of family-based enterprises these [characteristics] have been understood as *survival* strategies, a term employed frequently in the analysis of family-based farming enterprises (Redclift, 1986). A central theme of this literature is the unpredictability of the environment in which these enterprises operate, and the rationality of risk-minimisation in such circumstances. (Crow, 1989, p. 6)

However, following work by Ray Pahl (1984) and myself (see Pahl and Wallace, 1985), the idea of 'strategy' was generalised to apply to *all* households: any household could have a 'household work strategy', as we termed it. This helped us to explore the way in which households organised their work both inside and outside what at that time was termed the 'formal economy'. The advantage of this approach is that rather than just looking at the activities of individual actors in the labour market, we were able to see households as collective units. At that time in the 1970s the dominant academic paradigm in urban sociology had been Marxist structuralism, which saw individual actors as irrelevant or at best as reflections of dominant structural forces. The focus on household strategies allowed a more humanistic interpretation and enabled us to recognise the sources of power and rationality existing within households which could not necessarily be predicted from structural analysis. A further advantage was that this perspective enabled us to look at 'work' in a much wider sense, in terms of what people actually do rather than by examining insitutions in the labour market or some forms of formal employment. This radical shift in focus provided quite a different view of the meaning of work and social institutions from the 'bottom up', but it also implied a humanistic view of people's actions and consciousness:

> For many ordinary people, very little can be done at the workplace to improve their personal life chances . . . such activity is relatively marginal compared with the moving . . . to a house they own and on which they can work as they like. *They can express themselves more creatively in their own homes than they can in their employment.* (Pahl, 1984:323, emphasis added)

In this way, we could see the household as the determinant of its own actions rather than the helpless puppet of structural forces. This led us to ask questions such as: was it the change in household values which prompted social change rather than the 'objective' external forces of history? What was the relationship between household organisation and the external social context? Which features of the social context were the most relevant? This approach also opened the possibility of recognising contributions from different genders and generations in addition to the main 'breadwinner', although this was never really explored nor expanded at the time: 'People who want a better way of life for themselves and their families perceive that they can most readily achieve this through a distinctive mix of all forms of work by all members of the household' (Pahl, 1984:327).

However, the concept of household work strategies had inherent problems, some of which were soon manifest. Firstly, it implied a model of rationality – of people consciously making decisions about the sort of work they did. Secondly, it implied a model of collective decision-making in households which we cannot take for granted – did households really sit down round the kitchen table and work out a planned collective strategy for their work? Thirdly, in reacting against structural determination it perhaps over-emphasised the idea of voluntary action determining social consequences. Fourthly, it assumed a relationship between means and ends – that people had goals, that they perceived these goals and that they implemented strategies to achieve them. Finally, the concept did not take into account the opposing interests of different household members in the construction of a 'strategy', nor the fact that different household members may have different strategies. The household work strategy was assumed rather than explicitly deconstructed in terms of gender and generation. Thus we have a vision of households purposively planning their goals and mobilising resources: the kitchen table boardroom. Was this right? Perhaps they were forced to act in particular ways? Or perhaps they just muddled along from day to day without a strategic grand plan? How would we then explain their apparently irrational actions?

At the time we struggled with some of these problems and felt that 'strategy' was sometimes too strong a word for some of the activities which we were observing and we reverted instead at times to words such as 'practices' (Pahl and Wallace, 1985:199). The initial concern had been with economic behaviour and hence with exploring the economic, calculative rationality which lay behind statements from respondents such as 'it paid me to take a day off work to paint the house'. The problem became, however, to what extent households could be assumed to be undertaking a cost-benefit analysis of their own activities and the extent to which this could be generalised to other areas of social life where economic, calculative retionality was less obvious.

However, the term was being widely used as a convenient way of understanding the ways in which people negotiated the complex demands made upon them in their private and public lives. Graham Crow's (1989) article was the first concerted attempt to clarify the concept and to build a more coherent theoretical base. Crow traces the concept to 'game theory' and theories of 'rational choice' and explores it in these terms:

> The concept of strategy is, then, linked not only to questions of choice and power but also to patterns of interaction. The theoretical underpinning of the concept of strategic action lies in theories of rational choice, in particular game theory (Elster, 1983:13) and so it is not surprising to find strategies being discussed in situations which are, in some senses at least, game-like. (Crow, 1989:4)

In game theory, the concept implies making choices in a situation of risk or uncertainty. Crow asks us to look at who or what is the originator of the strategy; 'societies' cannot have strategies, he argues, but individuals or social groups or corporate bodies perhaps can. He looks at the ways in which strategies are used by subordinate or superordinate groups. However, he also defines some key elements. First, a strategy implies some model of choice as well as a rational agency – people need to be able to choose between alternatives to formulate a strategy. Second, it implies a notion of power – over resources or over others.

Taken to its logical conclusion, however, it is possible to see strategies everywhere. He argues that Thomas Szaz (1972, 1973), for example, could discern a strategy underneath even the apparently 'irrational' behaviour of hysterics. More importantly, Erving Goffman's sociology depends upon social actors adopting strategies of which they are not themselves entirely conscious (see, for example, Goffman, 1970). This raises the possibility that a strategy may actually be unconscious as well as conscious. However, Crow rejects this idea:

> A key problem which is encountered at levels of both the household and the individual is the problem of rationality. In various instances it proves difficult to speak of the rationality of household strategies, either because it is hard to detect anything resembling rational decision-making having preceded actions, or because there is no one standard of rationality by which it is appropriate to judge the strategies that have been developed. (Crow, 1989:12)

We are then faced with the problem of how to understand apparently non-rational or even irrational strategies. Thus a household trying to survive poverty may spend all or part of their money on some kind of conspicuous consumption such as a video tape recorder or a status car. This may not seem a very rational strategy in terms of a strict economically calculative model, and yet it could make sense in terms of a different rationality applied to a different set of goals in the real social and psychological world in which people live. We could see such choices in terms of 'substantive' rationality leading towards long-term goals or 'formal' rationality, meaning the technical means to achieve those goals (Habermas, 1969). The former can often be subordinated to the latter, whilst the former can also seem irrational in terms of the latter or vice versa.

> Game theory's presumption of rational behaviour on the part of players is undoubtedly one of its strengths, but it is also a weakness. Its strength lies in forcing us to question interpretations of actions which suggest them to be irrational or non-rational, but this questioning can become obsessive when it leads to a refusal to countenance the possibility of actions being non-rational, or rational according to some other standard unacknowledged by the observer . . . A further weakness relates to the way in which focusing attention on action can lead to a neglect of social structural constraints . . . There are further strengths and weaknesses to game theory in its emphasis on interaction as process: people's actions are frequently responses to a situation which is developing rather than static, but, to the extent that this is the case, these actions will be all the more difficult to predict and interpret. The more negotiation that is involved in the development of strategies, the harder the task of their analysis becomes. (Crow, 1989:14)

Crow analyses the problem of non-rational action in terms of interaction of rational strategies and structural constraints and here he chooses as examples partriarchal ideology and the Weberian idea of 'traditional' behaviour:

> Conflict between partners arises where economic rationality challenges tradition. Both economic rationality and patriarchy offer a basis on which household work strategies can be developed, but they are not easily combined, since there are serious tensions between the fundamental tenets on which they rest. Where negotiations are resolved in favour of a patriarchal solution, the absence of economic rationality in the adoption of a 'traditional' household work strategy does not necessarily reflect absence of rationality *per se*. The reason for this is that it may be rational in a very pragmatic sense, for those in positions of structural disadvantage to concede to the wishes of those with power. (Crow, 1989:15)

With respect to structural constraints, however, Crow argues we should look to structuration theory:

> Social structures limit the range of possible strategies an individual (or other agent) may follow, but in following these restricted strategies the constraints may be reproduced, possibly as an unintended consequence. Conventionally understood, 'an action is the outcome

of a choice within constraints' (Elster, 1983:vii) but this conventional wisdom breaks down with the recognition that constraints may be chosen, and the choices shaped by constraints. (Crow, 1989:17)

Crow therefore explores the limits of game theory in helping us to understand the use of 'strategy' in sociology. The main problem in applying the concept in this way lies in the relationship between choices and constraints and in understanding just what constitutes a constraint. Norms and traditions can be perceived as constraints, but as active agents, people also 'choose' the norms or traditions by which they are constrained. Their choice of strategy will depend upon their perception of these constraints. Norms can also represent habitual behaviour which may have not discernible rationale behind it. A further problem is that in the messy world of real life rather than in the clean and clinical world of abstract theorising, constraints are continually changing, as are the perceptions of them:

> Game theory implies each actor calculating and assessing the strategies of the other actors and the consequences of their own actions. However, in a dynamic situation the prediction of outcomes is not always possible.
> When considering a dynamic situation, the analysis is strengthened where the concept of strategies is supported by other elements of the game analogy, notably the concepts of tactics, moves, styles of play, resources, and information states . . . Distinguishing between strategies, tactics and practices . . . or between strategy and capacity . . . might usefully have come earlier into the labour process debate, for example, while in discussions of household strategies much conceptual clarification remains to be done. (Crow, 1989:19)

Crow makes the point that strategies are not necessarily based upon a consensus within the household. There will be different strategies originating from different household members which may or may not be in conflict.

Crow ends by asserting that it is dangerous for sociologists to read strategic motives into situations where the actors themselves may not have conceived of them in this way. Hence 'coping strategies' or 'survival strategies' may simply be ways of surviving and not rational plans to achieve a desired goal.

> A further potential difficulty in relation to labels arises when sociologists impute objectives which the actors to whom they are imputed would not necessarily recognise and may even object to. Thus, for example, the terms 'coping strategy' and 'survival strategy' are both open to the interpretation of being somewhat patronising by

those individuals or households supposedly parctising them, since
neither obviously makes sense as something sufficient to aim for.
(Crow, 1989:20)

He leaves us with the idea that 'strategy' cannot be applied to many kinds of
behaviour, although it can certainly be applied to some. He also insists that
we need to take into account the constraints which are operating as well as
the choices which actors may make.

This thoughtfully critical interpretation of strategy was followed by far
stronger attacks on the idea. Martin Shaw (1990), for example, argues that
the term did not originate in game theory. Rather, it originated in military
terminology and sociologists were merely absorbing the term. He traces the
concept to the history of the two world wars and the need to develop a
'corporate strategy' for weapons systems. This concept should not be
transposed from the military context into other social worlds, he argues. It
does not apply equally to individuals or households. Since there are many
limitations of 'strategic analysis' in any case, this flawed concept should not
be imported into other areas of social life where it would be even less
appropriate. Indeed we could go on to argue that a 'strategy' is how some
aspects of public policy (including military policy) are presented publicly
and therefore justified, but when we look at it more closely we may find that
they too are more irrational and random than they first appear.

The diffusion of strategic language to the non-military state and
private corporate spheres can be seen as a part of the general
expansion of state and corporate activities. With the increase in the
scale and forward planning of large organisations, it is under-
standable that their controllers should adopt linguistic devices which
express their tasks of coordinating complex activities towards concentrated policy goals . . . (Shaw, 1990:466)
Nevertheless, the diffusion of strategic language to the level of the
individual actor is a very significant social fact. Its origins almost
certainly lie in the incorporation of whole societies into the process of
total war, in the first half of this century, the penetration of strategic
concepts into society and the internationalisation of the military way
of thinking which this invited for individuals. But in its contemporary
forms, it is an even more recent phenomenon, perhaps essentially
one of the last decade. It reflects an increasing self-perception of
individuals, and basic social groups such as families, as embattled
agents, in constant tension with other individuals, groups and institutions, in a competitive social environment. It is interesting to investigate the extent to which the adoption of 'strategic' language can be
linked to the effects of state strategies which have exposed social

institutions, families and individuals to greater market pressures. (Shaw, 1990:467)

Shaw attributes the absorption of the concept of 'strategy' by British sociologists to the institutional pressures which they were under themselves in the 1980s. Faced with expenditure cuts and rationalisations in universities, sociologists have been forced to adopt 'strategies' and the language of business whether they like it or not, and this, he implies, seeped into their academic thinking and the ways in which they constructed the world:

> Within British academic institutions, certainly, it is in the current decade of financial crisis that it has become expected that every department or unit has a 'strategy'; for its future development. Similar pressures have been directed, if sometimes less formally, at units in a variety of institutions, and indeed at individual actors. In a market economy and society actors must constantly compete with others, and develop plans for successful competition. Much of the diffusion of 'strategic' language seems to be connected with the new vigour of market relations, and the individualisation of 'strategy' often appears as an internalisation of the imperatives of market relations. (Shaw, 1990:467–8)

Indeed, Shaw himself has been opposing the tendency to see war in terms of strategic studies in favour of a more sociological definition:

> An even more important lesson is that the study of wars as a social phenomena can never be reduced to the study of strategies and those actors (chiefly those controlling states and armies) who produce them. Wars are now generally momentous events for whole societies, for all social groups and institutions and for individuals. It may or may not be the case that those other actors have their own 'strategies' as distinct from the military strategies of armies and states ... It is surely devaluing the term to apply it to any partially conscious course of action by an individual or a group, when there are actors (in wars: states etc.) with much more articulate strategic postures. (Shaw, 1979:470)

David Knights and Glenn Morgan (1990) make the point even more forcefully; they argue that the idea of strategy came not just from military planning but very much from business as well:

> ... key elements of the military concept of strategy have been appropriated by business. The emphasis on the professional elite (strategic management), the total disregard of other actors in the organisations except as resources for, or means of, implementing the

strategy and the treatment of the external environment as a competitive obstacle/enemy to the organisation – all this served to create a discourse in which the 'captains of industry' are seen as the equivalent of generals in war continuously waging battle with the competition on a rough and unpredictable terrain. The rewarding of business leaders in Britain by knighthoods and peerages, traditionally granted by the monarchy for services in war, is further exemplification of the contemporary significance of economic competition as 'war by other means' (Knights and Morgan, 1990:478)

By seeing 'strategy' in terms of a Foucauldian 'discourse', Knights and Morgan analyse the use of the concept as a claim to truth. They argue that the term replicates the positivist and scientistic paradigm from which it originates and, further, that sociologists, in using it, are active in extending the discourse into people's ordinary lives. Sociologists actually play a role in constructing social actors according to the strategic discourse of the powerful. This is particularly the case where they impute a strategy to the actions of others and therefore reinforce the idea that individuals should act in a normative and rationalistic way:

Strategy is not the innocent concept that its current populist usage in sociology or anywhere else suggests (Knights and Morgan, 1990:475) . . . a concentration on sociological usage has a tendency to generate the illusion that the concept of strategy is somehow neutral with respect to the objects to which it is applied. Our argument is grounded in the opposite view and, moreover, a recognition that despite attempts to stigmatise and marginalise sociology, its discourse filters readily into – and has powerful effects upon – the cultures which the discipline merely seeks to study. The point we wish to make and demonstrate through our brief focus on military and business organisation is that the discourse and practice of strategy is distinctively a mechanism of power.

. . . it is necessary to confront a related . . . question of whether governments, armies, corporations, associations, households or individuals *actually* act in accordance with strategic plans or if a strategy is something *imputed* to their actions by the sociologist. Frequently sociologists draw either unconsciously or unreflectively upon explicit strategic discourse and practice that is prevalent within certain spheres of society and then apply it to areas where it is absent or assumed to be implicit. (Knights and Morgan, 1990:476)

Knights and Morgan analyse the development of the discourse of strategy in the context of business and particularly in business studies. They consider the ways in which this creates 'experts' who can intepret the discourse and help to diffuse it to ever wider areas of practice:

> Since 1947 the development of a discourse on business strategy is associated with two features. Firstly, it is linked to the overall expansion of managerialist ideologies and practices institutionalised through the business schools and other organisations claiming to provide a rational and scientific impetus to the development of management techniques and processes. . . .
>
> As with military discourse, a range of social relationships are constructed through strategy. At the academic level, it generates a set of experts – people who research strategy, who elaborate its 'inner meaning', who wrestle with its problematics and may be located within distinct schools of thought such as the rationalist of the processual approach to strategic practice (Morgan and Knights, 1989). Simultaneously, it generates an audience of students who will eventually 'go out into the world and apply the concept of strategy'. At the inter-organisational level, strategy discourse sustains another set of experts as well as another audience. These experts are the management consultants and analysts organised within their own particular companies or hidden inside large accountancy practices whose job it is to provide strategic analysis for the myriad of companies defined as lacking 'strategic skills'. Their audience in turn consists not just of the people within the organisation where consultancy expertise is exercised but also within the wider business community, in particular those who own or through the management of funds (e.g. with financial institutions) control the ownership of companies. Finally within organisations there are those managers who, learning from the business schools or from the experience of the consultants, take on the mantle of the strategists and work from the inside to implement the discourse; their audience is also partly inside the organisation, those who are subjected to the power effects of strategy or are competing for resources within the managerial hierarchy, and partly outside the organisation – the owners of the company and the analysts. (Knights and Morgan, 1990:478–9)

Furthermore, once the discourse of strategy has taken root it becomes self-perpetuating, since it constitutes the very terms in which people think and evaluate their actions:

> . . . organisations construct rational interventions in their 'environments' [and] there is no way of knowing whether or not the content of strategy makes a difference but it is a technique for transforming managers and employees into committed goal-oriented and self-disciplined subjects. And once subjectivity is defined in and through strategy, the discourse and practice becomes self-legitimating and

self-reproducing regardless of its effects . . . (Knights and Morgan, 1990:479)

. . . But from research we have recently been conducting on organisations it would appear that strategists are reluctant to admit failure; instead, they reconstitute their goals and end results of strategy so that it can be defined as a success (Knights and Murray, 1989). Mistakes and failures are relegated to the status of minor tactics and attributed to weaknesses in the organisation that can only be eradicated by invoking the discourse and practice of strategy. In this sense, then, strategy is self-fulfilling in its effects. (Knights and Morgan, 1990:480)

Knights and Morgan see a real danger in this discourse escaping from the world of business and starting to invade other areas of social life, especially if sociologists or anyone can claim to infer strategies from someone else or to speak on their behalf. In this way, those who are acted upon by business are constituted as subjects of the discourse as well as business itself:

. . . studies which impute strategic intent to actors may help to facilitate situations where people claiming to speak 'on behalf' of the actors concerned begin to articulate the strategy and appropriate ownership of it. This identification of an intended strategy sets up a new arena within which power is exercised in such a way as to transform individuals into subjects who are constituted though, and find their sense of identity in, strategy.

Examples of this abound in the area of labour markets; as new household work strategies are identified, for example centering on the propensity of younger married women with under school-aged children to go out to work, so firms develop working arrangements to allow this to occur. New specialisms arise within personnel departments to deal with the requirements of this group . . . In imputing strategies in this way, sociologists feed into the existing discourse. Their analysis legitimates strategy with reference to yet another 'expert' discourse, no matter how low in the hierarchy of expertise sociology may lie. In short, the uncritical adoption of the concept of strategy obscures the extent to which sociological accounts may themselves constitute knowledge that further enhances the strategic power of business corporations in providing them with additional techniques to control the labour market. (Knights and Morgan, 1990:480–1)

And the wider implication is that social behaviour in general starts to become classified in terms of the discourse:

In addition, sociological knowledge of this kind contributes to the 'normalisation' of subjects through reinforcing 'dividing practices' ... For in a world where strategic intent is taken for granted, those who lack it are seen as failures and labelled 'deviant'. (Knights and Morgan, 1991:481)

This leads Knights and Morgan to reject the use of the term 'strategy' altogether and to argue that we should find other ways to characterise social behaviour:

By taking on the language of strategy in an uncritical manner sociologists are contributing unintentionally to the spread and expansion of a multiplicity of these power discourses and practices. For there is little doubt that strategy operates as a power that normalises and individualises those who are subjected to it; not only does it force them to act strategically and take responsibility for their own strategies, it actually transforms individuals into subjects who secure their sense of meaning and reality through the discourse and practice of strategy. (Knights and Morgan, 1990:481–2)

... Nothing new is really added by talking the discourse of strategy; on the contrary, a limit is put on our understanding of the special phenomenon because we are forcing action into a particular rationalistic and individualistic framework. Moreover, as is clear from Crow's analysis, we do not escape the dualism between action and structure by imputing strategic intent to actions. Indeed we suffer the worst of both worlds since analysis either drifts into talking about collective strategies as if they were independent of subjective action (Silverman 1970) or imposes categories upon subjects that denies the integrity of the phenomena (Douglas 1970). (Knights and Morgan, 1990:480–1)

However, the Foucauldian vision of the ubiquitous diffusion of discourses is more useful for deconstructing ideas than for reconstructing them. The concentration upon how relationships of power and domination are spread from the top down tends to preclude certain areas of study – such as understanding the rationality of the day-to-day economic activity of households from the 'bottom up', as it were. The humanistic, grounded approach which was the original strength of the 'strategies' perspective is lost. Furthermore, the approach deriving from structuralism tells us nothing about how people outside of business actually perceive these discourses nor what other ways they may have of making sense of their lives.

William Watson (1990), by contrast, further elaborates the idea of rationality but from a more abstract perspective. He considers the concept in terms of Weber's classification of action, and looks at when action could be seen as strategic or non-strategic. He reconsiders the ideas of rationality raised by Weber but wishes to stretch the concept even beyond Weber's examples of 'non-rational' behaviour. Following his evaluation of Weber's account of anarcho-syndicalism, Szaz's account of hysteria, the Comintern strategy towards fascism, and Jeremy Bentham's Panopticon, he concludes that it is important to consider 'value figurative' relations which are misrepresented as rational means to specific ends:

> . . . a far more flexible understanding of the nature of *strategy* is required than is effectively suggested in the tacit or explicit linkage of the concept to some, typically Weberian, account of rationality. The development of a strategy is unlikely to be fully comprehensible to the sociologist if he or she starts out modelling the process as a complex sequence of quasi-syllogistic chains of inference linking ends to means. This simply reduces the symbolic character of human thought to a controlled and contained process of reference which, however philosophically mysterious it may remain, is practically circumscribed such that the symbolic is a mere medium for the development and sustenance of action processes. . . .
>
> What, then, is the effect of an acknowledgement of the *value figurative* relation for a definition of the strategic? The answer may lie, not in an assimilation of the strategic to the rational, but in a counterposing of the strategic to the 'traditional'. *The concept of strategy relates to the formulation and pursuit of aims and programmes, both conscious and unconscious, which are not reducible to the aims and programmes implicit in traditional action.* Such a definition does not beg the question of the forms of relation established in the development of a strategy and leaves room for the utilisation of elements of traditional or habitual action in the pursuit of strategies, insofar as the aims and programmes embodied in the strategy are not reducible to those implicit in these traditional components. One can go further and countenance the possibility of 'traditional strategies' where the selection of a course of action in the face of particular identified exigencies involves a process of *purposive selection* from a range of traditionally sanctioned actions, the strategic being given in the process of selection. However, the demonstration of an effective 'instrumentality' or 'rationality' implicit in traditional activities would not create the opening for an analysis in terms of strategy, which requires the recovery of empirical evidence which suggests that the subjects under investigation actually engaged in a process of aims/programmes construction. (Watson, 1990:495)

The feminist critique of the articles cited so far hinges on the fact that a 'malestream' view of strategy has been reinforced deriving from public domains – military planning and business – where masculine values predominate (Edwards and Ribbens, 1991). The argument is that this discourse reflects a malestream model of calculative, competitive rationality as being the dominant set of values, and this model of strategy seems inappropriate for studying household relations in the private domain.

Despite these criticisms, the concept was subject to various rescue attempts. David Morgan (1989), whilst recognising its limitations, argues that it gives us one possible way of understanding the 'complex dance' of agency and structure. He feels that 'strategy' need not be an entirely voluntaristic concept, but if used carefully can also incorporate a recognition of power, access to resources and structural constraint. He cites a number of examples in the sociology of the family where the concept has lead to fruitful and interesting insights: 'The real question is not one of whether a particular action is 'really' strategic but rather the more pragmatic one of the further insights we may or may not gain from such an application' (Morgan, 1989:28). The people who are most concerned to rescue the idea, however, are those doing studies of household work, for whom it has proved useful. Alan Warde (1990), for example, whilst critical of the way in which 'strategy' was used by Pahl and Wallace, feels that we can limit the idea to looking at the *outcomes* of household activity. We do not need to open the 'black box' of intra-household negotiation in order to be able to do this. He recommends that we should look at 'strategies' more in terms of 'socially constrained options' than in terms of choice. He outlines two senses in which the word can be used. One is the strong sense, that is, a rationally calculated set of actions. However, he feels this is difficult to sustain. Alternatively we can see 'strategy' in a weak sense, that households tailor their needs to resources in predictable ways and we can *infer* that these are strategies. However, since his own work is survey-based, there is no way of knowing what calculations people are making nor how they would perceive what they are doing. If 'strategies' are to some extent concerned with rational, purposive actions which actors can explain or justify, then survey research, by its very nature, is ill-suited to elucidate these. They can only be revealed by research methods which make the actor's consciousness an integral part of the study.

We could also make the criticism that we do indeed need to open the 'black box' of intra-household negotiation, since the outcomes would depend crucially upon these. To do so we need to take into account the inequalities within the household which were touched upon above. Graham Crow (1989) originally raised the idea that households do not represent a consensus strategy, but rather that there would be alternative or conflicting strategies based upon the power positions of people within the household and that these would be related in some way to gender and generation. This is consistent with a feminist view of the family as an arena of power relations in which women are dominated (Abbott and Wallace, 1990); however, it is also borne out in empirical studies of household relations, particularly that between spouses. Some authors have sought to unravel the different strategies existing within households (Wallman, 1984). Jan Pahl's work, ironically developed at the same time as the project on household work strategies, indeed seeks to unpack the 'black box' by looking in some detail at the internal workings of households from the point of view of women and concludes that there are a number of different ways in which resources can be allocated within households (see Pahl 1983, 1989, 1991; and also Sara Arber in this collection). Pahl considers this to be connected with power inequalities within marriage, and sheds an important critical light on the kitchen-table-boardroom model of the household. A similar but related point could be made with regard to generational differences within the household, which have been even more neglected (Jones and Wallace, forthcoming; and Sara Arber in this collection).

However, even these concepts of household strategy suffer from the fact that they imply a white, heterosexual view of the household: the heterosexual couple is the norm. The studies carried out have generally been of such households. The fact that there has been little attempt (with the exception of Wallman) to address the issue of ethnic diversity or still less to consider the strategies of non-heterosexual, non-couple households reflects the dominant view in sociology of what implicitly constitutes the 'norm' and thus what is worthy of study.

However, an alternative view is provided in the studies by Rosalind Edwards and Jane Ribbens. They argue that the idea of strategy can help to explain the way in which women as mothers manage to cope with the demands of private and public spheres and that, far from being patronising as Crow argues, the term actually dignifies women's efforts to resolve the tensions in their lives. They plead:

> . . . what other language are we to use in order to make visible the part played by individual interpretations in re/creating the larger social processes? It is because of the term's apparent ability to make visible both the individual and social processes that we have at times been drawn towards it in our own researches concerning women's lives. (Edwards and Ribbens, 1991:480)

They also make the point that although 'strategy' is a term derived from the public domain and applied to the private, we could instead start from domestic rationality and work outwards in our use of the concept:

> The reason for the application of the concept of 'strategy' to women's domestic and family lives may well be prompted by a concern . . . to steer a course between giving individuals a sense of agency whilst at the same time retaining a sense of the contextual constraints under which they live. (Edwards and Ribbens, 1991:478–9)

They thus take issue with Knights and Morgan's condemnation of the idea of strategy because it enables some to speak 'on behalf of' others. They argue that this is not necessarily a bad thing and can lead to an empowerment of the views which would otherwise be left voiceless:

> By using it [strategy] to describe the lives of individuals, sociologists may themselves be using a strategy (?) that seeks to legitimate and thus empower individual activities, including those which may at first sight appear irrational. But sociologists who do this must recognise that in applying the concept of 'strategy' to the lives of individual women in a shared situation (say, for example, the lone mothers with dependent children) they are imposing a particular, and a particularly loaded, pattern of order upon women whose lives, as we will argue, are founded upon a very different pattern. Indeed, they may also be imposing a pattern of order which may not fit even with aspects of male experience of the public world.
>
> . . . Whatever the intentions of the writers who use the concept (whether a conscious 'strategy' of empowering individuals and/or understanding their lives, or an unconscious form of self-aggrandisement), we must consider the reasons for their choice of this particular language. If researchers and sociologists are seeking to make individual activities visible and to legitimise them by describing them as 'strategies', what are the origins of the legitimating norms being invoked, and in what contexts is such empowerment being sought? We suggest that it is *audiences in the public domain* that are being addressed, particularly state and corporate policy makers concerned with women's domestic lives or women's employment issues. Furthermore, it is *public realm ideologies and norms* which are being invoked, using discourses derived from male-dominated spheres of activity, as the earlier articles have elucidated quite clearly. In this sense, the debate about 'strategy' raises broader questions of the relationship between sociological research (especially that which seeks to incorporate individuals' own perspectives) and social policy. Thus the ultimate effect of the use of the term 'strategy' in relation to women's lives in domestic settings may be to distort, undermine and ultimately erode their own understandings and priorities concerning

their activities. We are not suggesting that as sociologists we should never act as advocates for those whom we conduct our research on and about (and hopefully for). We are saying that we need to be careful that the bases for understanding on which we do so are not those which fit neatly with those of powerful public world organisations and institutions. To avoid this, our undertandings and analysis should be grounded in the world of people whose lives we are exploring – however difficult this might be. (Edwards and Ribbens, 1991:479–80)

In her own research on mothers in full-time higher education, Rosalind Edwards feels that 'strategies' did help understand what the women were doing:

I had felt that 'strategy' attributed to women some sense of dignity and control over their lives, which were governed by the often conflicting requirements of two very different institutions. However, strategy was not a word any of the women used themselves, or perhaps would have even recognised as appropriate in describing how they coped with moving between family and education. Indeed, very few of them recognised they were 'doing' anything other than just 'being' mothers/partners and students as they felt they should and to the best of their abilities. On the other hand, they were aware of the 'standards' and actions others required of them and those they required of themselves. They were both acting on an emotional, unconscious level and on a reasoned, conscious level at the same time. (Edwards and Ribbens, 1991:481)

In Jane Ribben's research on mothers with young children she felt similarly that 'strategy' was an appropriate term to use:

I have chosen these particular examples of behaviour outside the home because they are espcially tempting ones for the application of the concept of 'strategy' in a context where individuals are faced with wider social constraints which they may or may not seek to resist or negotiate in various ways. The concept of 'strategy' allows us to describe variabilities of social action at an *abstract* ideal-typical level – we can avoid classifying individual *people*, but can view them as moving between different *strategies* in different settings or at different times. Furthermore, its application invokes a sense of women rationally and purposively dealing in various ways with the tensions between individual children's behaviours and social pressures in non-domestic settings where they feel exposed to an impersonal public gaze. (Edwards and Ribbens, 1991:484)

These authors go on to argue that women's strategies should be seen as fundamentally different from male-oriented strategies of the public world in business and military planning:

> Set out in this way it becomes highly dubious to describe women's family lives by use of a concept which implies rational means-oriented activities within which individual people are treated as resources towards the achievement of larger goals. We suggest that women's family-based understanding are rooted in a concern with *processes* rather than goals; with activities and *ways of being* which are regarded as valuable in their own right, rather than as means to ends. Furthermore, it is precisely in the *concern with detail* rather than with overall 'strategic' end views that such orientation to process may be expressed. . . . This is not to imply that the public world is rational and the domestic/women are irrational – just that domestic 'rationality' has to be understood on its own terms as guided by both emotion and perception, with 'goals' that are linked to processes and to orientation . . . (Edwards and Ribbens, 1991:484, 486)
>
> . . . In rethinking these from women's private world understanding we may shed fresh light on what is obscured by such 'strategic' discourses in public settings also. There may indeed by permeations and overlaps between public and private understandings. As sociologists we ourselves need a vocabulary that allows us to illuminate these, rather than unquestioningly adopting a masculinized language of power in public settings.
>
> And yet we have sought in vain for an accepted and acceptable term (to the academic world and to ourselves) to apply to women's lives. We have found ourselves at something of a loss to know how to express such understandings for the purposes of public academic discourses. If we are not to use the concept of 'strategy' and other terms to connote rational action, what other vocabulary do we use? We have found ourselves turning to words and phrases such as 'different approaches', 'ways of coping', 'means of dealing with . . .'. This may not give the discussion the same flavour of grandeur and rational purpose as the term 'strategy', but in using this particular 'approach' we have been concerned to express the significance of women's lives without using a malestream conceptual filter. (Edwards and Ribbens, 1991:486–7)

It seems that those actually studying households are reluctant to abandon the term (although they may wish to transform it), whereas those looking at larger scale institutions are keen to reject it. The debate then came round full-circle to the issue of farming families once more, with an article by Steven Pile in 1991 which argues that the dairy farmers he studied exemplify the rise of work strategies. He analyses how farmers formulate their strategies, through his interviews with them. Hence, he is using 'strategies' in a different sense to Ribbens and Edwards, because his farmers are self-consciously forming policies for the business and for family transmission. Thus he is concerned precisely with the penetration of business (economically calculative) rationality into the private world of the family where different values may exist. He is untroubled by the extent to which the household strategy represents a consensus because he is concerned only with male respondents and their representation of the family. He therefore takes their patriarchal values – for example, that the farm must be transmitted through the male line – for granted. Given the preceding discussion, we cannot assume that this view represents a consensus strategy for all members of the household. Nevertheless, he sees this as an important way of understanding social processes from the 'bottom up' – of the way in which actors shape their circumstances as well as being shaped by them:

> From this perspective, the major problem faced by farmers is how to ensure the survival of family farming under conditions which are increasing economic and political contraints. Instead of assuming that farmers are caught in a web, this paper examines the ways in which farmers resist entrapment and in so doing choose strategies that tend to reproduce those webs. It is far too easy to suggest that farmers have no choice, no control over their conditions and that they fatalistically acquiesce to prevailing market structures . . . I suggest that farmers are, in part through their own actions, ensuring the web of relations in which they farm. That these farmers choose strategies within structural constraints and their choices tended to reproduce these structures, sometimes against their intentions.
>
> Social structures restrict the range of strategies but constraints may be chosen and constraints shape choices (Crow, 1989). . . . structural contraint operates through the active participation of people involved. I use the term 'survival strategy' to describe the complex relationships between structure and agency, constraint and choice, in a way that shows how structures are reproduced by the everyday practices of knowledgeable people . . . Farmers' experience is not 'neutral'; it comprises sets of relations which not only set particular 'choices' but also structure how these choices come about and how they are defined. In practice, these choices represent survival strategies, which are long term aims which lead to conscious rational decisions (Redclift, 1986:219). (Pile, 1991:255–6)
>
> For farmers, the world is historical, so reactions to uncertainty and complexity are bound up with their reading of the (involuntary)

labour treadmill that set the circumstances for the future reproduction of the *family farm*. In the 1980s farmers have been watching a
crisis situation developing. Farmers are not happy admitting that they
are in a poor position to cope with the economic crisis. Farmers are
concerned to secure their future but their survival strategies were
conditioned by their individual readings of the general circumstances
which they all face. The effect is that whilst each farmer picks an
individual route through the crisis, each route parallels those chosen
by others, producing similar outcomes. Survival strategies, in
practice, are the selective engagement and disengagement within
the labour treadmill. Farmers' *choice* of survival strategy, framed by
the social, economic and political circumstances which they read,
tend to reproduce those very circumstances which make farmers
choose a survival strategy. (Pile, 1991:272)

Thus strategies create structures, which in turn constrain strategies, in a
circular fashion. The sociologist must therefore look at the rationality from
which strategies are constructed, but also at the perceptions of constraint
and choice within which the rationality exists. We return here to the way in
which structure and agency relate, just as Morgan (1989) pointed out in his
original comment on Crow. Although some critics – such as Knights and
Morgan – feel this concept of strategy conflates structure and action, others
(such as Pile or Edwards and Ribbens) feel that, on the contrary, the
relationship between structure and action is elucidated.

Conclusion

How far can the concept of 'strategy' with its various origins be applied to
households? In the end I would conclude with the premise with which
Crow started. Namely that whilst: '. . . the term strategy is undoubtedly
appropriate in the analysis of many social relationships, it is equally
obviously inappropriate in others' (Crow, 1989:2). It would certainly seem
that under some circumstances people do pursue strategies, and these
strategies can represent an economic, calculative rationality. For example,
in order to pay off an overdraft and not go bankrupt, a farmer may well be
forced to formulate a strategy. In order to achieve a given desired goal such
as buying a house, a family or person may have to develop a strategy.
However, the strategy will reflect those persons' perceptions of what is
necessary and meaningful in their social world rather than an economic,
calculative rationality alone. Also this does not mean that the strategy is
necessarily realistic or successful.

What other circumstances are there in which 'strategies' are constructed by households? People do at least imagine that they act rationally, but they also mostly just act without excessive reflection. It could be that through the very act of asking questions, sociologists encourage respondents to develop a strategy or to think of what they do in terms of a strategy, which they might not have done otherwise. Alternatively, it could help them to make explicit a strategy which was perhaps implicit. In this way both the sociologist and the bank manager can encourage people to formulate their actions in a rational or strategic way in order to justify them to an outsider. Thus where there is some sort of rational calculation then we could infer a 'strategy', but not necessarily under other circumstances. The research method used must enable us to interpret how people are constructing this rationality.

One problem which remains, however, is the extent to which a 'strategy' can be assumed to be the property of a household rather than an individual. If it is the property of the household then it represents some sort of collective decision-making which has reached a consensus. To what extent does such a consensus actually exist? This assumption seems very problematic and the terms of the ensuing debate suggest that we can no longer look at household strategies without unpacking the 'black box' of intra-household relations.

However, we are also left thinking that we should be circumspect in our use of the concept. The use of any concept tends to open up some areas of investigation but also to close off others. The infusion of the concept with discursive meaning results in us constructing the world in particular ways. We should recognise that since the concept has become part of sociological knowledge, we are constructing households in terms of 'strategies' and perhaps encouraging our respondents to do so also.

Future directions

It seems evident that, despite attempts at demolition, the term 'strategy' will continue to be used in research on households because of its empirical usefulness. Indeed it has helped to shed some new light on the 'workings' of households (Morris, 1991). Perhaps in the end, as David Morgan intimates, the proof of the concept lies in how empirically helpful it is and continues to be. There are several expanding areas of research where it will probably play some part.

Firstly, the issue of household strategising is by no means dead, since the relationship between actors in the household and the economic circumstances in which they find themselves is continually changing and continues to be of crucial interest to sociologists. The emergence of non-nuclear family forms, of new patterns of employment for women, men, young and old, the development of social policies encouraging 'community care' by the family, all point to the fact that households are forced to adopt means by which to survive which involve some sort of calculation of risks and gains. These can and are still usefully analysed in terms of 'strategies'. These changes were the subject of the large-scale research on 'Social Change and Economic Life' which was sponsored by the ESRC and which encouraged detailed studies of the relationship between economic change and household life. In this research 'strategy' was a key concept (Anderson, Bechofer and Gershuny, forthcoming). Similarly, the large number of studies of household life under different employment conditions which have been spawned over the last decade will ensure that the concept enjoys a long run.

Secondly, the changing situation in Eastern Europe will no doubt inspire many studies as transformation to a capitalist economy takes place. The concept of strategy was already used to describe the ways in which households shuffled resources between different 'economies' to make ends meet under state socialism (Redclift, 1986; Rose, 1991). The introduction of privatisation measures will force many households to construct new 'strategies' for survival, as they are forced to become more self-conscious in the way they organise their work whilst their environment becomes increasingly risky and uncertain. The business vocabulary has already been imported by Western 'experts' who will assist in its diffusion. These changes may act in the same way as economic transformation in agriculture and in the cities of Latin America – to make people self-consciously strategic in their thinking about some of their activities and to encourage new inter-relations of economic and family life. However, it seems clear that future sociological use of the term should take cognisance of the debates around its use which have taken place in *Sociology*.

Acknowledgements

I would like to acknowledge the help of Sukumer Periwel, A. V. Wallace, Ray Pahl, Jan Pahl and the editors for their comments on this paper.

References

Abbott, P. and Wallace, C. (1990), *An Introduction to Sociology: Feminist Perspectives*, London, Routledge.

Anderson, M., Bechofer, F. and Gershuny, J. (eds.) (forthcoming), *The Social and Political Economy of the Household*, London, Oxford University Press.

Crow, G. (1989), The Use of the Concept of 'Strategy' in Recent Sociological Literature, *Sociology*, 23, 1–24.

Douglas, J. D. (1970), *Understanding Everyday Life*, London, Routledge and Kegan Paul.

Edwards, R. and Ribbens, J. (1991), 'Meanderings around "Strategy": A Research Note on Strategic Discourse in the Lives of Women', *Sociology*, 25, 477–90.

Elster, J. (1983), *Sour Grapes*, Cambridge, University Press.

Goffman, E. (1970), *Strategic Interaction*, Oxford, Basil Blackwell.

Habermas, J. (1969), *Towards a Rational Society*, Cambridge, Polity Press (1987).

Knights, D. and Morgan, G. (1990), 'The Concept of Strategy in Sociology: a note of dissent', *Sociology*, 24, 475–84.

Morgan, D. H. J. (1989), 'Strategies and sociologists: a comment on Crow', *Sociology*, 23, 25–9.

Morris, L. (1990), *The Workings of the Household*, Cambridge, Polity Press.

Pahl, J. (1983), 'The allocation of money and the structuring of inequality within marriage', *Sociological Review*, 31, 37–62.

Pahl, J. (1989), *Money and Marriage*, London, Macmillan.

Pahl, J. (1991), 'Money and power in marriage', in Abbot, P. and Wallace, C., *Gender, Power and Sexuality*, London, Macmillan.

Pahl, R. E. (1984), *Divisions of Labour*, Oxford, Basil Blackwell.

Pahl, R. E. and Wallace, C. D. (1985), 'Household work strategies in an economic recession' in Redclift, N. and Mingione, E. (eds.) *Beyond Employment: Household, Gender and Subsistence*, Oxford, Basil Blackwell.

Pile, S. (1991), 'Securing the Future; "Survival Strategies" amongst Somerset Dairy Farmers, *Sociology*, 25, 55–74.

Redclift, M. (1986), 'Survival strategies in rural Europe: continuity and change', *Sociologia Ruralis*, XXVI, 15–27.

Roberts, B. (1978), *Cities of Peasants: The Political Economy of Urbanisation in the Third World*, London, Sage.

Rose, D. (1991), 'Between state and market. Key indicators of transition in eastern Europe', Centre for Study of Public Policy, University of Strathclyde, Paper no. 196.

Shaw, M. (1990), 'Strategy and social process; military context and sociological analysis', *Sociology*, 24, 65–74.

Silverman, D. (1970), *The Theory of Organisations*, London, Heinemann.

Szaz, T. S. (1973), *The Manufacture of Madness*, Frogmore, Paladin.

Szaz, T. S. (1972), *The Myth of Mental Illness*, Frogmore, Paladin.

Warde, A. (1990), 'Household work strategies and forms of labour: conceptual and empirical issues', *Work, Employment and Society*,4, 495–15.

Wallman, S. (1984), *Eight London Households*, London, Tavistock.

Watson, W. (1990), 'Strategy, rationality and inference: the possibility of symbolic performances', *Sociology*, 24, 485–98.

Further reading

For an evaluation of what stage ideas of work and household have reached:
Morris, L. (1990), *The Workings of the Household*, Cambridge, Polity Press.

Anderson, M., Bechofer, F., and Gershuny, J. (eds.) (forthcoming), *The Social and Political Economy of the Household*, London, Oxford University Press.

For an account of survival strategies in Latin America:

Roberts, B. (1978), *Cities of Peasants: The Political Economy of Urbanisation in the Third World*, London, Sage.

For an account of work strategies in agriculture:

see *Sociologia Ruralis*, XXVI, 3/4.

For a good empirical study of family work strategies:

Hareven, T. K. (1982), *Family Time and Industrial Time*, Cambridge, Cambridge University Press.

For an account of household strategies in Eastern Europe:

Rose, R. (1991), *Between State and Market. Key Indicators of Transition in Eastern Europe*, Centre for the study of Public Policy, University of Strathclyde (there are a series of papers on this theme).

Inequalities within the household

The last twenty-five years have witnessed a paradigm shift in how sociologists conceive of relationships within the household, spurred by feminist sociological debate on gender inequalities and the private domain, previously largely invisible to sociologists. This chapter illustrates the changing contours of this debate through an analysis of key articles published in *Sociology*.

In the mid-1960s the household was considered a unitary concept, and involved collective decision-making. An implicit assumption was that all household members shared in the same standard of living. Sexism permeated all writing and research; it was unquestioned that women were the natural homemakers, responsible for domestic work and childcare, and men the natural 'breadwinners' who should control the household's financial resources. The sexual division of domestic labour was seen as unproblematic and inequalities in power and access to resources remained invisible.

This chapter illustrates how the nature of relationships within households became the subject of academic study in their own right. In the 1980s, the household became a key topic for feminist work: 'as the theatre of many aspects of the relationship between men and women' (Morris, 1988: 337). The initial focus was on the internal characteristics of households but later turned to how these were constrained by external influences, such as the characteristics of the local labour market. The 1990s is likely to see a shift in focus towards how inequalities of race and age, together with gender and class, structure relationships within the household.

The affluent worker studies and the sexual division of domestic labour

An appropriate starting point to exemplify this sea change in sociological concerns is one of the key empirical studies of the 1960s – *The Affluent Worker* (Goldthorpe *et al.*, 1967, 1969). This research aimed to test the 'embourgeoisement thesis' – whether skilled manual workers were taking on the characteristics of the middle class in terms of their norms, patterns of social relationships and their family lifestyle.

There was no questioning of the assumption that 'workers' were men only. Within the Affluent Worker research, women's involvement was limited to the joint interview with workers and their wives. Wives were conceptualised only in terms of having an influence on attitudes towards children's education, patterns of sociability of the worker and his family and the extent to which the family (the husband) was becoming more home-centred in terms of leisure activities. Unmarried women were entirely excluded from the Affluent Worker research.

Thus women were peripheral to testing the sociological theory of 'embourgeoisement'. They were only present as a vehicle through which other subsidiary parts of the theory could be tested. One of these was 'The analysis of the "jointness" and "segregation" of conjugal roles advanced by Elizabeth Bott (1957) . . . that working class couples tend to have more segregated roles and middle class couples to show more jointness.' (Platt, 1969: 287).

Jennifer Platt, the junior (i.e. fourth) author of the Affluent Worker publications, states:

> The degree of jointness/segregation was therefore an obvious dimension to measure in a study designed to test the hypothesis that affluent manual workers were in some sense becoming middle class; the less segregated their conjugal roles, the more 'middle class' they could be regarded as having become. (Platt, 1969: 287)

Thus, Platt's article in *Sociology* considers the division of domestic labour as a resource in order to test the theory of embourgeoisement, not as a topic for the investigation of gender inequalities in the domestic arena.

This early research did not intentionally study gender inequalities within households, and was oblivious of women's oppression within the family. There was no questioning of the assumption that the gendered division of labour was divided into 'women's work' and 'men's work'; Platt describes the research:

> Our interviews were with married couples seen together in their own homes. 229 husbands had manual and 54 had white-collar jobs. The

average interview took about three hours, and the questions relevant to conjugal roles took up a small part of this time and occurred at several places in the schedule; some of them were also designed for other purposes. These questions covered the following areas: '(a) who usually performed various household tasks (washing up, doing the main shopping, taking children out and putting them to bed; (b) who usually made certain household decisions (what to do for holidays, to buy something new and expensive for the house, what colour to have the paint and wallpaper when redecorating); (c) whether the couple had discussions together on various kinds of issue (how to spend their money, the children's education, whether the husband should go after promotion or his own business); and (d) who paid for various items of expenditure (regular bills, irregular bills, rent or mortgage, holiday and Christmas expenses). The answers to each of these questions were dichotomized into 'joint' and 'nonjoint'. The criteria on which this was done were to regard all cases where an activity was done by both husband and wife together, or by either equally, as joint; and to regard all cases as joint where the husband did what would be conventionally regarded as woman's work (e.g. washing up, putting the children to bed). (Platt, 1969: 288).

This crude dichotomy was premised on the assumption that 'jointness' was measured by *any* involvement of men in 'women's work'. This could hardly be considered evidence of equality in the domestic arena. There was no conception that the division of domestic labour might be contested between spouses and thus the assumption prevailed that it could be objectively measured through a single joint interview with a married couple.

An important conclusion from Platt's paper was that 'jointness/segregation is not here unidimensional' (Platt, 1969: 292). She recognised that jointness in one area of behaviour was not matched in any consistent way by jointness in other areas. The items of behaviour did not form a unidimensional Guttman scale of jointness.

Another important distinction drawn by Platt was between overt descriptions of behaviour (as measured in her article) and personal norms or role expectations:

In our research, respondents were always asked about their behaviour rather than about personal or social norms; thus our data refer overtly to role performance rather than to role definitions or expectations. The assumption was made, perhaps unjustifiably, that role performance is a fair indicator of norms, and that if reporting were inaccurate it would err in the direction of over-emphasizing conformity to norms. (Platt, 1969: 292).

Platt goes on to give an example of this which remarkably illustrates the gendered nature of sociology in the late 60s and its view of the household as a collective decision-making unit:

> Some items of behaviour may have different meanings for one couple from those they have for another, and issues may vary in their relative significance. If, for instance, a wife takes a job, this may be as part of a family plan to improve their shared standard of living, and so express jointness, or as an independent decision on her own part that she would *like an outside interest or more pin-money*, and so express segregation. Again, for one couple it might be regarded as a much bigger step for the husband to do the washing up than for him to take the children out, while for another the position could be reversed. (Platt, 1969: 293, my emphasis)

Gender inequalities remain unquestioned; women *are* the 'natural' carers of the home and children. If a woman's work conflicts with home-care, then she either has to give up her leisure time or her job:

> If a wife goes out to work this decision changes the family situation: *she* has less time for housework, and thus a constraint is present. She may have had time on her hands in any case, and then there is no problem; or *she may resolve it by allowing herself less leisure*, and if this solution proves unsatisfactory she may eventually give up her job. (Platt, 1969: 294, my emphasis)

Thus, Platt's writing illustrates the framework of male-bias in sociology in the 1960s. Despite being trapped by the paradigm of this time, Platt shows many insights, including the way forward: '[I]n matters where so many complex and often subjectively-defined variables are involved, it may as a matter of research tactics be more suitable to use qualitative and partly impressionistic measures, since the intervening variables may be so diverse that it will be impossible to hold them constant without an impracticably large sample'. (Platt, 1969: 295).

During the 1970s, Ann Oakley (1974) published her highly influential study of housework based on interviews with forty women with dependent children. This was followed by other small-scale studies which analysed the division of domestic labour (e.g. Edgell, 1980), and larger surveys, including Martin and Roberts (1984), Pahl (1984) and the British Social Attitudes Survey (Jowell *et al.*, 1988). In addition, time budget studies have documented the relative amounts of time men and women spend on various domestic tasks (Gershuny *et al.*, 1986). These surveys have measured the relative amount of domestic work performed by husbands and wives, but paid little attention to control, responsibility and manage-ment of domestic labour. Following Platt (1969), they remain locked into a concern with documenting inequalities in behaviour.

Large-scale survey approaches have neglected more fundamental issues of inequalities in the allocation and distribution of other resources within households, as well as issues of control and responsibility. These have remained mainly the province of smaller-scale qualititative research. It had to wait until the early 1980s before feminist-inspired qualitative research uncovered power relations, patterns of control and other areas of inequality within the household.

Gender inequalities in household resources

The early work on gender inequalities in resource allocation and distribu-tion within the household took place largely outside the pages of *Sociology*. Pioneering work was published by Jan Pahl (1983) in *Sociological Review*, which provided a springboard for much later work. Pahl conducted quali-tative research on household finances, and argued the need to distinguish three different functions, which vary systematically with gender. 'Control' refers to decision about the allocation of finances to different areas of expenditure and most commonly rests with the husband. On the other hand, 'management', which is concerned with implementing these control decisions, and 'budgeting', which is associated with spending to achieve minimal consumption levels within each expenditure category, are mainly the province of the wife. The household became seen as the site of conflicting individual interests, with these interests expressed particularly clearly through differential access to and control of various household resources, such as money, food and access to leisure.

Following Pahl (1983), it was no longer possible to take the household as the unit of analysis in terms of consumption of goods or expenditure or indeed of domestic labour. These studies of intra-household inequality have highlighted the traditional invisibility of women's poverty within households and their lack of access to valued resources. Path-breaking work was undertaken by the Resources within Households Study Group, culminating in a collection of important papers by Julia Brannen and Gail Wilson (1987).

Inequalities in the household became a topic for research in its own right as well as a vehicle for understanding gender relations. An example of this research genre published in *Sociology*, was by Nickie Charles and Marion Kerr (1986). This research goes beyond the documentation of gendered inequality and 'explore[s] the implications of 'proper' eating and the provision and consumption of 'proper' meals in terms of the reproduction (material and ideological) of the family' (Charles and Kerr, 1986: 412).

The preparation and consumption of food within the household is important because:

> [I]t symbolises the relation of men to the home and women's place within the home (Murcott, 1982: 693). Our own research has led us to conclude that the regular provision of a 'proper meal' (cooked dinner) which is consumed by the whole family (usually together) is an important part of the process of reproduction of the family as a cohesive social unit. (Charles and Kerr, 1985: 412)

Women are central in achieving this process of reproduction.

This research was not originally conducted to explore gender issues, but for health policy purposes, centring on the nutrition of pre-school children:

> The concerns of this paper arose during the course of a research project concerned with family feeding practices [Charles and Kerr, 1985, 1988]. Two hundred women with pre-school age children were interviewed on all aspects of feeding a family. The interviews were semistructured and each lasted between one and three hours, depending on how talkative the women were. The interviews were separated by a fortnight, during which time the women were asked to keep a record of all the food consumption of each family member; these we refer to as the dairy records.
>
> The sample was located in a specific geographical area, a northern town and its surrounding villages, and was randomly selected from district health authority records of all births. It was stratified by the age of the sample child in each family. Seventeen of the families were found at interview to be dependent on state benefit, and the analysis we present below relates to this sub-sample and to the main sample of 200 women. (Charles and Kerr, 1986: 413)

The *Sociology* article analyses gender differences in food consumption, and compares food consumption of women in single parent and two-parent families living on a low income.

Charles and Kerr's research demonstrated how socio-economic characteristics of the household influenced the nature and extent of gender inequalities within the household:

> We have shown elsewhere (Charles and Kerr, 1985) that differences in food consumption between men and women appear to be less in families where the male partner is unemployed than in families where he is in paid employment. However, there is substantial evidence, both from the diary records and from the comments of the women

themselves, that although the number of meals may be the same, men are consistently given larger helpings of food than women and children. (Charles and Kerr, 1986: 421)

[W]omen in [two-parent] families [living on state benefits] do without to ensure that their partners and children can eat adequately. Indeed it is *only* in families living on state benefit that children's meat/fish consumption is higher than women's; in all other families it is usually significantly lower . . . [C]hildren's meat consumption was especially high in single-parent families. This suggests that in these families children enjoy the special treatment that would otherwise be afforded to the male partner. (Charles and Kerr, 1986: 423)

Women in two-parent families living on state benefit were particularly disadvantaged in terms of meat/fish consumption. 'Women living with men tend to privilege the men at their own and their children's expense' (Charles and Kerr, 1986: 425). This contrasted with women in single-parent families living on state benefit where food consumption was no lower than among married women in the whole sample.

The authors conclude:

Among families living on state benefit, however, our data suggests important differences between two-parent and single-parent families. In the former, women's and children's consumption of certain food items was lower than the consumption of the same foods by women and children in single-parent households. In addition, women in two-parent families seemed less likely to eat 3 meals a day than women in single-parent households. Balanced against this, however, is the fact that two-parent families seemed to eat 'proper' meals more frequently than single-parent families. We suggest that these differences can be related to the presence of a male partner. Women feel that it is particularly important to provide a proper meal for a man, and one of the constituent elements of the proper meal is 'proper' meat, preferably of high status [i.e. fresh meat]. This is expensive and so if it is provided there is less money available for other foodstuffs. This affects the diets of all family members, and means that consumption of other foods is lower in the two-parent than in the single-parent families [living on state benefit]. (Charles and Kerr, 1986: 426)

Charles and Kerr's research not only provided a clearer understanding of the bases of gender inequalities in access to household food resources, but showed how married women living on low incomes are particularly disadvantaged. In such households, men are considered to have a right to spending money (Bell and McKee, 1985; Morris, 1988; Pahl, 1990) and money for leisure activities, thus a smaller sum is available for women to budget for food. Women's own food consumption is adversely affected by the cultural norm of providing high status meat for men and 'proper' meals; these are intrinsic to the process of reproduction of the family as a cohesive social unit.

Counter-arguments relating to gender inequalities within households

The growing body of feminist research on resources within households inevitably led to critics, such as Peter Taylor-Gooby (1985), who reported his empirical research in the pages of *Sociology*. He sought to address two issues:

> [F]irstly, it has been argued that the distribution of resources between partners in a marriage 'reflects broader patterns of inequality between men and women and between social classes' (Pahl, 1983: 251). If this is so, is it the case that women in married-couple households have a lower level of living than the men to whom they are married? Secondly, it has been suggested that women's involvement in paid work may actually reduce their command over resources, either because husbands tend to retain more of their own larger incomes for their personal use (Land, 1983; Reid and Wormald, 1982: 78; Hunt, 1978) or because women have more direct contact with needs in the home, are accustomed to ensure lower levels of consumption and have a more tenuous relation to personal consumption-based culture outside the home. Thus in dual-earner households husbands may pay less of the food bills and wives *prefer* to use their incomes to buy their children new clothes. (Taylor-Gooby, 1985: 273–4, my emphasis)

Taylor-Gooby states that his interests in this research stem partly from a concern with the effectiveness of the social security system:

> These issues merit attention for three reasons: Firstly, on a practical level, the social security system distributes resources on a household basis, largely to an assumed 'head of household' in the case of married couples. If resources are not distributed evenly to 'dependents', the capacity of the social security system to achieve desired living standards is impaired . . . Secondly, the more even spread of paid employment resulting from the influx of women, especially married women, into the labour market from the mid-sixties onwards (Martin and Roberts, 1984) may not result in any more even spread of living standards. Thirdly, it is unclear how far differences in men's

and women's living standards are matters of choice and how far they are matters of external coercion. It may or may not be the case that women (or men) *prefer to go without some things themselves because they derive more satisfaction from contributing to the enjoyment of others.* (Taylor-Gooby, 1985: 274, my emphasis)

Thus, his orientation shows remarkably little appreciation of feminist work on the ways in which women's identity is shaped by self-sacrifice for the benefit of other family members (Graham, 1983; Finch and Groves, 1983).

Taylor-Gooby re-analysed data from the 1983 Breadline Britain poverty survey, which interviewed a quota sample of nearly 1,200 individuals. He identified fifteen items of personal consumption, which he argued were 'items necessarily consumed on an individual basis' (1985: 275), and found that married women were significantly more likely to consume five of these items than married men, namely – roast meat weekly, meat or fish on alternate days, owning a dressing gown, owning a weather-proof coat and the household owning a car. Married men were significantly more likely than married women to have access to two items – cigarettes and new clothes. He summarised 'This indicates that, by the measures of standard of living used in the study, married women tend to have slightly higher standards in most respects than married men'. (1985: 277).

Although he warned 'It should be emphasized that the gender-differences . . . are relatively slight' (Taylor-Gooby, 1985: 278), his conclusion was clearcut:

Taken as a whole, the analysis does not confirm the view that inequalities of power between women and men in society at large are reflected in patterns of resource allocation within marriage in any simple way. However, there is some evidence that being in a low income household is associated with lower levels of living for a woman in a way that it is not for a man. It should be noted that this conclusion is reached through equations that take marital status, age and income into account . . . This, and the fact that paid employment is a strong influence on women's consumption but not on men's, indicates that there are inequalities in consumption in particular kinds of households. However, the marked association between being married and enjoying a higher standard of living for women shows that this is not the outcome of marriage itself. The argument that involvement in paid work does not increase married women's living standards because the household absorbs the extra money is not confirmed. For women both full-time and part-time work enhances living standards. In general, the analysis suggests that it is only in particular kinds of household that women tend to be significantly worse off than their husbands; married women in general enjoy rather higher standards of personal consumption than married men. (Taylor-Gooby 1985: 282–3)

Taylor-Gooby's conclusions flew in the face of virtually all other research, and it was not surprising that a debate ensued in the pages of *Sociology*. Anne McGlone and Stephen Pudney (1986) succinctly demonstrate the invalidity of Taylor-Gooby's methods and discredit his conclusions. Because of the importance of their critique, a lengthy extract is provided:

A recent paper by Taylor-Gooby (1985) makes an interesting attempt to analyse the differences between men's and women's living standards within marriage. However, it is our contention that any convincing attempt to do this requires very detailed information on the distribution of resources *within* the family – information that is not available from the 'Breadline Britain' survey, used by Taylor-Gooby.

Firstly, as pointed out by Taylor-Gooby himself, the married men in the survey are not married to the married women in the survey. This means that, even if details of personal consumption were available, it is tenuous to argue that intra-family patterns of consumption may be analysed using these data.

Perhaps more importantly, the data themselves do not reflect *individual* consumption at all well. The survey was conducted as an attempt to look at *families'* attitudes to living standards and, for this reason, details of individual members' consumption were not collected. The report by Peter Taylor-Gooby does try to take this into account by separating out 15 items deemed to be purely personal consumption. In fact, we would claim that 9 of these items were really enjoyed by the whole family. For example, three items relate to food consumption, yet it seems unlikely, for instance, that roast meat was cooked by the respondent for him or herself alone. Similarly, a respondent may have access to a car, but it seems most unlikely that the married women in the sample actually use the family car to the same extent as the married men. . . . In fact the items relating to clothing, cigarettes and a hobby are probably the only ones which could be said to be purely personal consumption items.

Moreover, Taylor-Gooby's method of constructing an index of 'access to consumption goods' – merely counting, for each respondent, the number of affirmative replies to these 15 questions – is very arbitrary . . .

Leaving these problems aside, it is interesting to try to compare married men's and women's access to these consumption items, using regression analysis . . .

Firstly, he states that 'being married is the most important single factor in determining a woman's level of living'. He does not point out that it is for men too.

Secondly, he states that 'In cases where a positive [regression] coefficient is larger for women than for men, the characteristic in question is a stronger influence in enhancing the level of living for women than for men'. This is very misleading. A larger coefficient means that the characteristic in question has a stronger effect for women – but it means that the difference between getting married and remaining single (or divorced or separated) is greater for women than for men. It does not *say* that married women are better off than married men, because the regressions for men and women are run separately. (McGlone and Pudney, 1986: 88–9)

McGlone and Pudney go on to argue that: 'A much sounder approach to the analysis of access and gender, using this data set, is to run regressions for married women, married men and all married people and then conduct a test to determine whether the same regression coefficients apply to married men as to married women' (1986: 89). They conclude:

[W]e *cannot* say that the coefficients on the equation for married women are significantly different from those for married men. Nor can we say that either gender enjoys a significantly higher personal standard of living on the basis of this evidence.

Our conclusion, that there is no detectable difference in living standards between married men and women, is really what we would expect from this survey. There is not enough detail to allow us to analyse differences in consumption behaviour in a proper manner, since most of the items in Taylor-Gooby's index are jointly consumed by the whole family and not by one individual.

This is not to say that we believe that married women and men have the same personal consumption patterns. Detailed data on use of the family car, how much each individual eats and so on might well paint a very different picture. (McGlone and Pudney, 1986: 90)

In one of these areas, namely car usage, Angela Dale (1986) conclusively demonstrates that women are disadvantaged: 'Nationally representative data from the General Household Survey (GHS) provide evidence that married women do not have greater access to a car than married men, as suggested by Taylor-Gooby' (1986: 91). Dale showed 'that married women are substantially less likely to hold a full driving licence than married men [36% compared with 75%] while, of those who do hold a licence, married women are, once again, less likely to use a car on a daily basis [57% compared with 79%] (1986: 91).

Taylor-Gooby's (1986) reply did not contest the findings of his critics, but he did argue that the divergence in findings reflected:

... [A] difference in focus. My primary concern is with the relationship between gender and power. The interest in consumption arises from the argument that relative levels of living may be a useful indication of differences in power between men and women. Women are oppressed in our society. Is this due to the superior power of men (as radical feminists argue) or do the operations of the capitalist labour market (in exploiting those in the weakest bargaining position) and the state (in structuring welfare around work and family ethics) play major roles (as Marxist and socialist feminists claim)? This question puts the debate crudely ... If our interest is primarily in the question of whether men oppress women within marriage the approach of [McGlone and Pudney], which restricts attention to married women, is appropriate. If we wish to consider marriage within a social context then the approach of my [original] paper, which contrasts married and unmarried men and women, seems more suitable. (Taylor-Gooby, 1986: 93)

Taylor-Gooby presents the original data in a new form and concludes: '. . . that married women tend to have slightly higher levels of [individual] consumption than married men, but that unmarried women have somewhat lower levels than unmarried men . . . the consumption gap between married and unmarried people is greater for women than men' (Taylor-Gooby, 1986: 93).

Thus Taylor-Gooby in his reply to some extent 'moved the goal posts'. He admitted the methodological defects of his earlier work, and downplayed the comparison between married men and married women, which he characterised as an interest of 'radical feminists'. He then emphasised the greater disadvantages in consumption experienced by unmarried relative to married women, than of unmarried compared with married men. This is an important finding, and is consistent with other work documenting the higher level of poverty faced by women without a partner, whether due to divorce, widowhood or remaining single (Glendinning and Millar, 1987).

The debate over Taylor-Gooby's paper highlighted the problem of relying on relatively small-scale qualitative studies, because of the difficulty of being confident about the generalisability of their findings. It also showed up the inadequacy of existing large-scale survey data: no surveys routinely record the personal consumption of *each* adult within the same household, so secondary analysis of existing data cannot be used to throw light on inequalities of resources within households.

Intra-household inequalities and the labour market

By the late 1980s the debate was beginning to take on a new form. Earlier in the decade the focus on gender inequalities and gender relations within the household was necessary in order to make visible what was previously regarded as an unproblematic 'black box' of the household. By the late 1980s the research questions were broader – to understand how the social and economic context in which the household is located impacts on gender inequalities in access to and control over resources within households. Thus the debate brought into the intellectual fold the labour market position of both partners, their class, their education and their income.

Jan Pahl (1990) has contributed to this newer debate in the pages of *Sociology*. She argues: 'First, it is important to see financial arrangements in terms of social processes, as dynamic rather than static. Secondly, it is important not to separate financial arrangements within the household from the social and economic context in which the household is located' (Pahl, 1990: 137). Her paper provides a useful summary of how the 1980s research on resources within households has changed assumptions and policies associated with the household:

> Traditionally, economists have treated the household as though it were an individual and have assumed that the same economic theories apply . . . they have created a black box in the space between earning and spending . . .
>
> In reality, of course, income is earned by individuals, not households, and goods and services are purchased not by households but by individuals. However, 'by a heroic simplification the separate identities of men and women are merged into the concept of the household. The inner conflicts and compromises of the household are not explored' (Galbraith, quoted by Land, 1983:49).
>
> By treating it as though it were an individual the household has become a sort of black box, within which the transfer of resources between earners and spenders has been rendered invisible. This has three important effects. First, it has blurred the distinctions between controlling, managing, spending and consuming . . .
>
> Secondly, the black box model has blurred distinctions between different sorts of spending . . . The distinction between *household spending* and *personal spending* is an important one here . . .
>
> Thirdly, the black box approach has led to a neglect of all the issues which surround the sharing of resources within households. The disparities in income between men and women . . . mean that there has to be some sharing of incomes . . . Traditionally policies related to income tax and income maintenance have assumed that married couples do share their resources . . . The move away from joint

taxation and towards independent taxation of married people is . . . often presented as an ideological shift towards greater equality between men and women and away from the inequality associated with financial dependence of wives on husbands. However, assuming that all adult members of a household are financially independent of each other does not make them so, especially when the household is located within social and economic structures which offer unequal opportunities for becoming financially independent. (Pahl, 1990: 120–1)

Pahl interviewed 102 couples with at least one dependent child, first together and then separately. She showed how the labour-market position of each partner was associated with the patterns of control and management of finances in these households:

. . . [T]he more the wife contributed to the household income the more likely it was that she should control household finances; this effect was particularly marked among pooling couples [nearly two-thirds of all couples]. Where wives' earnings were 30 per cent or more of their husbands' earnings, wives were twice as likely as husbands to control the pool; where wives had no earnings, husbands were three times as likely to control the pool. When neither partner was employed there was a tendency for wives to control finances; however, the term 'wife control' of finances seems a misleading way to describe what was essentially a struggle to make ends meet in very poor households.

The effect of social class was particularly marked among pooling couples . . . Where the husband was classified as middle class and the wife was working class, the husband always controlled the pool, or joint account. Where the wife was middle class and the husband working class, she controlled the pool in all but one instance. The same pattern occurred for qualifications. If one partner had more qualifications than the other he or she was likely to control finances; where both partners had gained some qualifications after leaving school there was a tendency for the husband to control finances.

. . . [W]here a wife controls finances she will usually also be responsible for money management; where a husband controls finances he will usually delegate parts of money management to his wife . . . There were no examples of this in the study sample, nor were there examples of . . . marriages where the husband both controls and manages the money. (Pahl, 1990: 124–5)

Regression analysis was used to assess the relative impact of the level of wives' and husbands' earnings on the amount spent on housekeeping. Her findings are dramatic and have clear policy implications:

The regression analysis suggested that

(a) the husband contributed most *absolutely* to housekeeping since on average his income was four times as great as that of his wife.

(b) the wife contributed most *relatively* to housekeeping; this meant that if incomes of wife and husband rose by the same amount 28 per cent of her increase would go to housekeeping compared with 16 per cent of his.

Put simply, if an additional pound entered the household economy through the mother's hands more of it would be spent on food for the family than would be the case if the pound had been brought into the household by the father . . . (Pahl, 1990: 129–130)

She continues by arguing that:

Though in absolute terms men may contribute more to the household economy than do women, in relative terms women typically contribute a higher proportion of their income to the household's basic needs, and especially the needs of children. Compared with men, women hold less back, both absolutely and relatively, for their personal use . . .

The best way to raise the living standards of poor children is to increase the amount of money over which their mothers have control. It is becoming clear that the financial dependence of women and children, far from protecting them, constitutes a major cause of their poverty (Glendinning and Millar, 1987). The results reported in this paper are therefore very relevant to current debates about poverty, about the future of child benefit and about changing patterns of female employment. Giving additional money to mothers, whether in the form of wages or social security payments, is likely to produce bigger increases in family living standards than giving the same money to fathers. (Pahl, 1990: 130–1)

A key aspect of Jan Pahl's work has been to highlight how women's employment participation influences resources within households, and to begin to address issues of class. In addition, her work has had profound implications for the ways in which social policy analysts conceptualise households, and indeed has influenced government policy. Writing elsewhere, Pahl (1992) discusses the ways in which different types of research can impact on policy, using examples from the health and personal social services area.

Pahl's research illustrates the value of going beyond very small-scale qualitative studies. Although her sample was still modest, it was sufficient to analyse how a woman's own labour-market position influenced resource allocation. Larger and more representative samples are required to further clarify the associations between patterns of control and social and economic variables.

One such study is the ESRC-funded Social Change and Economic Life Initiative (SCELI), which included interviews and self-completion questionnaires with each partner in about 1,200 married couples. Carolyn Vogler (1989) has analysed this six location data and shown how financial allocation systems are influenced by the class, employment status and income level of both partners, as well as demonstrating which household allocation systems are associated with greater financial deprivation between partners.

The work of Lydia Morris (1985, 1988, 1989a) has been central in extending the conception of inequalities within households to explicitly examine the interface between the public domain and what goes on within the private domain 'inside the household'. Morris studied local labour markets, first in South Wales following up the households of redundant steel workers (1985), and subsequently in North-East England (1988, 1989a, 1989b). She shows how access to and control over household resources are constrained by experiences in the local labour market. An important focus has been to understand how male unemployment affects resource allocation and patterns of power within households.

Future developments

Several dimensions have remained largely absent from the debate on inequalities within households, namely race, age and generation. These are likely to become salient research issues during the 1990s. Because the topic of resources within households arose from feminist sociologists' own concerns, and a central tenet of much feminist work is to research issues of direct concern to the researcher's own biography, much of the research focus has been on white women with dependent children.

Hilary Graham (1991) in *Sociology* provides an important critique of the preoccupations of white feminists in the area of domestic care, highlighting the neglect of race. She uses the literature on caring as a means of demonstrating ethnocentric bias:

> [C]aring is seen as all about gender. Because of the way in which care is defined, feminist research has constructed a uni-dimensional perspective on social divisions. Other social dimensions, like other kinds of care, are eclipsed . . .
> [B]oth mainstream and feminist [writing] has been constructed

within and out of white-dominated intellectual traditions and white-dominated societies. Feminist studies which have turned to personal experience as an alternative resource on which to build perspectives on women's lives are seen to reflect, rather than avoid, this problem (for example, Carby, 1982; Parmar, 1982; Dill, 1983; *Feminist Review*, 1984; Glenn, 1985). Articulating the interests and concerns of white (and middle class) women, these perspectives treat racial divisions as structures that only affect black women (Phoenix, 1988) . . .

[T]his critical current of work appears to have had little impact on the way in which caring has been theorised within British feminist literature. (Graham, 1991: 68–9)

Research which examines how racial divisions and alternative cultural practices influence resource distribution and control within households is overdue. Graham's critique of the caring literature could be equally applied to the literature on inequalities within households:

[T]his literature appears to have remained relatively unaffected by wider currents within feminism. It appears to have become rooted in the paradigms of the early 1980s, with current empirical work con-tinuing in the mould set by theoretical papers which marked out the field a decade ago. Subject neither to external scrutiny nor to internal critique, theoretical work on the concept of caring appears to have been suspended. As a concept, it is undertheorised. (Graham, 1991: 74)

Turning to issues of age and generation, we find that one or both of the partners are above retirement age in over a quarter of households con-taining couples; and yet sociology has systematically excluded such house-holds. Research on elderly people has focused on social problems, such as poverty, disability and ill-health, and the burdens for women of providing care to elderly people (Arber and Ginn, 1991a, 1991b). This neglect of elderly people as research *subjects*, as opposed to being the *objects* of research attention, is evident in the area of inequalities within households. After reviewing research in this area, Sara Arber and Jay Ginn conclude 'The scant attention paid to the situation of elderly people contrast strikingly with the number of studies about resource distribution in those households where the husband is unemployed (Morris, 1985, 1990; Bell and McKee, 1985; McKee, 1987; Leighton, 1991) – a numerically much smaller group' (1991a: 265).

There is some work on later middle-age, for example, Jennifer Mason (1987, 1988) examined how older women's leisure and domestic roles are constrained by the presence of their husband at home after retirement, and

Rosemary Deem (1986, 1987) showed how inequality within marriage constrained women's leisure at different stages of the life course. However, 'While these studies represent a new interest in the post-reproductive phase of women's lives they include few women over 65' (Arber and Ginn, 1991a: 266).

An associated concern which has recently begun to enter the research literature is inequalities between generations living in the same household. Research on inter-generational dynamics within households has focused on adult children, for example examining their consumption of resources and their financial and domestic contribution to their parents' household (Hutson and Jenkins, 1986; Wallace, 1987; Jones, 1992; Hutson and Cheung, 1992). Morris (1990, Chapter 8) provides a useful review of this research.

The inter-generational relationships between elderly parents and their middle-aged children living in the same household has largely been studied in terms of how frail elderly parents constrain the lives of their daughters (and daughters-in-law) (Lewis and Meredith, 1988; Nissel and Bonnerjea, 1982; Finch, 1989). There is also a need to consider household resource transfers from the point of view of the frail elderly person as well as from the viewpoint of the care-giver (Arber and Ginn, 1992). Elderly people tend to be defined as a burden rather than as providing care and support to others (Arber and Ginn, 1990). We know little of the contribution of elderly parents to the lives of their adult children and grand-children, although demographers, such as Richard Wall (1989, 1992), have been more active in this area than sociologists.

Conclusion

Articles in *Sociology* over the last quarter century illustrate how the literature on inequalities within the household has reflected intellectual developments within feminist empirical scholarship. At the start of the period, the topic was restricted to the sexual division of domestic labour and studied as a resource to test malestream theoretical propositions, such as the thesis of 'embourgeoisement'. It was not seen as a topic worthy of study in its own right, and wider issues of resource allocation and distribution within households were not part of the sociological agenda.

Inequalities in the sexual division of domestic labour have not only become a mainstay of many larger sociological enquiries (e.g. Pahl, 1984; Martin and Roberts, 1984; Jowell *et al.*, 1988), but also passed into public discourse, for example, the media debate on the existence of the 'New Man', who is defined as participating 'fully' in domestic work and childcare. However, inequalities in access to other resources, such as income and food, have largely remained the preserve of smaller-scale qualititative research. During the late 1980s, research developed to encompass a more dynamic approach to household resource distribution, taking into account the effects of the local labour market, and also how both partner's employment position, class and income, influenced inequalities within the household.

The period of the 1990s is likely to see the debate broadened to take into account other neglected dimensions, in particular race (Graham, 1991), age (Arber and Ginn, 1991a, 1991b), and intergenerational relationships (Jones, 1992; Wall, 1992; Arber and Ginn, 1992). Studying inequalities of resources within households has become a resource through which to better understand fundamental sociological issues, including the interface between gender relations and inequalities associated with class, race and age.

References

Arber, S. and Ginn J. (1990), 'The meaning of informal care: gender and the contribution of elderly people', *Aging and Society*, 10, pp. 429–54.

Arber, S. and Ginn, J. (1991a), 'The invisibility of age: gender and class in later life', *Sociological Review*, 39, pp. 260–91.

Arber, S. and Ginn, J. (1991b), *Gender and Later Life: A Sociological Analysis of Resources and Constraints*, London, Sage.

Bell, C. and McKee, L. (1985), 'Martial and family relations in times of male unemployment', in B. Roberts, R. Finnegan and D. Gallie (eds.), *New Approaches to Economic Life*, Manchester, Manchester University Press.

Bott, E. (1957), *Family and Social Networks*, London, Tavistock.

Brannen, J. and Wilson, G. (eds.), (1987), *Give and Take in Families: Studies in Resource Distribution*, London, Allen and Unwin.

Carby, H. (1982), 'White women listen! Black feminism and the boundaries of sisterhood' in Centre for Contemporary Cultural Studies, *The Empire Strikes Back: Race and Racism in 70s Britain*, London, Hutchinson.

Charles, N. and Kerr, M. (1985), *Family Food Practices and their Social Context*, Report for the Health Education Council.

Charles, N. Kerr, M. (1986), 'Eating properly, the family and state benefit', *Sociology*, 20, pp. 412–29.

Charles, N. and Kerr, M. (1988), *Women, Food and Families*, Manchester, Manchester University Press.

Dale, A. (1986), Differences in car usage for married men and married women: a further note in response to Taylor-Gooby', *Sociology*, 20, pp. 91–2.

Deem, R. (1986), *All Work and No Play: The Sociology of Women's Leisure*, Milton Keynes, Open University Press.

Deem, R. (1987), 'My husband says I'm too old for dancing: Women, leisure and life cycles', in P. Allatt, T. Keil, A. Bryman and B. Bytheway (eds.) *Women and the Life Cycle: Transitions and Turning Points*, London, Macmillan.

Dill, B. (1983), 'Race, class and gender: perspectives for an all-inclusive sisterhood', *Feminist Studies*, 9, pp. 131–50.

Edgell, S. (1980), *Middle Class Couples*, London, Allen and Unwin.

Feminist Review (1984), *Many Voices, One Chant: Black Feminist Perspectives*, Issue 17.

Finch, J. (1989), *Family Obligations and Social Change*, Cambridge, Polity Press.

Finch, J. and Groves, D. (eds.) (1983), *A Labour of Love: Women, Work and Caring*, London, Routledge and Kegan Paul.

Gershuny, J. et. al. (1986), 'Time budgets: preliminary analyses of a national survey', *Quarterly Journal of Social Affairs*, 1, pp. 13–39.

Glendinning, C. and Millar, J. (eds.) (1987), *Women and Poverty in Britain*, Brighton, Wheatsheaf Books.

Glenn, E. (1985), 'Racial ethnic women's labor: the intersection of race, gender and class oppression,' *Review of Radical Political Economics*, 17, pp. 86–108.

Goldthorpe, J. H., Lockwood, D. Bechhofer, F. and Platt, J. (1967), 'The affluent worker and thesis of embourgeoisement: some preliminary findings', *Sociology*, 1, pp. 11–31.

Goldthorpe, J. H., Lockwood, D. Bechhofer, F. and Platt, J. (1969), *The Affluent Worker in the Class Structure*, Cambridge, Cambridge University Press.

Graham, H. (1983), 'Caring: a labour of love' in J. Finch and D. Groves (eds.) *A Labour of Love: Women, Work and Caring*, London, Routledge and Kegan Paul.

Graham, H. (1991), 'The concept of caring in feminist research: the case of domestic service', *Sociology*, 25, pp. 61–78.

Hunt, P. (1978), 'Cash transactions and household tasks', *Sociological Review*, 26, pp. 555–74.

Hutson, S. and W. Cheung (1992), 'Saturday jobs: sixth-formers in the labour market and the family' in C. Marsh and S. Arber (eds.), *Families and Households: Divisions and Change*, London, Macmillan.

Hutson, S. and R. Jenkins (1986), 'Family relations and the unemployment of young people in Swansea', in M. White (ed.) *The Social World of the Young Unemployed*, London, Policy Studies Institute.

Jones, G. (1992), 'Short-term reciprocity in parent-child economic exchanges' in C. Marsh and S. Arber (eds.), *Families and Households: Divisions and Change*, London, Macmillan.

Jowell, R., S. Witherspoon and L. Brook (1988), *British Social Attitudes: the 5th Report 1988/89 Edition*, SCPR, Aldershot, Gower.

Land, H. (1983), 'Poverty and gender: the distribution of resources within the family', in M. Brown (ed.), *The Structure of Disadvantage*, London, Heinemann.

Leighton, G. (1991), 'Wives' and husbands' labour market participation and household resource distribution in the context of middle-class male unemployment' in S. Arber and G. N. Gilbert (eds.), *Women and Working Lives: Divisions and Change*, London, Macmillan.

Lewis, J. and B. Meredith (1988), *Daughters Who Care: Daughters Caring for Mothers at Home*, London, Routledge.

Marsh C. and S. Arber (eds.) (1992), *Families and Households: Divisions and Change*, London, Macmillan.

Martin, J. and C. Roberts (1984), *The Women and Employment Survey: A Lifetime Perspective*, Department of Employment/OPCS, London, HMSO.

Mason, J. (1987), 'A bed of roses? Women, marriage and inequality in later life', in P. Allatt, T. Keil, A Bryman and B. Bytheway (eds.), *Women and the Life Cycle: Transitions and Turning Points*, London, Macmillan.

Mason, J. (1988) " 'No peace for the wicked": older women and leisure', in E. Wimbush and M. Talbot (eds.) *Relative Freedoms: Women and Leisure*, Milton Keynes, Open University Press.

McGlone, A. M. and Pudsey, S. E. (1986), 'Personal consumption, gender and marital status: a comment on Taylor-Gooby', *Sociology*, 20, pp. 88–90.

McKee, L. (1987), 'Households during unemployment: the resourcefulness of the unemployed', in J. Brannen and G. Wilson (eds.) *Give and Take in Families*, London, Allen and Unwin.

Morris, L. (1985), 'Renegotiation of the domestic division of labour' in B. Roberts, R. Finnegan and D. Gallie (eds.), *New Approaches to Economic Life*, Manchester, Manchester University Press.

Morris, L. (1988), 'Employment, households and social networks', in D. Gallie (ed.), *Employment in Britain*, Oxford, Blackwell.

Morris, L. with S. Ruane (1989a), *Household Finance Management and the Labour Market*, Aldershot, Gower.

Morris, L. (1989b), 'Household strategies: the individual, the collective and the labour market – the case of married couples', *Work, Employment and Society*, 3, pp. 447–64.

Morris, L. (1990), *The Workings of the Household*, Cambridge, Polity Press.

Murcott, A (1982), 'On the social significance of the "cooked dinner" in S. Wales', *Social Science Information*, 21, pp. 677–96.

Nissel, M. and L. Bonnerjea (1982), *Family Care of the Handicapped Elderly: Who Pays?*, London, Policy Studies Institute.

Oakley, A. (1974), *The Sociology of Housework*, London, Robertson.

Pahl, J. (1983), 'The allocation of money and structuring of inequality within marriage', *Sociological Review*, 13, pp. 237–62.

Pahl, R. (1984), *Divisions of Labour*, Oxford, Blackwell.

Pahal, J. (1989), *Money and Marriage*, Basingstoke, Macmillan Educational.

Pahl, J. (1990), 'Household spending, personal spending and the control of money in marriage', *Sociology*, 24, pp. 119–38.

Pahl, J. (1992), 'Force for change or optional extra? The impact of research on policy in social work and social welfare', *Social Work and Social Welfare Yearbook*, Milton Keynes, Open University Press.

Parmar, P. (1989), 'Other kinds of dreams', *Feminist Review*, 31, pp. 55–65.

Phoenix, A. (1988), 'Narrow definitions of culture: the case of early motherhood' in S. Westwood and P. Bhachu (eds.), *Enterprising Women: Ethnicity, Economy and Gender Relations*, London, Routledge.

Platt, J. (1969), 'Some problems in measuring the jointness of conjugal role-relationships', *Sociology*, 3, pp. 287–97.

Reid, I. and Wormald, E. (eds.), *Sex Differences in Britain*, London, Grant McIntyre.

Taylor-Gooby, P. (1985), 'Personal consumption and gender: An analysis of national survey data on the relation between standards of living, gender, martial status and work', *Sociology*, 19, pp. 273–84.

Taylor-Gooby, P. (1986), 'Women, work, money and marriage: a reply to McGlone and Pudney and Dale', *Sociology*, 20 pp. 93–4.

Vogler, C. (1989), *Labour Market Change and Patterns of Financial Allocation within Households*, ESRC/SCELI Working Paper 12, Oxford, Nuffield College.

Wall, R. (1989), 'Leaving home and living alone: an historical perspective', *Population Studies*, 43, pp. 369–89.

Wall, R. (1992), 'Relationships between the generations in British families past and present' in C. Marsh and S. Arber (eds.), *Families and Households: Divisions and Change*, London, Macmillan.

Wallace, C. (1987), *For Richer, For Poorer*, London, Tavistock.

Further reading

Brannen, J. and Wilson, G. (eds.) (1987), *Give and Take in Families: Studies in Resource Distribution*, London, Allen and Unwin.

Marsh, C. and Arber, S. (1992), *Families and Households: Divisions and Change*, London, Macmillan.

Morris, L. (1990), *The Workings of the Household*, Cambridge, Polity Press.

Pahl, J. (1983), 'The allocation of money and the structuring of inequality within marriage', *Sociological Review*, 13, pp. 237–62.

Pahl, R. (1984), *Divisions of Labour*, Oxford, Blackwell.

Pahl, J. (1989), *Money and Marriage*, Basingstoke, Macmillan.

7 John Scott
Industrialism, modernity and revolution

For much of the period since the early 1950s, the principal theoretical debates in macro-sociology have been dominated by the theory of *industrial* society, a theory which derives from a particular interpretation – or, perhaps, a mis-interpretation – of the classical traditions of social theory (Giddens, 1976). This theory, seen as a counter to the Marxist theory of *capitalist* society, discounted such factors as property and class relations and emphasised instead the role which was played by technology in determining the overall direction of social development. The 'great transformation' which had been initiated by the industrial revolution was held to have introduced a period of 'self-sustaining' economic growth (Rostow, 1960) in which the overall pattern of social and cultural development was shaped by the requirements of an industrial economy.

This theory of industrial society was an integral element of the dominant framework of structural functionalism, which served as its principal theoretical support. Structural functionalism often emphasised the overweening importance of cultural norms and values in social life, but when it was geared to the explanation of substantive processes of social change – as in the theory of industrial society – it came close to a position of technological determinism. The clearest and most influential expression of this particular viewpoint is to be found in a major work of synthesis that was produced at the beginning of the 1960s by Clark Kerr and his associates. *Industrialism and Industrial Man* (Kerr *et al.*, 1960), a gender-biased title typical of its day, set out a synthesis of research findings from economists, sociologists, and political scientists, and aimed to elaborate a framework for further research. It became a fundamental point of reference, for sympathisers and for critics alike, for the most important sociological debates of the period.

Kerr and his associates constructed a theory of long-term social development which postulated that a 'logic of industrialism' was bringing about a progressive structural 'convergence' of all the advanced industrial societies. Despite their diverse origins, their differing rates of development, and their varying cultural traditions, all industrial societies would come to exhibit a uniformity in their core social institutions because of the 'imperatives' or 'prerequisites' of the industrial economy. The capitalist market economies and the communist planned systems, therefore, whould evolve towards a pattern of 'pluralistic industrialism', a pattern whose general outlines were already apparent in the United States of the 1950s.

In the sphere of social stratification, for example, the functional imperatives of advanced industry were seen as the driving force in an 'occupational transition'. This involved the increasing importance of tertiary sector occupations relative to both primary and secondary sector jobs, and a consequent increase in the levels of education and training required for the workforce. The greater opportunities for social mobility through education which were created by this occupational transition led to the dominance of educational achievement in processes of stratification. For these reasons, Kerr and associates saw the stratification systems of all industrial societies moving in the direction of greater mobility: towards an expanding 'middle class' and greater openness. And for related reasons, uniformity was becoming apparent also in the spheres of the family, education, political organisation, and so on.

In Britain, two principal lines of criticism were directed at this theory of industrial society. Marxist theory, of a fairly orthodox kind, reiterated the original tenets of the theory of capitalist society (Frankel, 1970; Aaronovitch, 1955 and 1961), but also provided a critical base for much non-Marxist research; it was particularly influential, for example, in the development of 'conflict theory'. The second and more influential strand of criticism was rooted in conflict theory itself and was associated with a 'voluntaristic' thesis that political ideologies and values had a critical and independent importance in the shaping of structural developments.

The leading figure in the development of this second line of criticism was John Goldthorpe, who set out his position in a now-classic paper delivered at the 1964 Annual Conference of the British Sociological Association (Goldthorpe, 1964). Goldthorpe pointed to the empirical inadequacy of the convergence theory, so far as its image of social stratification was concerned, and he outlined an alternative approach to industrial development. Social inequality, he argued, varied considerably in both its degree and its extent from one nation to another, and

Goldthorpe held that variations in government policy and in political outlook were the crucial determinants of these variations. Goldthorpe also previewed some of the concerns of the work he undertook for the 'Affluent Worker' project and elaborated its critique of embourgeoisement (Goldthorpe and Lockwood, 1963; Goldthorpe *et al.*, 1969). The emergence of a 'new working class' seemed to have involved gains in income and living standards by manual workers, but these were not matched by their acceptance, in status terms, as members of a growing 'middle class'. He also highlighted the continuing efforts made by members of the 'service class' to maintain their cultural distinctiveness from their subordinates in the administrative hierarchies of the industrial society. With respect to the question of social mobility, again previewing his later concerns (Goldthorpe, 1980), Goldthorpe argued that the increasing role that was played by education in occupational mobility had actually *diminished* the opportunities for social mobility for those with working-class origins: for those lower down the stratification system, industrial society had become less open than before. Comparative evidence showed, furthermore, that there were considerable variations in mobility patterns from one nation to another, and that differences in ideology and culture were the crucial factors in explaining these variations.

In a subsequent paper, Goldthorpe (1974) placed these criticisms in a wider theoretical context, contrasting those 'historicist' theories which drew their inspiration from nineteenth-century evolutionism, with his preferred 'anti-historicist' approaches, which were rooted in the works of Weber and Popper. The theory of industrial society and the concept of convergence were seen as part of a 'recrudescence' of historicism in social thought. Goldthorpe's anti-historicist alternative, closely allied with the then-fashionable conflict theory, held that the structures of industrial societies varied as results of the power struggles that existed between classes, interest groups, and governments. These struggles were informed by the political strategies which were pursued by organised social groups. Variations in political strategy were the results of differences in national culture, ideology, and religious belief.

Goldthorpe illustrated his preferred framework of explanation by pointing to the contrast between the advanced societies of the West and those of the then-powerful 'Communist World' of Eastern Europe. These formed two distinct types of industrial society, each having its own dynamic. While they may show certain superficial 'phenotypical' similarities, there were fundamental 'genotypical' differences (Goldthorpe, 1964:110). In the West, market forces were the crucial determinants of life chances, and so they could be regarded as 'class' stratified societies. In the East, on the other hand, political regulation by a 'totalitarian' elite was the determinant of life chances: instead of a class structure there was a politically organised system of inequality.

Goldthorpe therefore rejected the underlying logic of the thesis of industrial convergence, arguing that there is no inevitability in processes of social development. In particular, there is no reason to suppose that industrialism and totalitarianism were incompatible with one another:

> no serious grounds exist for believing that within Soviet society any
> . . . diffusion of power is taking place, or, at least, not so far as the key
> decision-making processes are concerned. The régime may be compelled to give more consideration to the effect of its decisions on popular morale and to rely increasingly on the expertise of scientists, technicians and professionals of various kinds; it may also find it desirable to decentralise administration and to encourage a high degree of participation in the conduct of affairs at a local level. But the important point is that all these things can be done, and in recent years *have* been done, without the Party leadership in any way yeilding up its position of ultimate authority and control. (Goldthorpe, 1964:115)

Goldthorpe was, of course, writing during the Kruschev era: pre-Brezhnev, pre-Gorbachev, and pre-Yeltsin. But the central point should not be misunderstood. Goldthorpe's contention was not that the Soviet Union would *never* change in a pluralistic direction, but that any such change would be the result of political choice and of political struggle and not of some ineluctable logic of industrialism.

In volume 9 of *Sociology*, Elizabeth Garnsey (1975) took up many of the issues raised by Goldthorpe. Garnsey accepted many of the points which Goldthorpe had made, but she held that his criticisms failed to reach to the heart of the convergence thesis. This, she claims, is the idea that the occupational structure itself was determined by economic and technical requirements. The occupational convergence thesis holds that an occupational transition to secondary and tertiary sector occupations, and an increase in the knowledge and skill requirements for occupations, are uniform features of industrial development. Garnsey, on the other hand, sought to show, using material from the Soviet Union, that occupational structures varied considerably from one industrial society to another.

Garnsey's initial claim is that the sectoral distribution of the labour force in the Soviet Union differed considerably from that found in other advanced industrial societies. In 1960, for example, two-fifths of the Soviet labour force was to be found in the primary sector, compared with a figure of just one-tenth in the United States. Similarly, the proportion in the tertiary sector was just under one-third in the Soviety Union and two-thirds in the United States. These differences cannot be explained simply in terms of differing levels of industrial maturity, but must take account of state policies directed at the establishment of a particular social division of labour. Ideological considerations and a strategy of economic growth, rather than a 'logic of industrialism', created a particular structure of employment:

> In recent years theories of the convergence of industrial societies have been subjected to criticism on a number of conceptual and empirical grounds. It has been quite widely accepted, however, even by critics of the convergence thesis, that the economic and technological requirements of industrial development have brought about marked uniformities in the occupational structure of advanced societies. The present paper points to inadequacies in this account of the process and outcome of occupational transformation with reference to features of Soviet experience.
>
> The Soviet case is of special interest because it is the only country in which attempts have been made over as long a period as half a century to transform the occupational structure by means of deliberate policy measures involving the training and planned allocation of manpower. The distinctive features of the Soviet occupational structure which have resulted from these policies have definite implications for the life-chances and mobility opportunities of those entering work in the Soviet Union. It follows that studies of the distribution of rewards and mobility patterns in state socialist societies which neglect the relationship between social stratification and occupational structure provide an incomplete and at times misleading account of their social structure.
>
> The question of the transformation of the occupational structure of the industrialised societies involves consideration of the distribution of the labour force both by sector of the economy and by occupational category, or level and type of skill. It is generally accepted that economic development tends, initially, to be marked by a decrease in the percentage of the labour force employed in the primary sector (agriculture, forestry, etc.) and an increase in the proportion employed in the secondary sector (manufacturing, etc.). With the further growth of the economy there is a rise in the percentage of the labour force employed in the tertiary sector (the service industries) and beyond a certain point an actual decline in the proportion employed in manufacturing has in some countries set in. Secondly, it appears that technological progress and economic growth are accompanied by the specialisation and upgrading of skills and a steady increase in the number and proportion of high level

occupational roles. In the writings of the convergence theorists the two processes tend to be accounted for by a similar explanation which assumes that these changes occur spontaneously under the impact of technological progress and the workings of market forces.

The convergence thesis and occupational structure

. . . Insofar as the theory relates to the common features of industrial societies, 'virtually no-one rejects the notion that industrial societies share a core set of social structures that together provide a kind of extended operational definition of industrialism itself' (Feldman and Moore, 1965:261). Once a particular concept of manpower structure is incorporated into the general definition of industrial society then it becomes indisputable, because tautological, that such an occupational composition is an attribute of industrial development. But this diverts attention from the fact that the industrial structures of developed economies differ according to the region's economic history and position in the international division of labour, and that there are corresponding variations in labour force distribution trends (Platt, 1964:139).

If instead of identifying the 'core set of social structures' which, in most general terms, could be said to characterise industrialism, one examines more specific indices of level of economic development, it becomes evident that the very notion of industrial society as a general category is ambiguous. Similar levels of gross national product per capita are found together with considerable variation in GNP per worker, in personal disposable income per capita, in level of urbanisation, in educational attainment of the population and other indices of economic development. These differences are associated with considerable variations in occupational structrue between countries which can all be classed as industrialised by one or more criteria (Kuznets, 1957 and 1962).

It is indisputable that certain features of pre-industrial societies – shortages of capital or skilled manpower, for example, and barriers to labour mobility arising from demand and supply factors – are incompatible with industrial development. In this sense economic and technological contraints are inherent in the process of industrialisation – indeed it is only if certain exigencies are met that the social structures by which industrial societies are defined come into being. But when we go on to specify in greater detail the mechanisms by which the transformation takes place, we come up against the problem of the causal primacy of various factors, economic, technological, political and cultural. The proponents of the convergence thesis in its best known form see the similarities in occupational trends and their outcome as representing one of the '. . . uniformities of industrialisation . . . arising out of the uniformity of the basic technology itself' (Kerr *et al.*, 1960:37).

But while the predominance of economic and technological factors in determining the distribution of rewards and opportunities in industrialised societies has been disputed, the notion that 'the structural and functional prerequisites of a developing technology and economy result in the occupational distributions of advanced societies being patterned in a fairly standardised way' (Goldthorpe, 1960:190), has not been seriously called into question. Goldthorpe . . . argues, drawing on Miller's data, that 'patterns of social mobility in industrialised societies cannot be understood simply in terms of occupational structures – or, one would add, in terms of any "inherent" feature of industrialism . . . It appears necessary, rather, to consider also the effects of other and more variable aspects of social structure – educational institutions, for example . . . and the part played by cultural values' (Goldthorpe, 1964; Miller, 1960). This statement does not actually challenge the notion that in its main features a certain occupational structure is an invariable and inherent feature of industrialism.

. . . My argument is that the occupational profiles characterising industrialised economies are more varied and less rigidly determined by technological factors than is commonly recognised in the sociological literature (Moore, 1964).

[The] evidence does not fit the convergence theorists' interpretation of the transformation of occupational structure. For example, the following account is given by Clark Kerr of the factors underlying occupational composition: 'The same industries in different countries use roughly similar technologies with roughly similar proportions of workers in jobs of varying skill and wage levels' (Kerr *et al.*, 1960:248). A technological explanation of this kind is also found in some of the manpower planning literature: 'Increases in output per worker . . . occur primarily as the result of changes in production techniques, and it is the latter that dictate the functional [i.e. occupational] composition of the workforce' (Parnes, 1968; Treiman, 1970).

The first objection to this account is that it assumes what it sets out to explain, viz. similarities in occupational composition resulting from industrial development. Convergence theorists have failed to investigate the range of variation in occupational patterns and the causes and effects of these variations. Secondly, the state of technology is treated as an autonomous variable, not amenable to political manipulation. But the level of technology prevailing in various industries can be determined by deliberate investment policies. Priority industries will then tend to be highly capital-intensive, while low-priority industries may still be at a craft stage. In this case, instead of being an independent variable in relation to occupational structure, technology becomes an intermediate variable, and occupational structure is seen to be the outcome of the investment and manpower policies of the authorities and not simply the product of the impersonal forces of industrialisation . . .

The notion that the redistribution of labour resources is brought about spontaneously by market forces, regulated by changing wage differentials, is inappropriate in many cases of directed industrial development. The forces of supply and demand do of course operate to a significant extent in the Soviet Union and other centrally planned economies, but the assumption about the sovereignty of the market and the primacy of technological factors in stimulating social change make the explanation put forward by the convergence theory particularly inapplicable to Soviet experience. In the Soviet Union manpower policy has led to accelerated and uneven rates of change in the distribution of the labour force and to distinctive skill profiles among the work force, with the result that occupational composition shows certain unique characteristics.

Occupational Structure and Social Stratification
A . . . detailed analysis of occupational patterns in the Soviet Union would reveal . . . that occupational structure cannot be viewed as an invariable feature of industrial society, nor simply as the product of technological advance and market forces. The occupational structure has been transformed as a result of policies which were adopted in part as a by-product of the broader strategy of economic growth and in part as the outcome of ideological considerations, usually but not necessarily in keeping with the aims of economic development (Nove, 1966; Lance, 1974).

The other countries of Easter Europe differed considerably among themselves in the occupational distribution prevailing at the onset of the period of Communist party rule. However, insofar as manpower policies were based on the Soviet model, occupational patterns were created which have certain features in common with the soviet structure. For example the proportion of agricultural workers in the majority of state socialist countries of Easter Europe is higher than that found in other countries with comparable levels of GNP per capital. The proportion of service workers is lower. The gap in commerce and public administration is especially marked. The skill structure of the labour force reflects the emphasis on the training of high level cadres, while lower grade white collar workers make up a smaller proportion of the labour force than in the West (Ofer, 1973, Chapter 8). . . .

Parkin (1971) has argued that the lower non-manual categories in socialist societies do not receive the same kind of status, material and social advantages over skilled manual workers as do their counterparts in capitalist societies, and that the major break in the stratification system comes between specialist and non-specialist . . .

Lane has disputed Parkin's thesis on the grounds that a reduction in income and consumption differentials does not entail a 'pro-letarianisation' of white collar workers, and that differences in life-styles between manual and non-manual groups persist in state socialist societies as in the West (Lane, 1971:78). From the point of view of the present argument, however, the main weakness of Parkin's thesis is that he does not at any point indicate that the 'lower categories of white collar workers' simply do not exist in most state socialist societies in the form in which they are to be found in the West. They perform a much more limited role in the broad division of labour in society . . . In the Soviet Union the size of the lower white collar category has been curtailed by restrictions on the growth of trade and public administration and by organisational features in industry and government. This is the outcome not so much of the immaturity of the economy as of ideological objections to the employment of non-productive personnel. . . .

We can now make some general observations on the relationship between occupational differentiation and social stratification. There is a tendency in many stratification studies to treat the division of labour as a parameter to which reference need be made only in passing to qualify certain generalisations. It is assumed that the study of social inequality is concerned with the question of differential access to rewards and resources, whatever the prevailing division of labour in society. But inequalities in the receipt of income and status stem in part from the distribution of marketable skills in society. For this reason the distribution of rewards cannot be analysed without reference to the system of occupational differentiation, which reflects the existing skill structure of the labour force. This is not to say that occupation is the only determinant of an individual's income, status and power in modern societies. The fact that a large proportion of personal wealth in modern capitalist societies is made up of inherited property in itself makes such a viewpoint untenable. Similarly, politi-cal position provides access to material rewards and income to political power to a greater or lesser extent in various societies. But the majority of comparative stratification studies focus on rewards channelled through the occupational system; here the proportion of the population found in various occupational categories and the relative availability of their skills are relevant issues. Even in centrally planned economies the material rewards and status commanded by members of occupational groups are related to the demand for and supply of their labour.

The study of social stratification is concerned not only with the distribution of rewards but with the structure of opportunities in society. The system of occupational differentiation constitutes a crucial set of variables when opportunities for social mobility are compared over time or between societies. Access to positions in society and to the rewards accruing to them is determined not only by the openness of the system but by the actual structure of positions. Mobility is affected not only by the extensiveness of social barriers to equal opportunity but by the state of demand for occupational skills. . . .

Occupational structure is not determined exclusively by economic and technological factors, but nor is it purely the product of deliber-ate manpower policies in any society. More work remains to be done on the diversity brought about by sociological factors (organisational patterns, labour relations, educational systems, career structure) in the occupational division of labour in industrial societies. (Garnsey, 1975:437–41, 450–2).

Industrialism and revolution

The criticisms of the thesis of industrial convergence which were made by Goldthorpe and by Garnsey had rejected the idea of an inexorable logic of industrialism. Both authors saw social change as the outcome of deliberate and purposive political action. Does this imply, however, that radical structural change can come about only through revolutionary action? This was an issue to which Krishan Kumar (1976) addressed himself in the pages of *Sociology*. In particular, he wished to discover whether industrial societies had already changed in such a way as to make revolutions of the classical type impossible.

The classical European revolutions had occurred, argued Kumar, where societies were predominently agrarian, where the military force of the state was not disproportionate to that available to insurgents, where political authority was imperfectly institutionalised, and where the traditional ruling groups were divided among themselves by the impact of social change. Kumar claimed that these conditions no longer held in the industrial world and that, therefore, revolutions of the classical kind could no longer occur. In a section of his paper not included in the extract below, however, Kumar considers whether a new concept of revolution might prove useful in the analysis of politics in industrial societies. His model for this new form of political action was provided by the 'events of May' 1968 in France.

Writing in 1976, Kumar saw these events as being the closest known approximation to a 'revolution' in an advanced industrial society. Nowhere else, he argued, had there been a 'serious revolutionary challenge, in a time of peace, and (apparent) stability, to the authority of the state in an advanced industrial society' (Kumar, 1976:245). Student protest had triggered worker occupations of factories and other forms of trade union action, including a general strike, to which the state leadership had responded ineptly. The government eventually proposed an economic package which ended a settlement of the worker demands, and ensured an ultimate failure to transform the political system. While this shows, Kumer argues, the impossibility of a revolution of the classical type, the 'cultural politicisation' which had been brought about by the anarchists and situationists pointed to the need for revolutionary action to direct its attention to the personal and intimate sphere of everyday life. The growth of industrial technology and of consumerism had already generated tendencies towards public concern over the size, complexity, hierarchy, and specialisation of bureaucracy and an emphasis on the importance of the small-scale groups found in the community and in the work place. In this respect, the May events comprised 'the compressed anticipation of the forces and strategies of social change of an already visible future' (Kumar, 1976:264). Revolutions, if they were to occur, would build on these tendencies and would be *permanent* revolutions rather than mere violent uprisings.

In 1992, following the radical political changes that have occurred throughout Eastern Europe and the former Soviet Union, this judgement must be in need of reconsideration. The nature of the Soviet occupational and stratification systems had been central to the criticisms of convergence which had been set out by Goldthorpe and by Garnsey, and the Soviet case also proves central to Kumar's contention that revolutions may indeed be possible in advanced industrial societies.

Kumar had argued that the political uprisings in East Germany (1953), Hungary (1956), and Czechoslovakia (1968) could not be regarded as revolutions. Nationalist risings against representatives of the Soviet 'Empire', he argued, 'disqualifies them from being considered alongside revolutions . . . where the principal dynamic has been the internal conflict of groups' (Kumar, 1976:246). The conditions for revolution had all but disappeared in Eastern Europe, though Kumar points to continuing sources of division within the ruling elites. While this offered the possibiity that radical groups within the old order might appeal to the populace for support for change, 'the absence of the other conditions . . . makes it unlikely that any change that takes place would resemble the classic European revolutions' (Kumar, 1976:256). 'Liberalisation' rather than 'revolution' would be the likely outcome in these societies.

The comments of P. K. Edwards and Roger Penn on Kumar's paper (Edwards *et al.*, 1978) have pointed to some of the difficulties with his conception of the conditions for a classical revolution, and these authors have suggested that some of the East European cases that Kumar discussed might usefully be regarded as 'revolutionary', despite having been unsuccessful. Penn argues, for example, that a revolution can be seen as 'a political seizure of state power and a subsequent tranformation of the previously dominant class structure' (Edwards *et al.*, 1978:327). On this interpretation, then, there can be little doubt that the 'events' of Eastern Europe in the period 1989–91 can be seen as revolutionary and that, therefore, Kumar's position is in need of reformulation.

Revolution and industrial society: Kumar's view

... It is possible to list, in a simple and schematic way, certain basic factors that were present in the pattern of past European revolution. (1) The agrarian or rural factor – in all cases revolutions occurred in societies in which only a minority, often a very small minority, of the population, lived in towns and cities. While these were not necessarily peasant societies in the strict sense of the term, they were largely agrarian societies; and the support of the rural classes was a necessary ingredient of success. (2) These were societies where the technical means and organization of coercion possessed by governments were never so totally superior to those of the insurgents that the insurrections were doomed from the start. The arms available to the revolutionaries were, roughly speaking, not so very different from those available to the governments – and they were reasonably portable. (3) These were societies where the integration of political authority, even at its best, was never very complete. There were always large areas where the writ of the ruler ran very little if at all; where the 'opposition', however conceived, could collect its forces and bide its time, waiting for the most favourable conjunction of circumstances or, simply, for a chance opportunity. (4) These were societies which for a variety of reasons were changing in such a way as seriously to divide the traditional ruling groups among themselves. (In other words, Plato's condition was satisfied: 'In any form of government revolution always starts from the outbreak of internal dissension in the ruling class. The constitution cannot be upset so long as that class is of one mind, however small it may be' (Plato, 1941:262). Quite apart from whether discontent was stirring among the other classes, it was the fact of fundamental discontents within the traditional ruling stratum that seems to have been the main dissolving force. There is here a clear relation to condition (3): the rebellious sectors of the upper classes needed time to develop in consciousness and strategy, and the fact of imperfect political integration – or the lack of effective sovereignty – gave them both time and 'space'.

No claim is made here that these conditions are all of the same logical order, or that they are weighted in terms of causal priority, or that they amount to a list of sufficient or even all the necessary conditions. They are simply, and rather loosely, general conditions associated with the successful revolutions of the European past, and they are a helpful starting point.

If we ask now whether revolution of the classic type is still possible in the industrial societies of the present, we have to see which of these conditions still obtain. Three positions – at least – can be held. Either: to argue that most of these conditions still obtain, hence a revolution in the classic style is still possible, no doubt given a number of incidental conditions which would need to be specified. Or: to argue that these conditions have mostly disappeared, so that the achievement of revolution, in anything like its traditional sense, is no longer on the agenda, and that any contemporary group currently pursuing a revolutionary strategy on the inherited model needs to give very good reasons why this course is not suicidal. The third position is of a different order. It agrees that the conditions that gave rise to revolutions in the past no longer exist. But, it argues, this does not matter, because the sort of revolution possible (or inevitable or desirable) in contemporary industrial society is so different – qualitatively different – from anything experienced in the past that quite different conditions and agencies must be discussed in contemplating it. A corollary of this position is that a new concept of revolution is needed. . . .

So far as the first two are concerned the evidence seems to speak clearly in favour of the second. In the conditions of contemporary industrial societies neither the social forces nor the technical means exist for the occurrence of revolution in the classic European form. Camus was right when he said that '1789 and 1917 are still historic dates, but they are no longer historic examples'.

Consider, first, that the industrial societies are now all overwhelmingly urban. Any rising that took place would lack the support of that vast reservoir of rural population and resources that has been crucial to all revolutions to date. In fact there has not been a single successful purely urban insurrection so far. The lesson has been taught repeatedly: in 1848, when the urban risings in Paris, Berlin, Vienna, Budapest, Milan, and elsewhere, were all defeated, often with peasant support for the counter-revolution; in the urban insurrections after the First World War; in 1871, when the Paris Commune was crushed after a three-week war with the govenment, having failed to take an early opportunity to secure itself by taking the struggle outside the city; in the risings of Shanghai and Canton in the late 1920s, when the Chinese Communists were massacred, and which taught Mao to quit the towns for the countryside; and perhaps finally one might instance the failure of the rising in Algiers from 1954 onwards, and the crushing of the Budapest rising in 1956 by Soviet tanks – not to mention the repeated failures of urban riots in the black ghettoes of the United States.

Unless supported by non-urban actors, all urban risings have failed. Second, as early as 1895 we find Engels arguing that revolution in the old style, with street-fighting and barricades, has become obsolete (Engels, 1895). He pointed out that developments in military technology, in communications (especially the railway system), and in such matters as the planning of cities on the principles of counter-insurgency, had all worked in favour of the authorities and against potential insurgents. Arguably the conqueror of the Communards in 1871 was not Thiers but Baron Haussmann. Victory on the barricades, always a precarious matter for even the revolutions of the past, was now a dangerous myth. The point was not simply the increased power and precision of the new weapons' technology: that could work in favour of revolutionaries as much as of governments. The important thing was that most of the new developments depended for their operation on the complicated products of big industry; they could not be manufactured *extempore* with the time and materials commonly available to the population. . . .

Again, some of these developments, e.g. two-way radio, can benefit insurgents as much as counter-insurgents. But Engels' main point stands even stronger today. The enormous spending by governments on the research and development of counter-insurgency weapons and tactics, the high level of specialisation and skill involved in the manufacture of the new weapons, and, perhaps above all, the great increase in flexibility and mobility of police and troops brought about by advances in communication: all these factors tip the balance decisively in favour of the powers that be, to the extent that the civilian population of the industrial societies are effectively disarmed.

But it is when we turn to the third general condition under which past revolutions have occurred that we see the most fundamental and far-reaching change. This is the overall framework of political authority and the new constitution of political society. That looseness in political integration which seems to have been a pre-requisite of all past revolutions has disappeared. Political sovereignty has in the course of the last one hundred years become an accomplished fact.

Ironically it was those very revolutions that were largely responsible for bringing this about. Alexis de Tocqueville showed how the French Revolution of 1789 had continued and consolidated prerevolutionary tendencies in the direction of a strengthening of state power and the elimination of remaining autonomous sectors. The same lesson was taught by all revolutions since the eighteenth century. As Marx remarked: 'All revolutions perfected the state machine instead of smashing it. The parties that contended in turn for domination regarded the possession of this huge state edifice as the principle spoils of the victor' (Marx, 1852:332–3). Increasingly the strong centralised state came to be assumed, as much by revolutionaries as others, as the political framework within which aspirations were conceived and demands made. All attempts to change society either assumed the agency of the state in effecting the changes or, despite initial intentions, ended up by relying on the state and expanding its scope and power. Occasionally, as with the risings after the First World War, defeat in a long drawn-out war could weaken the state temporarily to the point where a power vacuum was created, in which the revolutionary parties postured briefly. But they seemed both incapable and unwilling to tackle the structure and power of the modern state as such, and were crushed as soon as the state recovered its confidence. The revolutionary parties of the Left were as much dazzled by the potentialities of the new state as the conservative parties of the Right. Even where they remained formally revolutionary the programme and strategy of the working-class parties were shaped to a predominant extent by day-to-day bargaining with the institutions of the state, which imposed their own patterns on the parties. Increasingly, as Michels demonstrated, the structure of leftwing parties came to mirror the structure of the state, ensuring that even if they did make a successful bid for power they would simply substitute the rule of another bureaucratic elite for the existing one (Michels, 1915).

Political centralisation, the rapid expansion of bureaucracy, both public and private, and the establishment of larger, professional standing armies, were the developments that offered the most serious obstacles to a recurrence of revolution on the classic pattern. . . .

The point can be put more generally as follows. The centralisation and integration of political authority, whether or not itself originally accomplished by revolution, takes away that looseness in the structure of society which previously allowed revolutionary groups to 'take shelter' in the interstices of society, among its unco-ordinated parts. Perhaps the most difficult problem for modern revolutionaries is where to find sufficient geographical and social 'space' in urban-industrial societies: areas, activities, and organisations, that is, that are uncontaminated by dependence on the bureaucracies of the wider society, and which can sustain themselves for long enough to develop different values, different practices, and different authority structures. So far, at any rate, no group seems to have discovered such space. The difficulty is compounded by the problem of finding sufficient 'psychological space' to develop alternative needs and values. As Marcuse has forcefully argued, industrial society has not been content to shape and control men's [sic] behaviour simply from the outside; in its later stages, through its cultural institutions, its schools, mass media, and advertising systems, it has invaded men's psychic life so totally that they are incapable of conceiving alternatives to the existing order (Marcuse, 1964). . . .

There remains the fourth and final condition of past European revolutions: a divided ruling class. Of all the general conditions this is probably the most difficult to assess at any given time, and it may be only possible in retrospect. It is prior to the English Revolution of 1640, the French Revolution of 1789, and the Russian Revolution of 1905 and 1917 – to name only the best known and studied. But, putting together the relevant evidence, and considering this century as a whole, a reasonably uncontroversial picture can be presented. And here what appears as initially the most interesting feature is a divergence in the positions of the ruling classes of East and West, of the industrial societies under Communist rule and those under capitalist rule. Somewhat paradoxically it might be that, because of the particular structure of the ruling groups, there is greater prospect for some kind of revolutionary change in the Communist East than in the capitalist West.

In the evolution of Communist rule, a period of concentration, consolidation, and unity at the top, has been followed by one which has revealed serious strains and conflict (Parkin, 1972). This process has parallelled fairly closely the curve of industrialisation: the conflicts within the ruling groups are the expression of the difficulties of managing and developing an advanced industrial society with a ruling structure basically adapted to the conditions of a revolutionary seizure of power and rapid industrialisation from on top. Especially since the Second World War there has been observable a process of what Parkin calls 'elite differentiation', a certain fragmentation of interests and of ideology within the ruling stratum. The most important divergence is probably that between the 'old guard', the political officers and bureaucrats, exercising an old-style domination based on their control of the military and bureaucratic apparatus of the state; and the more recently developed intelligentsia – cultural, scientific, technical, and 'entrepreneurial' – whose claims are based on their control of knowledge and of much of the legitimating symbols of the social order. There is posed here the possibility of a radical and chronic conflict, with the opposing groups perhaps being prepared to make open appeals for support to the rest of the population, with the acutely destabilising consequences that such a pattern exhibited before the earlier French and Russian Revolutions. Something of the kind seems to have happened during the 'Czech Spring' of 1968.

But that episode also reveals the limits of the possibilities in

Eastern Europe. Empires can and do last for long periods of time despite quite serious 'internal contradictions'. Moreover a divided ruling class is only one condition of a successful revolution: the absence of the other conditions noted earlier makes it unlikely that any change that takes place would resemble the classic European revolutions. At best probably the replacement of the old guard by the new would result in a degree of 'liberalisation' in the political and economic realms, for reasons of greater efficiency – a very far cry from the aspirations of the men [sic] of 1789, 1848, 1871, or 1917.

Still by contrast the position of the ruling class of western capitalist societies has been and seems still remarkably secure. There is a homogeneity, a consensus of interests and outlook, that has confidently resisted all attempts to divide it by infiltration or direct intervention. Property ownership, political office-holding, educational and technical expertise, cultural ideals, all have for a long time formed a pattern of concentration and congruence, a dense system of overlapping and thickening circles of common membership and common experience. Such an integrated elite can afford a degree of tolerance, a variety of deviant behaviours and sub-cultures, a level of 'permissiveness' in moral and cultural life, that is quite unthinkable to the elites of Eastern Europe. Rightly, from the point of view of the latter, such behaviour is seen as politically and ideologically sensitive, always liable to become the material or the focal point of opposition by disaffected counter-elites. In the capitalist West, lacking so far any genuine threats from counter-elites, this attitude can only be the result of paranoia, delusions of the lunatic fringe of both Left and Right. (Kumar, 1976:251–257)

Industrialism and post-industrialism

Kumar's starting point for his reflections on revolution had been an investigation of 'post-industrialism' and the future of industrial society. The 1975 Annual Conference of the British Sociological Association was organised around the theme of 'Industrial Societies', and in his contribution to this conference Kumar (1977) had looked at some of the ways in which the idea of 'post-industrialism' had come to the fore in theoretical discussions of industrialism. The theory of industrial society had, for many writers, been associated with a particular view of structural transformation. The pluralistic industrialism to which the logic of industrialism was leading, it was argued, involved the creation of a very different kind of society, a 'post-industrial' society whose features could be glimpsed in contemporary America (Bell, 1973). This was a society in which education would be the driving force, and in which manufacturing industry would play a progressively less important part. The new technologies of computing and telecommunications epitomised this enhanced importance for knowledge and information, and they reduced the relevance of classical sociological theories. Such theories might no longer be of any help in underdstanding the emergent post-industrial society of the future. This view was criticised by such commentators as Kumar (1978), who argued that the supposed characteristics of 'post-industrialism' were, in fact, long-standing features of industrial society which had been discussed by the classical sociologists.

Nevertheless, the idea of the centrality of knowledge and communication to social development struck a chord in many sociologists, and these debates were given a further impetus by the rapid strides in computing technology which were made during the early 1980s. The introduction of micro-processor technology and the radical transformation of information processing spawned a popular literature exploring concern over 'the silicon chip' and its implications for the future of work. Academic reflections on these developments re-invigorated the old debate over industrialism, with hard-fought debates over such issues as 'post-Fordism' and the 'flexible firm'. Much of the writing on 'postmodernism', looking at cultural developments in art and architecture and at their economic and political correlates (Harvey, 1989), reiterated the concerns of the theorists of the post-industrial society. David Lyon's (1986) 'Trend Report' for *Sociology* on developments in the debate over information technology stressed that Kumar had been correct to reject the idea of post-industrialism, but held that there were, nevertheless, a number of important trends at work and that the idea of 'the information society' was a useful but imperfect attempt to grasp them. These developments in information technology and mass communications were not the result of a technological determinism – as implied in many popular accounts – but were the outcome of the political strategies which had shaped technology.

Post-industrialism: Lyon's view

> The rapid introduction and widespread diffusion of information technology (IT) within the advanced societies raises numerous questions of great interest for sociology. Among them is the broad question of whether we are at the threshold of a new kind of society. Naturally enough, this issue features prominently in futurist television shows, popular paperbacks, and the press. But the kinds of claims made – such as that we are constructing a 'wired society' (Martin, 1978) or experiencing a 'third wave' (Toffler, 1980), dependent on the 'wealth of information' (Stonier, 1983) – warrant more systematic social analysis.

Among the concepts put forward to encapsulate what is going on, the 'information society' is clearly a leading candidate. Given the newness of the technologies, and the relatively recent realisation of their potential to affect all areas of life, it would be surprising if sociological debate were already crystallising around a single concept. But the growing number of references to the 'information society' (or to related categories, such as 'information workers') makes it a suitable focus for discussion of research on the social dimensions of the new technology, and the specific question of whether we should revise one of our basic means of characterising 'society' today.

The emergence of this concept within serious social analysis is explicable. Firstly, the social (not to mention economic and political) significance of information technology is rapidly being established as a phenomenon worthy of social investigation (sometimes on dubious grounds, as we shall see). Secondly, whereas 'post-industrialism', the only previous potential usurper of 'industrial society' concepts, was *negatively* and thus rather vaguely defined, 'information society', promises concrete clues as to the dominant features of the burgeoning social formation. Thirdly, just as Daniel Bell more than any other single contributor placed 'post-industrialism' on the sociological agenda, so he has also put his weight behind the 'information society' concept. . . .

(a) The roots of the information society idea

The roots of the information society idea are intertwined in a fairly complex manner. It is hard to disentangle the diverse strands of attempted social prediction, government policy, futuristic speculation and empirical social analysis. . . . One strand that is readily identifiable, however, is the idea of post-industrialism, especially the version associated with Daniel Bell. Several writers refer hopefully to the 'information society' future (for instance, Nora and Minc, 1981), but frequently fall back on the language of post-industrialism. In essence, this is the view that, as 'agrarian' was replaced by 'industrial' society as the dominant economic emphasis shifted from the land to manufacture, so 'post-industrial' society emerges as a result of the economic tilt towards the provision of services. The increased part played by science in the productive process, the rise to prominence of professional, scientific and technical groups, plus the introduction of what we now call 'information technology', all bear witness to a new 'axial principle' at the core of the socio-economic system. This 'axial principle', the 'energising principle that is the logic for all the others', is the centrality of 'theoretical knowledge' (Bell, 1974:14).

Bell argues that the information society is developing in the context of post-industrial society. He forecasts the emergence of a new social framework based on telecommunications which 'may be decisive for the way economic and social exchanges are conducted, the way knowledge is created and retrieved, and the character of work and occupations in which men [sic] are engaged'. The computer plays a central role in this 'revolution' (1980:500).

Bell also sketches other significant features of information society. Information and telecommunications, as they shorten labour time and diminish the production worker, actually replace labour as the source of 'added value' in the national product. Knowledge and information supplant labour and capital as the 'central variables' of society. He comments on the 'pricing' of information, and the way in which the 'possession' of information increasingly confers power on its owner. Bell acknowledges but sidesteps the amiguities involved in identifying a 'service sector' by proposing that economic sectors be divided into 'extractive, fabrication, and information activities.' This way, he claims, one may monitor the penetration of information activities into more traditional areas of agriculture, manufacturing and services.

Bell underlines what he sees as the expansion of these areas in the wake of information technology. He foresees major social changes resulting from the establishment of new telecommunications infrastructures. These in turn will intensify concern about population distribution, national planning, centralisation, privacy, and so on. The 'fateful question', when all is said and done, is whether the promise will be realised that 'instrumental technology' will open 'the way to alternative modes of achieving individuality and variety within a vastly increased output of goods. (Bell, 1980:545).

Of course, Bell's is not the only version of the post-industrialism thesis. Alain Touraine's European alternative, for instance, takes account of the same socio-economic trends as those isolated by Bell, but views the post-industrial society as a somewhat less harmonious product of them. Arguing that our image of class has been too deeply bound up with the 'era of capitalist industrialisation', Touraine challenges the bland post-industrial assumption that class struggle is a thing of the past, and invites us to consider the 'fundamental importance of class situations, conflicts and movements in the programmed society' (1974:28). He identifies the major new cleavage between on the one hand the technocats, and on the other a more disparate grouping whose livelihood and lifestyle is governed by their practice. The princial opposition between the two great classes or groups of classes hinges not so much on property-ownership but 'comes about because the dominant classes dispose of knowledge and control *information*' (Bell, 1974:61).

During the 1970s a number of theories appeared, purporting both to document the emergence of 'new classes' – 'the knowledge class'

(Gouldner, 1979) or the 'professional–managerial class' (Ehrenreich, 1979) – and to bid 'farewell to the working class' (Gorz, 1980). Novel class alignments, it appeared, were bound up with changing technologies and shifts in educational qualification and skill. As we shall see, however, the effort to identify new lines of class cleavage has sometimes deflected attention from those which still opeate within societies adopting IT, namely, property relations. . . .

(b) The critique of 'information society'
The 'information society' concept has inherited several symptoms of the troubles which beset 'post-industrialism'. The post-industrialisists failed to justify the significance given to trends such as the growth of theoretical knowledge and 'services'. Their idea of a leisure society, based on automated manufacture, and a vast array of services, with a cultural system embodying self-expression, political participation, and an emphasis on the quality of life, does not seem to have materialised, at least not for the majority of the populations of the advanced societies.

Much of the exaggeration and sociological sleight of hand involved in post-industrialism has been adequately exposed (most economically in Kumar, 1978). For instance, the *quality* of research and development (R & D) in a given economy tells us nothing about the social *role* of scientific and technical knowledge, the price put on it, or the power of those who mainipulate it. The fact that R & D is often financed for political rather than social reasons, and developed for military rather than economic purposes, gives the lie to any idea that universities may have become crucibles of power in the new world. (Add to this the current squeeze on university funding, plus the politicisation of science and technology policy, and the notion of 'powerful' universities becomes even more of a chimera.) The so-called 'new-class' is probably less strong than some post-industrialists imagined, either as an enlightened elite or as an exploitative class (see further, Badham, 1984).

Kumar, whose work draws together diverse strands of the critique of post-industrialism, concludes that a qualitatively different social world has not appeared. When one has distingished between 'white collar' and 'service' work, shown that some 'professionalisation' in fact involves 'relabelling' (the plumber becomes a 'heating engineer'), and deflated the idea that more PhDs means a bigger stock of social knowledge, the claims about a 'new social transformation' begin to wear somewhat thin. The agenda of questions for post-industrial society, say Kumar, is remarkably reminiscent of the agenda for *industrial* society, In his words,

Beneath the post-industrial gloss, old scarred problems rear their heads: alienation and control in the workplaces of the service economy; scrutiny and supervision of the operations of private and public bureaucracies, especially as they come to be meshed in with technical and scientific expertise. Framing all these is the problem of the dominant constraining and shaping force of contemporary industrial societies: competitive struggles for profit and power between private corporations and nation states, in an environment in which such rivalries have a tendency to become expansionist and global. (1978:231).

Kumar points out that the early sociologists foresaw in *industrialism* exactly those trends which are now touted as signs of post-industrialism, such as Weber's observation of the increasing application of calculative rationality to the productive order. Something not dissimilar applies to 'information society' as well. . . .

(c) Information society as a problematic
Given the massive alterations in the way of life and in patterns of social, economic and political relationship which actually and potentially accompany the diffusion of information technology, focusing sociological attention on these is clearly a priority. The danger (in view of who pays for research) is that the scope of such studies will be restricted to the social *consequences* of new technology, and on 'adaptation to change'. It is a danger because the technology is then taken as given, rather than as the outcome of economic, political, and technical choices (although the socially-constraining effects of those choices should also be analysed).

So what concepts should we use in attempting to analyse these changes? My own suggestion is that, rather than discarding the 'information society' concept, we should grant it the status of a 'problematic'. A 'problematic' is a 'rudimentary organisation of a field of phenomena which yields problems for investigation' (Abrams, 1982:xv). What would its features be?

Firstly, it must be very clear what 'information society' does *not* involve. The technological determinism lying not far beneath the surface of some accounts is rejected. Likewise the idea that a new 'technocracy', in which power resides with a knowledgeable or 'information-rich' class, is vulnerable to critique from both within and outside of Marxism. Also, any view which ignores the palpable fact that no social-economic development takes place today in isolation from the *world* economic system must be subjected to severe criticism.

Secondly, alternative explanations must be offered. Technological determinism may be countered with analyses of the *social shaping* of new technology, the diverse contributions of governments, labour unions, corporations, universities, and consumers (see MacKenzie and Wajcman, 1985). Predictions about the growing power of intellectuals or, rather, the technically knowledgeable, are thrown in doubt by the continuing salience of property relations to the analysis of IT. The same economic activities are also inherently *international* in scope.

Negatively and positively, then, such criteria alert us to significant features of the 'information society' problematic. Two final comments are in place. Firstly, social analysis must grapple with the social implications of the *fusion* of technologies represented by the phrase 'information technology' (as begun, for instance in Bannon, 1982; Bjorn-Andersen, 1982; and Forester, 1985). This involves eroding the conventional division of labour between 'communication studies' on the one hand, and 'computing/automation studies' on the other. For instance, issues raised by the decline of public service broadcasting are no longer relevant only to 'communication and media studies'. The burgeoning of communication between computers, and the emergence of the commercial database brings 'public service' questions to the heartland of computing. . . .

Secondly, as social analysis exposes *alternative* options in the adoption of new technology which are in fact available to governments, industry and the public, discussion of strategies for *shaping* new technology will become more relevant. Such analysis can serve to indicate the conditions under which ethical considerations and social hopes might be released. The yawning credibility gap between futurist dreams and the hard realities of government, transnational, and military involvement in IT demands a sense of urgency about research within the 'information society' problematic. It also indicates a vital role for serious social analysis within the policy-making process. (Lyon, 1986:577–9, 581–2, 585–6).

Conclusion

The starting point for this review was Goldthorpe's 1964 critique of technological determinism and his defence of purposive-social action as the fundamental force in social change. Twenty-two years later, Lyon's commentary on information technology shows this issue still to be alive. Determinism *vesus* voluntarism, or 'structure' *versus* action, remains a central dilemma in sociological explanation.

Despite this continuity in its central theme, however, the debate has failed to keep up with other developments in the mainstream of sociology. The central actors in these debates have been classes, as collective agents, and individual members of social classes. There is very little consideration of issues of gender and ethnicity which have drawn many of the central debates in sociology since the 1960s. Writers such as Habermas (1971) have explored the implications of industrialism and 'late capitalism' for patterns of class relations, emphasising the increasing part played in social changes by the students', women's, and green movement. While Kumar addressed the issue of the students' movement and its relationship to the centrality of 'knowledge' in the post-industrial society, none of the authors' considered has given satisfactory attention to any of the other non-class dimensions of analysis.

Interestingly, Goldthorpe has been drawn into a detailed elaboration of his views on the relationship of gender to class analysis (see Helen Roberts' contribution in this volume), but these arguments have not been reflected in more recent considerations of the question of 'convergence'. The emergence of new class relations in Eastern Europe and the Soviet Union suggests fruitful issues for sociological investigation, but perhaps changing patterns of gender relations in capitalist society pose equally important questions.

References

Aaronovitch, S. (1955), *Monopoly: A Study of British Monopoly Capitalism*, London, Lawrence and Wishart.

Aaronovitch, S. (1961), *The Ruling Class*, London, Lawrence and Wishart.

Badham, R. (1984), 'The sociology of industrial and post-industrial society', *Current Sociology*, 32, pp. 1–13b.

Bannon, L., Barry, V. and Holst, O. (eds.), (1982), *Information Technology: Impact on the Way of Life*, Dublin, Tycooly.

Bell, D. (1973), *The Coming of Post-industrial Society*, New York, Basic Books.

Bell, D. (1980), 'The social framework of the information society', in T. Forester (1985).

Bergson, A. and Kuznets, S. (1962), *Economic Trends in the Soviet Union*, Cambridge, Mass., Harvard Univesity Press.

Bjorn-Anderson, N. *et al.*, (eds.), (1982), *Information Society: For Richer, For Poorer*, Oxford, North-Holland.

Blaug, M. (1968), *Economics of Education*, Harmondsworth, Penguin.

de Kadt, E., and Williams, G. (1974), *Sociology and Development*, London, Tavistock.

Edwards, P. K., Penn, R., Kumar, K. (1978), 'Debate: "Revolution in Industrial Society" ', *Sociology*, 12, pp. 325–31.

Engels, F. (1895), preface to Marx (1850).

Feldman, and Moore W. E. (1965), 'Are industrial societies becoming more alike?' in Gouldner and Miller (1965).

Forester, T. (1985), *The Information Technology Revolution*, Oxford, Basil Blackwell.

Frankel, H. (1970), *Capitalist Society and Modern Sociology*, London, Lawrence and Wishart.

Garnsey, E. (1975), 'Occupational structure in industrialised societies: Some notes on the convergence thesis in the light of Soviet experience', *Sociology*, 9, pp. 437–58.

Giddens, A. (1976), 'Classical social theory and the origins of modern sociology', *American Journal of Sociology*, 81, pp. 703–29.

Goldthorpe, J. H. (1964), 'Social Stratification in Industrial Societies', in P. Halmos.

Goldthorpe, J. H. (1966), 'A Reply to Dunning and Hopper', *Sociological Review*, 14, pp. 187–95.

Goldthorpe, J. H. (1971), 'Theories of Industrial Society', *European Journal of Sociology*, 12, pp. 263–88.

Goldthorpe, J. H. (1980), *Social Mobility and Class Structure*, Oxford, Clarendon Press.

Goldthorpe, J. H. and Lockwood, D. (1963), 'Affluence and the British Class Structure', *Sociological Review*, 11, pp. 133–63.

Goldthorpe, J. H., Lockwood, D., Bechoffer, F., and Platt, J. (1969), *The Affluent Worker in the Class Structure*, Cambridge, Cambridge University Press.

Gorz, A. (1980), *Farewell to the Working Class*, London, Pluto.

Gouldner, A., and Miller, S. M. (1965), *Applied Sociology*, Free Press, New York.

Gouldner, A. (1979), *The Rise of the Intellectuals and the Future of the New Class*, London, MacMillan.

Habermas, J. (1971), *Towards a Rational Society*, London, Heinemann.

Halmos, P. (ed.), (1964), *The Development of Industrial Societies*, Sociological Review Monograph, No. 8.

Harvey, D. (1989), *The Condition of Postmodernity*, Oxford, Basil Blackwell.

Kerr, C., Dunlop, J. Harbison, F., and Myers, C. A. (1960), *Industrialism and Industrial Man*, Cambridge, Mass, Harvard University Press. (Page references are to the reprint: Harmondsworth, Penguin, 1973).

Kumar, K. (1971), *Revolution*, London, Weidenfeld and Nicolson.

Kumar, K. (1976), 'Revolution and industrial society: A historical perspective', *Sociology*, 10, pp. 245–70.

Kumar, K. (1977), 'Continuities and discontinuities in the development of industrial societies', in Scase (1977).

Kumar, K. (1978), *Prophecy and Progress: The Sociology of Industrial and Post-Industrial Society*, Harmondsworth, Penguin.

Kuznets, S. (1957), 'Quantitative aspects of the economic growth of nations', *Economic Development and Cultural Change*, 5, Supplement to No. 4.

Kuznets, S. (1962), 'A comparative appraisal', in Bergson and Kuznets (1962).

Lane, D. S. (1971), *The End of Inequality?*, Harmondsworth, Penguin.

Lane, D. S. (1974), 'Leninism as an ideology of Soviet development', in de Kadt and Williams (1974).

Lyon, D. (1986), 'From "Post-Industrialism" to "Information Society": A new social transformation', *Sociology*, 20, pp. 577–88.

MacKenzie, D., and Wajcman, J. (1985), *The Social Shaping of Technology*, Milton Keynes, Open University Press.

Marcuse, H. (1964), *One Dimensional Man*, London, Routledge and Kegan Paul.

Marsh, R. M. (1963), 'Values, demand and social mobility', *American Sociological Review*, 28, pp. 565–75.

Martin, J. (1978), *The Wired Society*, Harmondsworth, Penguin.

Marx, K. (1850), *The Class Struggles in France, 1848–1850*, Moscow, Progress Publisers, 1952.

Marx, K. (1852), *The Eighteenth Brumaire of Louis Napoleon*, in Marx-Engels, *Selected Works in Two Volumes*, Moscow, Foreign Languages Press.

Matthews, M. (1972), *Class and Society in Soviet Russia*, Harmondsworth, Allen Lane.

Miller, S. M. (1960), 'Comparative Social Mobility', *Current Sociology*, 9, pp. 1–89.

Moore, W. E. (1964), 'Changes in Occupational Structure', in Smelser and Lipset (1964).

Nora, S., and Minc, A. (1980), *The Computerisation of Society*, Cambridge, Mass, MIT Press.

Nove, A. (1966), 'Ideology and Agriculture', *Soviet Studies*, 17.

Ofer, G. (1973), *The Service Sector in Soviet Economic Growth*, Cambridge, Mass, Harvard University Press.

Parkin, F. (1971), *Class Inequality and Political Order*, London, McGibbon and Kee.

Parkin, F. (1972), 'System Contradiction and Political Transformation', *European Journal of Sociology*, 13, pp. 45–62.

Parnes, H. S. (1968), 'Manpower Analysis in Educational Planning', in Blaug (1968).

Plato (1941), *The Republic*, (trans. F. M. Cornford), London, Oxford University Press.

Platt, J. (1964), 'Comment', in Halmos (1964).

Rostow, W. W. (1960), *The Stages of Economic Growth*, Cambridge, Cambridge University Press.

Scase, R. (ed.) (1977), *Industrial Society: Class, Cleavage and Control*, London, George Allen and Unwin.

Smelser, N. J. and Lipset, S. M. (1964), *Social Mobility in Economic Development*, London, Allen & Unwin.

Stonier, T. (1983), *The Wealth of Information*, London, Thames and Hudson.

Toffler, A. (1980), *The Third Wave*, London, Pan.

Touraine, A. (1974), *The Post-Industrial Society*, London, Wildwood House.

Treiman, D. J. (1970), 'Industrialisations and Social Stratification', *Sociological Inquiry*, 40, pp. 207–34.

Further reading

Goldthorpe, J. H. (1984), *Order and Conflict in Contemporary Capitalism*, Oxford,

Clarendon Press.
Harvey, D. (1989), *The Conditions of Postmodernity*, Oxford, Basil Blackwell.
Kumar, K. (1987), *Utopia and Anti-Utopia in Modern Times*, Oxford, Basil
    Blackwell.

Ethnomethodology

The discipline of sociology in Britain has been characterised in the past two decades by a profusion of theoretical initiatives and invasions, aiming in some cases at the entire renewal and refounding of the subject. This process seems connected with the rapid rate of expansion of study in the subject since the 1960s, and the opportunities this created for new academic generations to attempt to make their mark by defining distinctive intellectual projects for themselves (similar tendencies and conflicts can be seen in the equally-rapidly growing fields of literary and cultural studies and also within academic feminism). The earlier part of this period, influenced by the campus upheavals of 1968, was ideologically high-charged as well as experiencing rapid growth. The new sociological currents of this time, such as those associated with the National Deviancy Symposium, the Centre for Contemporary Cultural Studies, and feminist sociology, both aimed to develop new theoretical positions and to give a voice to under-represented or suppressed groups in society, in ways that were closely linked. At the same time, a 'globalisation' of social science was taking place (before this came to be theorised as a phenomenon in its own right) and sociologists in Britain found available to them a huge variety of newly-imported or translated theoretical models and manifestos, deriving both from the United States and from the Continent, or both together, to use as resources in their own work. Sociology was host in this period to many new endeavours to make theoretical sense of the social world, its preoccupations in this direction also being influenced by the fact that far more new resources were being made available for teaching students than for empirical research. In many fields of substantive sociology, teaching texts were rapidly recast to take account of various new perspectives, often with a slender base of recent empirical work to support novel theorisations.

One of the most important of these new theoretical initiatives was that of the 'ethnomethodologists'. In a context where much theoretical debate had an explicitly or implicitly political aspect, ethnomethodology was distinctive for its professionalism, 'purist' and discipline-centred, even though the ethnomethodologists fervently disavowed that they were sociologists! The attention of the ethnomethodologists was concentrated largely on the methods and procedures of sociology itself, since they argued that unless these methods could be shown to be sound, no generalisations or con- clusions based on them could have validity. By this shift of the ground of discussion from substantive positions and findings to the epistemological grounds of sociological investigation, the ethnomethodologists effectively removed themselves from the many ideologically-contested fields of sociological debate of the time. However, they brought to their proposed long-term project to 'refound' sociology on a methodologically valid basis a single-minded dedication reminiscent of the outlook of their contemporary rivals in the domain of doctrinal purity and renewal, the Althusserian Marxists, whose aim was to establish an authentic Marxist social science on purified foundations.

What then did the ethnomethodologists put forward as their main methodological contribution to social science? Crucially, they proposed a change of sociological 'optic'. They argued that specific attention be given to the procedures of classification and interpretation inherent in all social action. A primary concept for understanding these procedures was *indexicality*, developed in the work of their most original theorist, Harold Garfinkel (Garfinkel, 1967; Garfinkel and Sacks, 1984; Heritage, 1984, 1987). Indexicality refers to the large element of the implicit found in all social uses of language, that is to say to the background and taken-for- granted assumptions which are not normally (indeed cannot be) spelled out in routine activity and communication, but which these nevertheless pre- suppose.

This concept encapsulated the complexity of routine language-use, since the latter could be shown to depend on the competent understanding and use for purposes of interpersonal understanding of an almost infinite body of implicit assumptions. The complexity of routine communication was then displayed as a topic of sociological interest in its own right.

How everyday understandings were maintained, in conversations and exchanges of various kinds, was identified as a hitherto uninvestigated precondition of social order. Without this everyday competence, there could in fact be no social order. The generalised common meanings and values of the world-view of Porsonian sociology were re-examined, in this perspective, through a 'microscopic' lens and in the temporal context of their continual construction and deconstruction. Ethnomethodology required sociologists to attend to the moment-by-moment processes by which social action was constituted, and gave a quite new salience to the present participle – 'doing', 'accomplishing', 'bringing off', 'glossing' – as a descriptor of social behaviour, because of ethnomethodological concern to grasp the ongoing constitution of social phenomena in real time. This insight led to the view that the 'order' of shared or 'typified' meanings is a precarious one, requiring continuously to be 'accomplished' and 'negotiated' by competent social actors if it is to survive. Garfinkel's famous 'breaching' experiments, in which he arranged for his students to test to destruction the commonsensical preconditions of everyday social order (for example, the routine presuppositions which students and their parents took for granted as the basis for living in a family household), were intended to expose these implicit foundations of common social understandings.

Sociology published many theoretical and methodological papers on ethnomethodology. This first selection illustrates debates which took place on some of its key concepts. The extract from Jeff Coulter's article characterises the essence of the ethnomethodologists' approach to social reality, insisting on the centrality of natural language to this investigation. The second selection, from an article by John Phillips, gives an exposition of the key concept of indexicality, the dense and opaque system of pre-suppositions on which communication and social interaction depends. Social order depends at the micro-level on negotiated agreement about the meaning and reference of ordinary expressions. The study of how such negotiation takes place is an important part of the ethnomethodologists' programme. Finally, in this section, one of the most influential exponents of these ideas, John Heritage, takes issue with Phillips' attempt (made later in his article) to identify a formal system of rules underpinning cognitive order. In an argument truer to the general spirit of ethnomethodology, Heritage argues that typification is relative to an indefinite diversity and particularity of context. This liability of perceptual and communicative frames confers an evolutionary and cultural advantage on those species which possess it, Heritage argues, here linking ethnomethodology to an implicitly libertarian and voluntarist world-view.

> Ethnomethodology currently generates rather more heat in sociological discussions than any competing paradigm in the discipline. It appears to do so largely because of the many radical claims made for it, and because of the novel styles of sociological analysis which it has introduced. Defending some of its basic research-guiding tenets would take up rather more space than I can

afford, so I shall restrict myself to a few initial remarks before moving on to the main considerations of this paper – language, meaning, and methods for their elucidation.

In posing as its central task the investigation of the commonsense cultural knowledge and procedures used by members of a society in constructing their communicative relationships, ethnomethodology starts out from the assumption that social reality is known by members, lay and professional, only from within situations constituted through the interactional use of natural language. That is, in contrast to most prevailing theoretical and methodological perspectives in sociology, ethnomethodologists generally deny that social phenomena are construable as inert wholes, bounded or determinate in their parameters. Further the goals of literal measurement and literal description of social processes and social 'facts' are precluded as logically unattainable due to the 'interpretive' nature of any dealings with humanly constructed organizations of interaction. Explanations in sociology of a deductive-nomological or disparity-reducing kind *either* impose arbitrary operational constructions on variably inter- pretable social categories, assume an isomorphism of relevances between researcher and members, *or* compete with lay accounts of the same order of phenomena rather than take such accounts as phenomena of interest in themselves. In accord with the arguments of Lonch and others that human actions cannot logically be explained in terms of causal (and causal-probabilistic) laws, ethno- methodologists tend to argue that 'explanations' of social phenomena are idealizations permissible only for practical purposes (their variety itself being considered examinable with respect to their features of practical reasoning). What kind of 'investigations', then, are pro- posed by ethnomethodology? Fundamentally, they are descriptive investigations of members' methods of producing the social struc- tures of everyday life. Since, as I have remarked, these social struc- tures are generated by means of the interactional use and under- standing of natural language – for example, giving instructions, making complaints, transmitting information and so on – the sociologist who wishes to obtain a fuller understanding of them (of their 'possibility') must take seriously the claim that language is his [sic] paramount phenomenon. (Coulter, 1973: 173–4)

The notion of 'indexicality', which is quite central to Garfinkel's argument, demonstrates immediately the connection between a focus on the 'subjective' and an interest in language. If we compare his approach on this point with more orthodox 'phenomenological' sociology, the connection between 'indexicality' and 'subjectivity' becomes clear. Consider, for example, Berger and Luckmann; their interpretation of language has it that the successful use of some term in language for the characterization of an event adds up to the subsumption of essentially unique personal experiences under an 'intersubjective typification' (Berger and Luckmann, 1966: 71–4). The 'order' or 'rationality' of an event for Garfinkel lies in the (attempted) replacement of 'indexical' by 'objective' expressions. Similarly, where they write

great care is required in any statements one makes about the 'logic' of institutions. The logic does not reside in the institutions and their external functionalities, but in the way these are treated in reflection about them. Put differently, reflective consciousness superimposes the quality of logic on the institutional order' (Op cit., 1966:82)

they imply the identity of 'member' and 'theorist', engaged in the same kinds of investigation to the same end: 'finding' or 'constructing' 'order' and 'meaning'. Garfinkel deepens and clarifies this identification, stressing that the investigation and theorizing are to be located in normal 'talk' about 'everyday' events. Social 'order' or 'structure' is a 'reflexive' consequence of the investigation and theorizing that are thus located.

This does not mean that 'indexicality' should simply be equated with 'subjectivity'. Rather, that if we were to search recent thought on language from the 'phenomenological' perspective the notion of 'indexicality' would carry immense promise for deepening and making researchable a Schutzian approach. Thus for any – possibly unacceptable – 'mentalistic' overtones of 'subjectivity', 'indexicality' substitutes a stress on meaning-in-context; indexical terms are originally those which depend on those who said them, on what occasion and in what place, for a definite reference. Their original specification, however, rests on a contrast between indexical terms, such as 'this', 'him', and 'here', and terms which by contrast either specify some referent uniquely, or general terms which are good for whole classes of referents. Garfinkel instead sets the question: what terms and combinations of terms in the language does the characterization of 'indexicality' exclude? For does not an 'understanding' of the 'meaning' of all talk and language depend upon answers about where, who, which, and what, in the same ways as the initial specification of indexical terms? Thus he extends the term to cover the possibility of differentiated hearing of sentences, or discourses, and ultimately to the observation that all uses of natural language are indexical.

It is characteristic of 'theory' or of 'formal' language, by which Garfinkel refers to the formulation of general statements about phenomena which are of wide validity under specifiable limiting conditions, that they should 'encounter (indexical) expressions as obstinate nuisances'. To 'work' they have to replace 'indexical' by 'objective' expressions, a process Garfinkel calls the 'repair' or 'remedy' of indexicality. Again, this notion is extended, until the repair of indexicality becomes more than the elimination of occasional nuisances, rather representing the central and general task of all theorizing. The underlying suggestion here would seem to be that the task of any theory is to bring the phenomenon concretely before us now, in its phenomenal uniqueness, under some general proposition or law. In the case of the social world, this is then the task of 'anyone', and constitutes their routine activities. 'Social order', 'structure', 'normality', etc., thus rest in the member's or members' finding that some rule, law or generalization applies in the present case. But as the uniqueness of each new case would suggest, there can be no question of a simple 'identification' or 'reading off' from a rule. The 'fit' of the rule or generalization to the present situation must always be 'problematic', and a successful demonstration of 'fit' a member's achievement. Further, to imagine that 'fit' can be demonstrated by any unchallengeable 'matching' is to forget that all the terms and uses of a language are indexical. Hence the repair can never succeed in any 'final' sense; the repair . . . *preserves in specifics the features for which the remedy was sought' (Garfinkel and Sacks, 1970:356).*

The repair of indexicality, the discovery of the rational properties of indexical expression, is hence never achieved finally, but only 'for all practical purposes'. But given this indefiniteness, how is this to be known? For Garfinkel, the answer must be a matter of 'social agreement', a constant process of negotiations about normality and order. The achievement of the demonstration of the rational properties of indexical expressions – which is also the demonstration of generality, clarity, consistency, rationality, and objectivity – is a matter of 'socially organized artful practices'.

'. . . *every feature of sense, of fact, of method, for every particular case without exceptions, the managed accomplishment of organised settings of practical actions'. (Garfinkel, 1967:64)*

It may very well be that there are substantial problems with this generalization and transformation of the meaning of 'indexicality'. For example, in changing the force of the term from its concern with the referential function of certain terms of the language, to a general approach to how any talk can 'mean', the original linguistic distinction is collapsed. Further, a very particular view of the role and nature of 'theory' and 'theorising' is implied. Rather than pursue these questions directly, I propose to concentrate on the way in which a theory of 'meaning' is implied by the approach.

In brief, the theory rejects any notion that the achievement of 'meaning', the successful use or understanding of a term, could happen 'by rule' or by any mechanical and determinate recognition procedure. Instead, Garfinkel suggests that what he had asked his students for was a set of rules for reading the conversation, so '*I had persuaded them to take on the impossible task of repairing the essential incompleteness of any set of instructions . . .*' *(Garfinkel, 1967:29).*

Our attention is therefore directed to the unknown ways in which talkers use their situation and their situated knowledge to achieve completeness and definiteness. These are members' 'methods' or 'practices' for the repair of indexicality, and they are the subject matter of ethnomethodology (Phillips, 1978: 56–8).

In this section, I wish to summarily note certain fairly obvious interventions in a variety of debates in sociology which would flow from the perspective presented in this paper.

1. Indefinite typification among animal species has clear evolutionary advantages even when it is confined to perceptual and cognitive processing capacities and not reflected in communication systems. Perceptual and cognitive processing which (assuming it were conceivable) was built on the paradigm series learning process (discussed by Phillips) characterised by highly defined paradigms would eventuate in extremely stereotyped and inflexible behaviour. One major advantage of indefinite typification at the cognitive level is to allow flexibility in conduct without the use of temporally and energetically 'expensive' 'look up' systems for memory retrieval. The extension of such properties to the communication system in the form of a descriptive apparatus with 'context-free/context-sensitive' characteristics can only accentuate the possibilities for flexibility in the co-ordination of human conduct. At the same time, the stabilization of 'context-free/context-sensitive' descriptors is, as we have indicated, a complex matter requiring 'expensive' multimode co-ordination at the various levels of communicative organization and sequential organizations for the checking and repair of sense.

2. Indefinite typification in perceptual, cognitive and linguistic processes makes personal change conceivable. For example, the elimination of indefiniteness from the operation of 'rules' would seem in principle and *per impossibile*, to render Piagetian assimilation and accommodation impossible.

3. Indefinite typification in natural language provides a straightforward basis on which cultural and linguistic change can be conceptualized. As Culler persuasively puts it from another perspective:

'*if there were some essential or natural connection between signifier and signified, then the sign would have an essential core which would be unaffected by time or which would at least resist change.*' *(Culler, 1976:35)*

Yet Phillips recommends that this essential connection be conceptualized as 'finite and definite' rule. However, having established such 'finite and definite' rules, it is difficult to provide for such meaning shifts as that of the term 'individual' which meant 'indivisible' (from the whole)' four hundred years ago but currently means 'unique or single' (Williams, 1976: 133–6) or of the meaning of the term 'cattle' which once meant 'property in general' and progressed through meaning 'four footed property' to 'domesticated bovines' (Culler, 1976:22).

4. In parallel with (3) above, cultural relativism of the Winchian variety can never be absolute. The view of description developed in ethnomethodological studies cuts powerfully against any tendency to reify 'language games' or 'forms of life' into fixed, untranslatable and unlearnable entities.

5. The conventionally given availability of collections of descriptors to characterize states of affairs, together with their indexical and reflexive properties, implies that the commonsense conception of social actors as *agents* cannot be undermined by social scientists. For, at the minimum, much of social action cannot be conceived otherwise than as mediated by a process in which actors select the features of the social world which they will make available to one another in contexted ways.

Perhaps it is unnecessary, at this stage in the argument, to note that Phillips' hopes for a rule-governed semantics actually purchase hermeneutic consensus, security and certainty at the (extortionate) cost of the theoretical impossibility of personal and cultural change, inter-cultural understanding and the phenomena of agency and choice.

At the conclusion of his paper, Phillips comments that:

'An ethnomethodologist might, justifiably, think that this paper has avoided the main issues with which he [sic] is concerned. It can very well be argued that the notion of indexicality basically involves the permanent availability of alternative characterisations and their reflexive aspects rather than those I related to "experienced licensed implications".'

One objective of this paper has been to assert just that. I have sought to indicate by example and analysis that 'the permanent availability of alternative characterizations and their reflexive features' is rendered unavailable if the notion of 'indexicality' is eliminated from the ethnomethodological corpus. Phillips' desire to separate 'finite rules' from 'experience licensed implications' ultimately derives from a moribund attempt within linguistics (promulgated by Bloomfield and Chomsky alike) to separate knowledge of the rules of language from knowledge of the world and this attempt, in its turn, derives from an over-extension of 'empiricist' metaphysics (in Bloomfield's case) and 'rationalist' metaphysics (in Chomsky's case). For my own part, I would prefer to follow

Lenneberg in avowing that *'grammar in general, and syntax in particular, interact inextricably with general problems of knowing' (Lenneberg, 1975:23)* and I would assume that, with the possible exception of Cicourel, all ethnomethodologists would share this view.

If this view is correct, it creates serious problems for the kind of enterprise espoused by Phillips. Moreover, a tacit orientation to these problems is evidenced by some rather extensive bet-hedging in the Phillips formulation. Thus we read of his hopes for the discovery of a: *'finite (but extensible) set of interlocking devices underlying social interaction and social relations'* and we discover that he would find ethnomethodology acceptable to the extent that it accepts *'finite and definite mechanisms which are in themselves both context-free and yet responsive to context'.*

In this paper, I have tried to raise the question of whether, or in what possible sense, 'finitude' co-exists with 'extensibility' or 'responsiveness to context'. In answer to this question, I have proposed, in programmatic, abstract fashion, that the ethnomethodologist is not a rule-sceptic but one who is sensitized to the multiplex arrays of indexical particulars which rules address. The concrete answer to this question, of course, is the corpus of ethnomethodological research. Both answers, I believe, restore a sense of 'moral' to the notion of 'rule' which would be eliminated by Phillips' proposal.

There is, as Mates has pointed out, a 'wearying platitude' which suggests that ' *"you can't separate" the meaning of a word from the entire context in which it occurs'* " *(Mates, 1971: 128. Cited in Giddens, 1976:44).* Yet this 'wearying platitude' must be thoroughly appreciated and understood before the extent of its challenge to sociology can be firmly grasped. Insofar as ethnomethodological observations are grounded in the insights of the 'ailing philosophies' (Giddens, 1976:34) of phenomenology and ordinary language philosophy, these insights must be absorbed deep into the heart of sociology – as indeed they have been so absorbed in other disciplines. To absorb the lessons of phenomenology, ordinary language philosophy and gestalt psychology into sociology undoubtedly implies, as Martins has rather testily pointed out (Martins, 1974), that sociology must undergo a 'cognitive revolution'. I see nothing to fear in such a revolution which has, after all, been effected with dramatic results in molecular biology, ethology, and psychology and, of course, stands at the very inception of artificial intelligence studies. In this paper, I have sought to illustrate the immense fruitfulness of such a revolution for sociology. (Heritage, 1978: 95–7).

These insights enabled the ethnomethodologists to identify programmatically an almost infinite new field of investigation, namely the study of how all manner of routine and non-routine social interactions were 'accomplished' or 'brought off'. The relationship between language and experience was quite central to these investigations. Social relationships and contexts, from the apparent triviality of an ordinary telephone conversation to the complex processes which lead to the production of a published scientific paper, were constituted by distinctive forms of language use. To understand these forms of social relationship required a much more complex view of language and its functions than sociologists had hitherto concerned themselves with. Whereas sociology had mostly found it adequate to think of language as a reliable, if to some extent socially-conditioned, representation of social reality, the ethnomethodologists drew on a variety of philosophical sources, including phenomenology, 'speech act' theory, and Wittgenstein's 'ordinary language philosophy', to call in question this view of a language as (on the whole) a reliable representation of the world. Language-use was perceived to function as a means of maintaining social relationships and contexts, not merely of representing them descriptively. Fundamentally for this perspective, even the process of representing experience through language was far from straightforward, and was usually governed as much by subscription to implicit norms and codes on which plausibility and social acceptance depended as by rational criteria of validity or truthfulness. The descriptions which social actors give of their experience are to be understood as largely the outcome of 'accounting-procedures' which aim to establish the plausibility or acceptance-worthiness of an actor's experience or action, in the eyes of the audience significant to him or her. There is no understanding such 'representations' or 'accounts', it was one of the main insights of the ethnomethodologists to point out, unless one understands the implicit rules and conventions which govern representations and accounts in the specific contexts of their production and reception. One might say that in this view of communication, coherence and consensus-maintenance take precedence as organising principles of utterance over correspondence or truthfulness. Sociologists thus needed to give as much attention to uses of language intended to establish consensus, context, plausibility, and influence, as to those which were representational in function.

Ethnomethodology was thus a new form of sociological relativism, seeking to demonstrate that actors' representations of situations were constrained by contexts of discourse which shaped what were acceptable or plausible utterances and what were not. The ethnomethodologists had in this way succeeded in identifying the speech-forms of everyday life as socially-constructed and contextually-dependent, achieving a radical 'sociologisation' of phenomena, such as those of normal language-use, which sociologists had hitherto tended to regard as universal and transparent means of understanding and communication, rather than as phenomena that needed sociological interpretation in their own right. In this respect the ethnomethodologists achieved a significant and challenging enlargement of the scope of sociological explanation, however in the 'inward' direction of self-reflexiveness and interiorisation rather than of outward scope.

This development can be seen to have been wholly consistent with the evangelising claim to be engaged in a 'demystification' of the social world that had been one of the main inspirations of the growth of sociology, especially interactionist sociology, of the 1960s. The ethnomethodologists could legitimately claim to have brought hitherto unrecognised and (in a non-Freudian sense) unconscious aspects of social behaviour into the realm of conscious awareness. What the ethnomethodologists' studies were revealing, however, was a dimension of action which lay outside the sphere of rationality, or at least which required its redefinition not as the discovery or instanciation of a pre-given order (whether materialist, cognitive, or psychodynamic), but as the *making* of order from the hitherto-disordered particulars of context-bound experience. They showed that at the point at which classifying frames or concepts were chosen for the phenomena of experience, or accounts of actions constructed, there was an element of undecidability, borderline territories of the social mind not without their *de facto* importance, but not themselves reducible to rational percept or model. Previous sociological demystification has sought to disclose unseen structures of mind or external constraint shaping and deceiving everyday consciousness (the Marxist theory of ideology is one case in point, but structuralist models of mind are another). The ethnomethodologists' demystifications worked in the opposite direction, since they purported to show that beneath the most apparently rationalistic models, whether of actors' rule-following or social scientific discovery, there was an essentially arbitrary and indeterminate core. From the point of view of the dominant sociological world-view (which one can perhaps define as a belief in enhancing human freedom through rational understanding in its many variants) to disclose the hidden power of reason was one thing, to point to its limits and boundaries was quite another.

In any case, many of those outside the ranks of the ethnomethodologists were too shocked by their disregard for social explanation at the social structural level to be very impressed by its claims to a new sociological radicalism directed inwards at the cognitive foundations of social being. These differences of perspective therefore gave rise to deep and painful misunderstandings. The ethnomethodologists believed themselves to be

bringing an unprecedented sociological rigour to phenomena which had
hitherto escaped sociological investigation even though they lay under the
sociologists' very eyes, and in effect were constituting aspects of their own
scientific work. Their mainstream critics, on the other hand, thought the
ethnomethodologists' attention to the everyday transactions of social life as
an irresponsible diversion from sociology's substantive responsibility to
understand the larger social world and the human problems to which it
gave rise. One element in this misunderstanding (there were others) was
probably the resistance of those whose intellectual formation had been
within the major sociological paradigms (whether functionalist, Marxist or
symbolic interactionist) to take the weight of a stringent but valid demand
to reflect on what had hitherto not seemed to need reflection.

As well as publishing work by ethnomethodologists and those close to
them, *Sociology* also gave space to critiques of this perspective, from which
the two following extracts are taken. The first of these, from Peter
Worsley's Presidential Address to the BSA, attacked ethnomethodology in
the name of a radical sociology committed to the idea of social and
historical coherence, a project more widely contested (and abandoned) in
this post-modern era than it was when Worsley was writing. The second
extract is from John Goldthorpe's more measured critique, in which the
primary target is the ethnomethodologists' polemical claim to have effected
a 'revolution' or paradigm shift in sociology. Goldthrpe's cool assessment is
that ethnomethodological insights into the density and complexity of members' understandings can quite well be assimilated within the theories and
methods of other sociologies, and constitute no fundamental challenge to
them. It is clear from this extract that the ethnomethodologists' more
extravagant claims aroused some irritation at the time, though the balance
between polemical boldness, pressing an argument to its limits, and
sectarian excess, is hard to judge.

The most denuded types of sociology do not deal in development at
all. They do not even have any image of society. Their lexicon of the
social contains only two terms: the 'situation' and the social actor or
member. The 'situation' is abstracted from any kind of wider
integument. Symbolic interactionists and ethnomethodologists, in
particular, have no explicit conceptualization of the supra-
situational, of social structure or culture, as societal phenomena,
even less of inter-societal cross-cultural or world-systemic relations
– the proper macro-context, rather than the 'nation-state'. In dealing
with the internal ordering of society, familiar intermediate categories
like 'institution', 'class', 'level', 'domain', 'primary' and 'secondary' –
notions widely used by 'members' – are not conceptualized explicitly,

though they are often smuggled in because life has a habit of spilling over the edges of inadequate theoretical boxes. Nor is there any worked-out temporal framework: development, history, and evolution become non-problems, because history has to be the history of some substantive entity, such as a society, and evolution the evolution of *types* of society in successive *epochs*. To work with social theory that – *mirabile dictu* – has no concept of society as an entity (however much we need to avoid 'systems' theory assumptions that underplay internal inconsistency and overemphasize the liminality of external boundaries) makes it impossible to produce a sociology which can answer to most of the major problems of understanding social life. Only a decade after Homans had had to argue for bringing *men* [sic] back into *sociology*, we have to plead for bringing society back in. (Worsley, 1974:9)

A crucial issue – and one on which the present discussion will concentrate – must therefore be that of whether or not the ethno-methodologists' claim to have made, or at least to have made imminent, a revolution in sociology is in fact a compelling one. If it is, then a crisis does indeed confront sociology; if it is not, the situation is presumably the less dramatic and more normal one in which the interest of new thinking may be expected to lie as much in comple-mentarities and developments as in oppositions and disjunctions. An evaluation made on the basis of the two volumes here considered must lead to the conclusion that it is the latter, apparently less exciting, prospect that is to be thought the more likely: in other words, to the conclusion that one need *not* accept that the objective of a 'paradigm shift' in sociology has been achieved or even is in sight. However, providing one is not as captivated by fashionable *dis-continuiste* philosophies of science as are the ethnomethodologists themselves, such a conclusion in no way implies a rejection of their position *in toto*. It is quite consistent with appreciation of the force of certain methodological and theoretical arguments that are integral to this position, and of the possibilities for a significant expansion of the field of sociological enquiry which these arguments would suggest. In what follows, an attempt is made to provide the grounds for this particular stance.

Ethnomethodological criticism of conventional sociology has as its major focus what are taken to be the 'positivistic' assumptions and practices upon which the latter rests. In regard to such criticism, however, an important distinction needs to be made, and one which is in fact acknowledged at the outset of a valuable contribution by Thomas P. Wilson to the Douglas collection (subsequently cited as D). That is, the distinction between (a) criticism of methodological and technical shortcomings in particular pieces or styles of research, or of conceptual weaknesses in particular theories – criticism, in fact, of a kind which might well come from among conventional sociologists themselves; and (b) criticism of a more fundamental character aimed at calling into question all forms of conventional sociology, no matter how well, on their own terms, they may be conceived and executed. In the chapters in the Filmer volume (subsequently F), which have a primarily critical intent, this discrimination shown by Wilson, and in effect by most of Douglas's collaborators, is unfortunately absent. Thus, while the authors of these chapters – David Walsh and Michael Phillipson – write in a highly polemical tone, much of what they have to say is of very uncertain relevance to their programmatic purposes. The main objection to which their contributions are open is not that some of the criticisms they advance are ill-conceived (although this is the case) but rather that many of them could quite readily be accepted as valid – and without damaging consequences – by adherents of various positions *other than* the ethnomethodological one. The point that Walsh and Phillipson seem not to appreciate is that if 'conventional sociology' is to be treated as a residual category – as including everything apart from ethnomethodology – then in seeking to maintain the claim that they have accomplished a paradigm shift, it will not do for ethnomethodologists to concentrate their critical attention on what would be quite widely regarded as bad research practice, or on the writings of Lundberg, Homans, the structural-functionalists and systems theorists. What, rather, is crucial is that they should demonstrate how *in principle* ethnomethodology differs radically from, and transcends, even those varieties of conventional sociology which would appear *prima facie* to have most in common with it.

Thus, in the Douglas collection it is not accidental that Don H. Zimmerman co-authors one paper (with D. Lawrence Wieder) which demurs at an attempt by Norman Denzin to represent ethnomethodology and symbolic interactionism as convergent perspectives; and another (with Melvin Pollner) which seeks to establish one quite general, defining characteristic of conventional sociology – and one by reference to which ethnomethodology may be clearly set apart – namely, the systematic confounding of 'topic' and 'resource'. The thesis that Zimmerman and Pollner here advance is also utilized by Wilson and is at various points alluded to by Walsh and Phillipson and their colleagues. It may in fact be considered as one of two lines of argument which are of a *kind* adequate to sustaining the revolutionary critique and programme that ethnomethodologists would wish to launch, and to which therefore one's attention must be chiefly directed.

In its essentials, the argument in question is the following. The ways in which conventional sociologists define their problem areas ('race relations', 'formal organisation', 'juvenile delinquency' etc.), collect their data (by interviews, use of records, official statistics etc.) and seek to explain 'what happens' (through hypotheses and theories) *all* necessarily involve them, if only through their use of language, in drawing on a vast array of everyday commonsense meanings and understandings. These meanings and understandings, they assume, are ones which they largely share with others – their respondents, informants, collaborators, readers or whoever; and such an assumption is obviously fundamental to their entire enterprise – the crucial resource for the social activity which is 'doing sociology'. Yet this resource remains quite unexplicated; it is simply 'taken for granted'. Thus the ironic situation arises that the conventional sociologist proceeds with, as it were, a most remarkable and fascinating social construction beneath his [sic] feet which alone sustains him yet which he does not notice or at least leaves unexamined. The consequence is, then, that conventional sociology fails to attain any significantly higher level of theoretical awareness than that possessed by the lay members of society themselves. While topic and resource remain so confounded, sociology can never be more than an eminently 'folk' discipline.

This analysis of the predicament of sociology as normally practised is, as will be seen, open to challenge in a number of particular respects. Nonetheless, the most obvious response to it is not to seek to deny its basic validity but rather to raise a simple question: so what? Such a response is indeed one that Zimmerman and Pollner anticipate – but this only underlines their inability to produce replies which are adequate to their purposes. Although they imply that it is in some way untoward that professional and lay sociology should be 'oriented to a common fact domain', they appear to offer only one argument in direct support of this view: that in so far as sociology is a folk discipline, it must be 'deprived of any prospect or hope of making fundamental structures of folk activity a phenomenon' (D, p.82) – which is true but hardly devastating. What they do not counter is the contention that, even accepting all they have said, one can still have good grounds for regarding conventional sociology as something clearly *more* than just one folk construction among others. For example, even if the data collection activities in which the sociologist engages do not give him information that is qualitatively different from that available to the actor in everyday life, they can, and do, provide him with significantly more, and more reliable, information on the topics he investigates. And this in itself, as suggested below, may lead to greater theoretical awareness than is available to lay members. Further, even if sociological theories are addressed to essentially the same sorts of problems as are lay theories, there is still a far from trivial difference which remains: namely, that the former theories, unlike the latter, must, in order to perform their intended function, conform to certain standards of logical consistency and exposure to empirical test. Thus, when sociologists place the results of their enquiries and their explanations in competition with members' accounts and seek to 'remedy' these, the basis on which they may properly do so is not primarily – as Zimmerman and Pollner seem to think – a claim to greater objectivity and freedom from bias. It is, rather, that they are able in this way to open up possibilities for discussion of a better grounded and more consequential character. (Goldthorpe, 1973:450–1)

Among the accounting procedures brought into critical focus by these new methodological insights were those routinely used by sociologists themselves. The ethnomethodologists pointed out that the typified descriptions of the world constructed by sociologists were themselves the outcome of classifying and accounting procedures whose validity should not be taken for granted. Frequently, for example in social research which depended on official statistics, the classifications and descriptive accounts of lay persons (coroners or police, for example, in the generation of instances of suicides or prosecutions) were the primary data source. Ethno-methodologists and their immediate precursors were able to demonstrate convincingly that the biases of selection and interpretation inherent in the production of such social facts as delinquency or suicide rates justified investigation in their own right. (Cicourel, 1968; Atkinson, 1968; Atkinson and Drew, 1979; Bittner, 1967). The ethnomethodologists' programmatic demand was thus to treat as 'topics' for investigation what had formerly been regarded uncritically as 'resources' of social science. To ask that the implicit coding and decision-procedures involved in the production of classifications of social data (such as responses to questionnaires) or typified social descriptions (the summaries of observations which become condensed into narrative or ideal-typical accounts) seemed a legitimate demand for empirical rigour. The accounts of social realities produced by sociologists should not be privileged above all others, especially not where they made uncritical use of 'lay' data sources and merely imposed a further layer of selective and classifying procedures upon this already unreliable base. There was invariably an element of the arbitrary in the construction of typified accounts of all kinds, since raw phenomena do not automatically classify themselves under one concept or another. This element of the arbitrary, and the implicit conventions which govern the construction and practical operation of classifying schemes themselves, were what justified the ethnomethodologists in their critique of non-reflexive sociologies which had not taken note of these presuppositions and preconditions of data-production. However, though it was easy to demonstrate the existence of 'borderline cases' in every system of data-collection and classification, the conclusion that the ubiquity of such borderline cases threw general doubt on the products of all such sorting procedures was less persuasive.

The ethnomethodologists used their critique of the methodology and epistemology of much conventional sociology (Cicourel, 1963, 1964) as a form of counter-attack against critics who attacked them for the sociological irrelevance and substantive triviality of their own findings. Insisting on standards of data production which took note of their own critical methodological insights became a way of discounting the relevance of other and earlier sociological accounts, which more or less by definition lacked these kinds of epistemological self-awareness. In these ways the 'substantive sociologies' based on concepts such as social class or stratification were displaced as topics of interest, not by supplanting them with alternative macro-sociological models, but rather by demanding that sociological investigation first of all be set on a methodologically adequate foundation. The implication was that once this methodological refoundation had been accomplished, then reconstruction of larger maps of the social world might subsequently be able to proceed. Most members of the sociological profession were not prepared to adopt this 'born again' attitude to sociological truth.

So much importance was attached, within this new view of sociology, to the procedures by which meaning and understanding are constructed by actors in living time, that it was deemed necessary to rebuild the whole field of sociology on methods which took proper account of this essentially temporal and cognitive process. Because of this overriding imperative, some ethnomethodologists thought it justified to give priority to establishing the philosophical foundations of their study of language, via the works of Wittgenstein or Searle, before proceeding to substantive researches. Others concentrated on exploring the foundations of social action in exemplars of everyday social routines and acts of communication (Atkinson and Heritage, 1984), believing that in exposing the competencies and accomplishments inherent in these they were establishing the 'building blocks' from which investigation of larger social structures and social relations might eventually come. In practice, however, the priorities given both to philosophical and linguistic ground-clearing, and to forms of conversation ('conversation analysis' as it was called) as elementary units of social action seem to have had disappointing results, and to have limited the influence of ethnomethodology on other sociological research. Sociologists have required to be convinced by evidence that their substantive models of the social world would be challenged and called in question by this new approach, and have not been overly impressed by ethnomethodological writings which appeared to by-pass this challenge or postpone to an indefinite future.

Sociology also published a number of articles based on empirical studies undertaken from an ethnomethodological perspective. These in some cases vividly evoked the practical negotiations and improvisations of social life. The first of these extracts, by T. Pinch and C. Clark, is a report of an investigation of the persuasive strategies of street traders, of which the researchers became engagingly a part. The more serious argument of this article was that the structure of contrasts employed in these face-to-face sales pitches are consistent with other forms of selling, and disclose the implicit assumptions underlying behaviour in markets. The second extract is from Dorothy E. Smith's analysis of an interview which described how a student came to be defined by her friends as mentally ill. It subtly demonstrated that the common attribute of the various descriptions given of her behaviour was their apparent inconsistency and incoherence. It was the inability to identify a rational pattern in her behaviour which led to her being seen as mentally ill rather than deviant. 'K is Mentally Ill' shows how communicative order is maintained in everyday life, by exploring a significant instance of its breakdown.

It is the contention of this paper that it is the largely informally grounded aspects of economic activity which are important in understanding selling and the achievement of sales. Our aim is to start to explore how informal economic reasoning is generated in the constitution of bargain and the management of sales.

The difficulty faced by the analysis of the part played by informal economic reasoning is that it is very hard to impute. The claim here is that this difficulty can, to some degree, be overcome through an examination of 'naturally occurring' sales routines, and in particular ones where members' economic reasoning is made more explicit than usual. In this paper we examine the sales rhetoric employed by market 'pitchers' who attempt to sell their goods through a sales 'spiel'.

Such traders regularly announce that their goods are bargains in order to sell them:

(1)P: We'll give yuh *more* value for money *now*, (0.5) in the *next two minutes*, (0.4) than them shops 'an stores'll give yuh up there in *two* years.

(2)P: tuh make it the *biggest* an' *best* bargain on the market tuhday.

Thus pitchers explicitly refer to, and take account of, what the audience is 'after' – bargains.

Our aim is to show how bargains, and related notions of worth, value, price and so on are constructed by market traders in their talk. The things that consumers take into account as the basis for making purchasing decisions are dealt with, managed and exploited in the pitchers' selling routines. Their rhetorical interventions between product and purchaser in one of the most elementary forms of economic exchange – selling in the market place – is taken to demonstrate that sales are fundamentally interactional accomplishments.

We take the existence of the repeatedly used selling strategies which we document to play a large part in confirming that notions of 'bargain', 'good value', and the like can be treated as rhetorically constituted interactional accomplishments. As we shall show, it is not the inherent qualities of the goods, nor their 'objective' status as bargains, but the manner in which the goods are presented for sale through some discursive process which results in sales activity. Therefore, we believe that pitchers (and perhaps sellers in general) should not be seen as merely another set of retailers working within a preconstituted economic system with its own set of inalienable economic laws but, rather, as the exemplary instance of 'patter merchanting'. For them it is talk that sells the product; in this, a real market, the only law appears to be that there are no laws by which products will sell themselves.

The study
We have conducted a study of a number of markets in the north of England. For comparative purposes we have also looked at a small number of markets in other regions of the UK as well as one market in the Netherlands.

Most market traders do not attempt to sell their goods orally; they tend instead to rely upon signs which state the price of the goods on offer. Pitchers refer to these traders by the pejorative terms 'gazers' or 'lurkers'. On occasions such traders will shout out the price of their goods in order to attract custom. Pitchers clearly differ from these traders in that talk is the main means by which they sell their products. Most pitchers sell only one type of product (e.g. toys, crockery, or household linen) but usually there is a variety of goods on offer within that type (e.g. in the case of household linen we may see a mixture of towels, sheets, bedspreads and so on). Some pitchers sell a much narrower range, or a single product, such as pens or perfume. Also to be found on markets (or in the vicinity) are the 'fly pitchers' or 'street hawkers', who attempt to sell their products by a similar use of an extensive oral sales routine but who have no legal site or 'gaff'. Fly pitchers often work for a short period before moving on or being moved on by the police or market inspectors. Usually they sell only one type of product and their goods, of necessity, have to be portable. Often they are such as can be carried in a briefcase (e.g. jewellery).

We have obtained a corpus of video and audio recordings of market pitchers (and fly pitchers) selling their products. We quickly encountered the extremely opportunistic selling skill of the pitchers. They welcomed and made use of the presence of the research team, with all its audio-visual hardware, by regularly announcing to their audience that advertisements were being made for a TV company:

3(P) *all* we're gonna do tuh get us going', (0.9) ah've got *all* sorts of oddments that ah'll charge yuh *coppers* for (0.5) for the *television* advert (0.5) right? We'll be on television (.) from *now* till Christmas, (0.6) so if yuh wanna get yer face on the box, nows yer chance.

Such references to the video equipment appeared to enhance both the pitchers' credibility and the bargain status of the goods. This was rather satisfying from a methodological point of view, not only as it facilitated data collection, but also because we became an integral part of the selling process itself. This entry into research quickly enabled us to build up contacts with the pitchers such that after a short time our presence (with, of course, the equipment) was requested for a Christmas perfume sales promotion, we were given 'trade secrets', and we were asked to post as 'ricks' (front men/women) to 'get in on the action and find out what it's all about'. (Pinch and Clark, 1986:170–1

. . . I suggest as a principle that rather than trying to identify a set of rules that are breached when people are recognised as mentally ill, or when behaviour is recognised as m.i. [mental illness] type behaviour, we place this indeterminacy at the heart of the problem and suggest that the phenomena of mental illness, including the organisation of social action to deal with that as a problem, are concerned precisely with creating an order, a coherence, at those points where members of a cultural community have been unable or unwilling to find it in the behaviour of a particular individual.

So I want to write a rule for assembling this collection which says that 'for this collection, find that there is no rule'. There is a visual analogy to the effect I'm trying to specify. Paintings such as Ben Cunningham's combine different perspectival instructions. The looker in imagination must be continually shifting her position in relation to the events in the painting. She is never permitted to adopt a decisive relation which resolves them into a single perspectival direction. I am looking for an analogue of that here.

There are indications from other descriptions of how people come to be categorized as mentally ill that this indeterminacy may be an essential preliminary phase to arriving at that label. The process described by the teller of the tale when 'Trudi and I found ourselves discussing (K's) foibles in her absence. I still tried to find explanations or excuses . . .' (100–101) suggests that not being able to find them may be a regular feature of the process . . . The kind of process I am trying to bring into focus as a fundamental feature of the account is that process described above, whereby alternative rules are sought and discarded or extenuations and excuses are sought and discarded. Treating the collection as a whole means that a rule of extenuation found for any item, must also hold for other items.

A microcosm of the process is exhibited in the passage describing K's behaviour at Angela's mother's home. The incident of the wrong breakfast is explained first of all by Angela's mother as a misunderstanding. That is an extenuation rule which removes any particular significance from the episode. But that principle cannot be extended to the following episode of the teapot cover. One cannot, so to speak, misunderstand a teapot. The previous extenuation is removed once it is held that the two episodes must be treated as 'a collection' such that a rule that is found for one must also hold for the other. I think that there are probably many instances of items in this collection for which it would be easy to find extenuations or alternative rules and that it is the stipulation 'one rule for all' which messes them up when the items themselves aren't already anomalous and serves also to fix the weaker anomalies.

Take for example the household passage . . . of the interview. If the instructions to read the following behaviour as 'queer' are removed and if certain of the items are also removed, the passage reads as incompetence rather than mental illness. As follows:

'she would wash dishes, but leave them dirty too. They would try and live within a strict budget, and take turns in cooking dinner and shopping for it, each for one week. K (frequently) overshot the budget by several dollars. She would buy the most impractical things . . . she would burn practically everything . . . She did not seem to absorb the simplest information regarding the working of the stove or other household implements'.

This could add up to K just being a hopeless housekeeper. Adding the items which don't precisely fit that categorization, namely the bathing religiously item, the food fads, the bland denial when things go radically wrong, makes it difficult to fix the explanation under the stipulation that any explanation you find must serve for all.

Similarly weaknesses in the construction at the level of individual items are worked up by setting them into multiple constructions which just make it harder to find a simple rule which provides for the whole. For example in the above passage:

'They would try and live within a strict budget, and take turns in cooking dinner and shopping for it, each for one week. K invariably overshot the budget by several dollars. She would buy the most impractical things, such as

a broom, although they already had one, 6lbs of hamburger at one go, which they would have to eat the whole week'.

This works I think by the cumulation of small things, the invariance of K's overshooting the budget displays a failure to recognise its strict terms, but that isn't very strong in itself, so that added to that is how it was overstepped – namely by the broom, already discussed, and the 6 lbs of hamburger. Even so the whole item in itself is rather weak and given a different frame it would be easy to filter out the anomalies. (Smith, 1978:47–9)

There have thus been significant fields of empirical investigation in which ethnomethodology has been able to demonstrate its power to generate new findings and insights. Particularly, these have been in substantive areas of study of institutions or professions where discovering and laying bare implicit rules and consensus-maintaining procedures has challenged conventional assumptions. Merely to demonstrate that there are such implicit rules and procedures underpinning everyday life was not seen in itself as major news by many sociologists. To show that certain conventions (of mutual identification, turn-taking, reassurance that a respondent is still listening, etc.) are necessary to sustain ordinary telephone conversations, for example, does not do much to change our view of the social world. This is because whilst we might have not have been aware in detail of such operating conventions, their identification does little to modify our conventional view that conversations are in any case social and norm-governed affairs. But in certain areas, understanding the implicit and taken-for-granted rules of social action did make a significant difference to our understanding, since it challenged rationalistic views of institutional behaviour, or identified hitherto unrecognised ways in which institutional practices were socially determined and constrained.

Thus demonstrating that forensic, judicial or classifying practices like those of coroners, juvenile courts, educators or police departments (Atkinson, 1978; Cicourel and Kitsuse, 1973; Cicourel, 1968; Bittner, 1965) are founded on implicit assumptions about just desert, social plausibility or probable guilt has modified the ways in which we think about powerful institutions. What this disclosure of implicit rules of classification has done is to show that the formal procedural rationality of legal or penal practices does not extend quite as far as was thought. It was shown that to be entered as a prospective case of suicide worthy of investigation, to be hauled in as a 'suspect', or be accused of a more or less serious charge, involved routine procedures of assignment and classification outside the public domain, but nevertheless regulated by the consensual norms and *de facto* understandings of practitioners. The nature of these norms and understandings, and the possible working preconceptions, assumptions, and biases composing them, could be shown to make up a significant level of institutional practice. In these cases, investigating the procedures and habits of mind by which cases are classified under one principle, criterion or rule or another makes a difference to our understanding, since the principles, criteria and rules which are supposed rationally to govern these activities depend on such prior activities of interpretation. In these cases, prising open the space that exists between formal categories and rules, and their matching with specific cases and instances, and examining how this fitting of cases to criteria takes place (the phrase 'fitting up' used pejoratively of criminal cases is apposite here), has generated authentically new knowledge.

In the area of forensic sociology it has been the disclosure of built-in 'biases' against the socially vulnerable, unsupported or disreputable which have perhaps been of the greatest significance, suggesting the continuity of ethnomethodologically-influenced sociology with the radical sociologies of deviance of the 1960s and 1970s. But in the application of these ideas to the field of the sociology of caring professions, what has been of most interest has been less determined by overt considerations of structural bias, and more by interest in routine organisational practices. Robert Dingwall and his colleagues' (1983) study of childcare disclosed not so much the weight of conventional assumptions of social status and power exercised through routine decision-making and classifying procedures, as a pervasive lack of clarity of definition of task, and the absence of routine applications of anything one could reasonably call 'professional knowledge'. Social workers, studied in large numbers, were shown to have followed above all a 'rule of optimism' – which entailed, roughly speaking, that whilst there is co-operation from the client, there are grounds for hope of improvement, and drastic statutory interventions are where possible to be avoided.

This study showed the priority given in practice in this field of highly-pressured work to the mundane problems of managing the workload, avoiding unnecessary conflict, resisting direct challenges to professional authority, maintaining consensus among colleagues, in situations of great uncertainty. Here the (perhaps unintended) effect of this study of routine decision-procedures was to expose the lack of a credible basis in professional knowledge for the work which social workers engaged in statutory childcare duties in fact did from day to day. The authors were at pains to refrain from criticism of their subjects, and indeed commended the quality of much of the work that they saw. This judgement, however, seems in some contradiction with the evidence of drift, unsystematic and ungrounded thinking, and improvisation, that was revealed in the practice of the social workers studied. The dependence of procedures of classification on the specific practical concerns or coping strategies of organisational participants (in this case in hospitals) was also brought out strongly in Sudnow's (1967) *Passing On: The Social Organisation of Dying.*

A third area of professional study which has been greatly influenced by ethnomethodological approaches and which has deservedly enjoyed considerable prestige and influence has been the sociology of science. Here the main point of critical leverage has been a contrast between a received, rationalistic and in fact manifestly ideological model of what laboratory-based scientists do, and the evidence of what observational studies show them in practice to be doing as they conduct experiments, classify their findings, and report them to the scientific community. A number of researchers – Barry Barnes (1984), Nigel Gilbert and Michael Mulkay (1984) Bruno Latour and Steve Woolgar (1979), Karen Knorr-Cetina and Michael Mulkay (1983) – were able to demonstrate the complexity of the contextual presuppositions and consensual assumptions on which laboratory science and its productions depended. Experiments did not usually produce unambiguous findings, automatically translating themselves into conclusive confirmations or refutations of theories. They depended on hosts of implicit assumptions about the validity and reliability of measurements, their relevance to the theoretical issues at hand, and the discountability of anomalies and imperfections.

To a considerable degree, what was demonstrated by these field studies was the high degree of 'craft skill' and tacit understanding involved even in the practice of the 'hard sciences', though these aspects of scientific work were routinely filtered out from the standardised and strictly impersonal form of their scientific reports. This ethnomethodological work in the sociology of science gave significant empirical support to relativistic approaches to scientific knowledge recently developed in the philosophy and history of science. These had stressed the role in scientific practice of procedures for achieving and maintaining institutional consensus, and because they had revealed a socially-constructed dimension to what had previously presented itself as a sphere of knowledge which was above social constraint, these perspectives had been popular and influential within sociology. Furthermore, because the model of knowledge-generation they presented was essentially pluralistic and relativistic, they offered some legitimation of different varieties of sociological investigation itself against the criticism of stricter 'positivist' and Popperian approaches to scientific method. The effect of this work was not of course to refute or invalidate the rationalistic claims of science, but to displace normative and essentially legitimatory accounts of its procedures with factual and empirical description. This showed the scientific community in a less idealised reflection of itself than that which it had usually been given by its interpreters and advocates within the discipline of philosophy. But bringing within the compass of scientific investigation and description a field of social activity which had usually been seen as the source rather than the empirical object of such norms of investigation was a real advance for empirical sociology, for which the innovations of ethnomethodology can take considerable credit.

The interest of the ethnomethodologists in the nature and function of language in social life – 'the linguistic turn' in sociology – was one which it shared with a number of other contemporary movements in sociological theory. The fields of structuralism, structural linguistics and semiotics, whose main origins lay in the French culturalist traditions of Durkheim and Saussure, was a parallel development, in this case providing theoretical and methodological resources chiefly for the study of cultural and media 'texts' hitherto difficult to analyse sociologically in ways which respected their own autonomy and complexity. A still closer convergence can be seen with the influence of Foucault on sociology, because of the focus in his work on 'discourse' as the constituting element of social life, parallel in some ways to the ethnomethodological interest in linguistic routines and accounting procedures as the elements of social action. Foucault, like the ethno-methodologists, perceived that forms of social classification construct social being, rather than merely reflect or represent it. Foucault to be sure was largely interested in the historical evolution of major new schema of classification, including those which he argued established 'man' [sic] and 'the individual' as recognisable entities and objects of value. The ethno-methodologists' aims were in essence more limited, being concerned with the micro-processes by which categories become assigned to their objects, not with the broader historical outcomes of these.

However, both Foucaldian sociology and enthnomethodology have through their core ideas been able to illuminate major new areas of social structure and process, each in a distinctively reflexive way. These areas significantly overlap. Foucault identified the ways in which social scientific classifications, especially as these were embedded in professional people-processing practices, constituted new kinds of social subject, and became new instruments of social control in the modern world. To understand the classifications and classifying procedures of medicine, psychiatry or penology and the professional activities legitimised by these, is to under-stand a substantive and powerful set of modern social institutions, and one in whose practices sociologists themselves are highly implicated. Foucault was in this way the author of a new institutional sociology, as well a more abstract social theorist and philosopher. Ethnomethodologists were more interested in the uncertain fit between classifications and their mental objects than in the systems of classification or their wider social significance. But they have also helped to construct a new area of substantive sociological study, identifying an important dimension of activity of institutions – in some cases institutions similar in function to Foucault's – which was hitherto hardly visible. Foucault's position was more overly polemical and committed – his models of surveillance and discursive power identified a dominated, victimised or resistant subject as an object of latent value in his schema. Ethnomethodology rather illuminated the *ad hoc*, negotiated, consensual character of social reality than its oppressive side. Its main emphasis has perhaps been to expose the less rationalistic face of the democratic dialogue between different subjects recommended by Richard Rorty as the only reasonable basis for a social ethics and politics. Like the Wittgensteinian study of ordinary language on which it has drawn, ethnomethodology tends, having exposed unrecognised complexities and spaces for decision in the conduct of social life, to leave the world as it is, rather than judging it by some ulterior standard of truth or enlightenment. The point, we might say, is *not* to change the world, but rather to understand it.

The absence of any transcendental meanings or values beneath the conversational surfaces painstakingly exposed by its investigations reveal ethnomethodology to have been a form of 'postmodernism' almost before the term was invented. Sociology has often, in its 'modernist' modes, sought to reveal deep structures of determination, and an underlying directionality or narrative of emancipation beneath the commmonsense social world. Ethnomethodology shows individuals merely to be making sense of things as best they can, producing utterance and explanations which are acceptable within their communities, on the whole covering over the many moments of uncertainty, ignorance and indecision they experience in their encounters with the world. It has offered, in truth, a somewhat quietist view of social life, except in the intransigence it has sometimes shown, as a movement, towards other elements of the discipline of sociology. To some degree this intransigence, and the scale of the ambition of ethnomethodology to refound and reconstruct the entire field of sociology, has been harmful, since it has inhibited the dialogue which might have led to the larger assimilation of ethnomethodological methods and perspectives into the many fields of substantive sociology to which they would be highly relevant. The sometimes inward-looking approach of this school has also diminished its own capacity to focus its research in those fields and topics where its findings would have the greatest effect.

References

Atkinson, J.M. and Heritage, J. (eds.) (1984), *Structures of Social Action: Studies in Conversation Analysis*, Cambridge, Cambridge University Press.

Atkinson, J.M. and Drew, J. (1979), *Order in Court: The Organisation of Verbal Interaction in Judicial Settings*, Basingstoke, Macmillan.

Atkinson, J.M. (1984), *Our Masters' Voices: Studies in the Language and Body Language of Politics*, London, Methuen.

Atkinson, J.M. (1978), *Discovering Suicide: Studies in the Social Organisation of Sudden Death* Basingstoke, Macmillan.

Attewell, P. (1974), 'Ethnomethodology since Garfinkel', *Theory and Society*, 1, pp. 179–210.

Barnes, B. (1984), *T.S. Kuhn and Social Science*, Basingstoke, Macmillan.

Bauman, Z. (1973), 'On the philosophical status of ethnomethodology', *Sociological Review*, 21, pp. 4–23.

Bittner, E. (1967), 'The police on skid row: a study of peace keeping', *American Sociological Review*, 32, pp. 699–715.

Cicourel, A. (1963), *Cognitive Sociology*, Harmondsworth, Penguin.

Cicourel, A. and Kitsuse, J. (1963), *The Educational Decision-Makers*, New York, Bobbs-Merrill.

Cicourel, A. (1964), *Method and Measurement in Sociology*, New York, Free Press.

Cicourel, A. (1968), *The Social Organisation of Juvenile Justice*, New York, Wiley.

Coulter, J. (1973), 'Language and the conceptualisation of meaning', *Sociology*, 7, pp. 173–89.

Dingwall, R., Eekelaar, J., and Murray, T. (1983) *The Protection of Children*, Oxford, Blackwell.

Douglas, J. (1971), *Understanding Everyday Life*, London, Routledge and Kegan Paul.

Garfinkel, H. (1967), *Studies in Ethnomethodology*, Cambridge, Polity.

Garfinkel, H., and Sacks, H. (1970), 'On formal structures of practical actions', in J.C. McKinney and E.A. Tiryakian (eds.) *Theoretical Sociology*, New York, Appleton Century Crofts, pp. 338–66.

Gilbert, N. and Mulkay, M. (1984), *Opening Pandora's Box: An Analysis of Scientists' Discourse*, Cambridge, Cambridge University Press.

Goldthorpe, J. (1973), 'Review article – a revolution in Sociology', *Sociology* 7, pp. 449–62.

Heritage, J. (1978), 'Aspects of the flexibilities of language-use', *Sociology*, 12, pp. 79–103.

Heritage, J. (1984), *Garfinkel and Ethnomethodology*, Cambridge, Polity.

Heritage, J. (1987), 'Ethnomethodology', in Giddens, A. and Turner, J. (eds.), *Social Theory Today*, Cambridge, Polity Press.

Knorr-Cetina, K., and Mulkay M. (eds.), (1983), *Science Observed*, London, Sage.

Latour, B. and Woolgar, S. (1979), *Laboratory Life: The Social Construction of Scientific Facts*, London, Sage.

Maynard, D.W. (1991), 'The diversity of ethnomethodology', *Annual Review of Sociology*, 17.

Phillips, J. (1978), 'Some problems in locating practices', *Sociology*, 12, pp. 55–77.

Pinch, T. and Clark, C. (1986), ' "Patter merchanting" and the strategic (re)production and local management of economic reasoning in the sales routines of market pitchers', *Sociology*, 20, pp. 169–91.

Sharrock, W. and Anderson, R. (1986), *The Ethnomethodologists*, London, Tavistock.

Smith, D. (1978), ' "K is mentally ill": the anatomy of a factual account', *Sociology*, 12, pp. 23–53.

Sociology (1978), *Language and Practical Reasoning*, special issue 12(1).

Sudnow, D. (1967), *Passing On: The Social Organisation of Dying*, New York, Prentice-Hall.

Turner, R. (ed.), (1974), *Ethnomethodology*, Harmondsworth, Penguin.

Worsley, P. (1974), 'The state of theory', *Sociology*, 8, pp. 1–17.

Further reading

The canonical starting point is Harold Garfinkel's (1967) *Studies in Ethnomethodology*. John Heritage's essay 'Ethnomethodology' in A. Giddens and J. Turner's (1987) *Social Theory Today*, and his longer *Garfinkel and Ethnomethodology* (1984) provide good introductions to Garfinkel and his influence. Also of great influence has been the work of A. Cicourel (1963, 1964, 1968). Among critical articles are those by Z. Bauman (1973) and P. Attewell (1974, and useful reviews of the field are by W. Sharrock and B. Anderson (1986) and by D. W. Maynard (1991). Good collections of articles from this tradition are R. Turner (ed.) (1974), *Ethnomethodology*, J. Douglas (ed.) *Understanding Everyday Life* (1971), and J.M. Atkinson and J. Heritage (1984), *Structures of Social Action: Studies in Conversational Analysis*. The special issue of *Sociology* (1978, 12, (1) *Language and Practical Reasoning*, is also a useful collection.

Leading examples of applications of etnomethodological approaches to empirical topics are J.M. Atkinson (1978), *Discovering Suicide: Studies in the Social Organisation of Sudden Death*, and his (1984) *Our Masters' Voices: Studies in the Language and Body Language of Politics;* A. Cicourel (1968), *The Social Organisation of Juvenile Justice;* R. Dingwall, J. Eekelaar, T. Murray (1983), *The Protection of Children;* D. Sudnow (1967), *Passing On: The Social Organisation of Dying;* B. Latour and S. Woolgar (1979), *Laboratory Life: The Social Construction of Scientific Facts*, and N. Gilbert and M. Mulkay (1984), *Opening Pandora's Box: An Analysis of Scientists' Discourse*, Cambridge, Cambridge University Press.

The uses of the concept of power

1 The concept of power

The discussion of power in the pages of *Sociology* has dealt with three principal issues. The first is the insistence, exemplified in the writings of Parsons, that power is to be understood as legitimate regulation in a society characterised by agreement on common values. Against this it was argued that power is exercised in conflicts of interest and ideals. The second is the question of whether it is possible to talk of someone's interests being violated if they themselves do not actively or vocally resist. Is there in other words what Steven Lukes called a 'third dimension' of power, where the powerful get their way be preventing disagreements from ever being expressed. The third issue is the attempt to make something of the arguments of Foucault that, in effect, all social life is the result of the exercise of power, and that even the individuals or subjects who are represented as resisting power are themselves created by it. The examination of each of these issues occupied, more or less, a distinct time span within the pages of *Sociology*.

Despite their capacity to both constrain and make possible understanding, concepts have more of an historical than an ideal or abstract life. They arise not at random, but in particular historical circumstances, and out of particular intellectual contexts. The debate over power developed in the 1960s and 1970s at a time when social scientists were questioning the benevolence and universal legitimacy of existing political and social arrangements, but did not want to have to rely on old concepts of class in order to do so. The intellectual oppressiveness of functionalism and pluralism was matched by the social oppressiveness of the arrangements which they appeared to justify. The orthodoxies, centralisations of power, and gerontocracies of Eastern Europe seemed to go hand in hand with a kind of official Marxism, just as those of the capitalist West seemed to keep company with functionalism, pluralism, and systems theory. The one might stress conflict as the characteristic feature of social life, and the other consensus, but the end result seemed to many to be remarkably similar.

Power was an especially appropriate concept for sociologists to concern themselves with at such a time. It was a combative term, almost all of whose connotations were negative: 'power hungry'; 'power politics'; 'power trip'. The intention of controlling others is always regarded with suspicion, however noble the motive. The concept of power promised to transcend the limitations of any theory which saw all inequalities as arising from class, since power could be political, or intellectual, as well as economic. It might equally well be sexual or racial. Its operation could even be both masked and justified by the relative or apparent freedom from material inequalities of those subject to it. So the concept of power was used to question the optimistic judgement which had been passed on western societies, and to draw attention to the hidden structures of liberal democracies, the agenda setting and policy making that was not necessarily reflected in formal constitutional systems. The formal accounts were criticised as either giving a misleading version of what actually went on, or as positively contributing towards its concealment. The debate over power was not about who got what, but about how they got it, and at whose behest. It was a debate about who was in charge. This is apparent in the many books which do not discuss the concept but which employ the title. All the volumes of 'Power in . . .' set out to show who really pulled the strings, who actually gave the orders and ran the show. To talk of power being exercised or enjoyed was to assert, if only by implication, that something was being done or left undone by somebody which would otherwise not have been done or left undone.

2 The debate in *Sociology* A) The criticism of consensus

Discussion of power in the pages of *Sociology* starts with the publication in 1968 of Anthony Giddens's discussion of Talcott Parsons (Giddens, 1968). Parsons had criticised Charles Wright Mills for his zero-sum notion of power (Parsons, 1960a, 1960b, 1963a, 1963b, 1964, 1966). The view that to the extent to which one party had power, another does not, had been employed by Mills in a radical criticism of contemporary American politics and society (Mills, 1956). Parsons was hostile to the use of the term power to identify the more or less systematic victory of one set of interests over another set. Giddens argues that Parsons, in trying to present social systems as based on justifiable principles, falls into the error of envisaging all power as derived from the legitimate pursuit of common interests:

Parsons's critique of the 'zero-sum' concept of power does contain a number of valuable contributions and insights. There is no doubt that Parsons is correct in pointing out that the 'zero-sum' concept of power sometimes reinforces a simplistic view which identifies power almost wholly with the use of coercion and force. Such a perspective tends to follow from, although it is not at all logically implied by, the Weberian definition of power, which has probably been the most influential in sociology. In Weber's familiar definition, power is regarded as 'the chance of a man [sic] or of a number of men to realize their own will in a communal action even against the resistance of others who are participating in the action'. Such a definition tends to lead to a conception of power relations as inevitably involving incompatible and conflicting interests, since what is stressed is the capacity of a party to realize its *own* (implicitly, sectional) aims, and the main criterion for gauging 'amount' of power is the 'resistance' which can be overcome.

As Parsons correctly emphasizes, this can be extremely misleading, tending to produce an identification of power with the sanctions that are or can potentially be used by the power-holder. In fact, very often it is not those groups which have most frequent recourse to overt use of coercion who have most power; frequent use of coercive sanctions indicates an insecure basis of power. This is particularly true, as Parsons indicates, of the sanction of force. The power position of an individual or group which has constant recourse to the use of force to secure compliance to its commands is usually weak and insecure. Far from being an index of the power held by a party, the amount of open force used rather is an indication of a shallow and unstable power base.

However, to regard the use of force in itself as a criterion of power is an error which only the more naive of social analysts would make. But it is much more common to identify the power held by a party in a social relation with the coercive sanctions it is *capable* of employing against subordinates if called upon to do so – including primarily the capacity to use force. Again Parsons makes an important comment here, pointing out that a party may wield considerable power while at the same time having few coercive sanctions with which to enforce its commands if they are questioned by subordinates. This is possible if the power-holding party enjoys a broad 'mandate' to take authoritative decisions ceded or acquiesced in by those subject to the decisions – i.e., if those over whom the power is exercised 'agree' to subject themselves to that power. In such circumstances, the party in power depends, not on the possession of coercive sanctions with which it can override non-compliance, but sheerly upon the recognition by the subordinate party or parties of its legitimate right to take authoritative decisions. The latter in some sense acquiesce in their subordination. Thus when subordinates 'agree' to allow others to command their actions, and when at the same time those who receive this 'mandate' have few coercive sanctions to employ if their directives are not obeyed, then there exists a situation of power not based upon control of means to coerce. It is because of such a possibility that Parsons emphasises that the question of 'how much' power a party holds, and the question of what sanctions it is able to bring into play in case of disobedience, are analytically separable. And it must be conceded that lack of capacity to command a defined range of sanctions does not necessarily entail a lack of power; the 'amount' of power held by a party cannot be assessed simply in terms of the effective sanctions it is able to enforce if faced with possible or actual non-compliance. At the same time, it should be pointed out that 'amount' of power wielded in any concrete set of circumstances, and the effective sanctions that can be used to counter non-compliance, are usually closely related. Studies of all types of social structures, from small groups up to total societies, show that power-holders always do command or develop sanctions which reinforce their position; in any group which has a continued existence over time, those in power face problems of dissensus and the possibility of rebellion. The very fact of possession of a 'mandate' from those subordinated to a power relation allows the dominant party to use this 'good will' to mobilize sanctions (even if only the scorn, ridicule, etc., of the conforming majority) against a deviant or potentially deviant minority. If a power-holding party does not possess sanctions to use in cases of disobedience, it tends rapidly to acquire them, and can in fact use its power to do so. . . .

But, at any rate, Parsons's own analysis shows an ingenuous tendency to see nothing beyond the processes which are overt. Parsons's account of how political support is derived, for example, is given in terms of a *prima facie* comparison between government and banking:

. . . political support should be conceived of as a generalized grant of power which, if it leads to electional success, puts elected leadership in a position analogous to a banker. The 'deposits' of power made by constituents are revocable, if not at will, at the next election . . .

Thus those in positions of political power have the legitimized right to 'use' the power 'granted' to them by the electorate in the same way as a banker can invest money deposited with him. Parsons is presumably only arguing that these two processes are 'analytically' parallel, and would no doubt recognize the many substantive differences between them. But nevertheless his anxiety to develop formal similarities between the polity and economy, and correspondingly between money and power, seems to have blinded him to the realities of political manipulation and the role which power itself plays in begetting more *sectional* control. Parsons's account of power and the electoral process reads like a description of normative democratic theory in general, and often like an *apologia* for American Democracy in particular. (Giddens, 1968:261–3, 267–8)

T. H. Marshall's article, written in 1969, takes the concept of power and applies it to racial politics in North America, to student politics in the universities, to Paris and to Prague. It tries to distinguish the differing efficacies of political, social, and civil rights and powers in these cases. But the discussion was inconclusive, and was not one that was pursued in later issues of the journal. Marshall's contribution is distinguished not only by its sense of humour, but by being the only contribution at the time which engages the historical circumstances in which the debate on power had emerged, and the only one which attempts to employ notions of power to illuminate those circumstances. It attempts to connect the theory of power with the inequalities, and particularly the inequalities of ethnicity and 'race', with the contemporary world of the observer:

My interest in power stems from my earlier interest in rights. It struck me, as it must have struck most observers, that whereas the outstanding achievement of western societies in the 19th century (suitably extended at both ends) was the establishment of the rights on which free democratic systems are based, the most striking phenomenon of the 20th is the development of new forms of power, or of old forms in new settings. It is well known that the possibility, or even probability, of the democratic process going into reverse at a certain stage in its career was foreseen long ago, and the most famous exponent of this view, since Plato and Aristotle, was Alexis de Tocqueville. The least adventurous form of this theory is content to argue that, when democracy becomes total, its defences against the assults of would-be tyrants or oligarchs are weakened; mass democracy is *vulnerable* to authoritarian rule. In the light of European history in this century it is hardly possible to refute this very modest proposition. Its interest lies in the explanations offered to account for this vulnerability. These generally stress two points.

First, it is asserted that a mass society is 'amorphous' or even 'structureless' – I am citing the words which are actually used. It lacks those intermediate repositories of interests and values – whether political, religious, economic or social – which have always been the main centres of resistance as well as the sources of positive action. That autocrats have many times in the course of history deliberately smashed intermediate centres of interest and potential power in order to consolidate their own position is obvious, and Bendix has made a more sophisticated study of the subject in his analysis of the role of 'plebiscitarianism' in nation-building. Speaking of the Soviet system, he says that the principles of totalitarian rule 'implement the plebiscitarian ideology by effectively suppressing the organization of interests arising from the differentiation of the social structure'. But this refers to what dictatorship can do to society after it has achieved power, whereas the vulnerability theory maintains that mass society prepares itself as a victim for the sacrifice by 'de-structuring' itself in advance. This is a much more doubtful proposition and has been hotly rebutted by Shils. Mass society, he says, is 'inevitably a differentiated society, differentiated in function, outlook and attachments. The complete homo-geneity which the critics of mass society perceive is an impossibility'. There are some who disagree with Shils on this point. the anti-university, we hear, started a class to study ways of 'destructuring' society, which went on, very properly, to consider how to 'destructure' the anti-university and finally the class itself.'

The vulnerability theory grows more interesting when it explicitly includes social classes among these intermediate groupings on which democratic freedom depends for its continued existence. For it is arguable that classlessness is a state towards which democratic mass society naturally tends, even if it does not quite arrive there. I am thinking of that curous passage in Hannah Arendt's chapter on 'A Classless Society' in her book on *The Origins of Totalitarianism*. She there argues that the class system in Germany prevented the growth of a universal sense of personal responsibility for the way the country was governed. So, when class collapsed (as she maintains that it did), there was nothing to take its place. 'The fall of protecting class walls transformed the slumbering majorities behind all parties into one great unorganized, structureless mass of furious individuals', and the Nazis swam into power. I have tried hard to visualize the scene depicted by these words, but have failed to do so. However, we should remember that Raymond Aron once used very similar words in a different context, that of the Soviet Union. Here, he said, was the only kind of classless society we are likely to see, and it is ruled by a 'unified élite', as distinct from a ruling class. In such circumstances as these 'a classless society leaves the mass of the population without any possible means of defence against the élite. But this, again, is a case of the deliberate destruction of intermediate bodies by a dictatorship already in being. It does not refer to the effects of the spontaneous development of mass democracy towards the elimination of class loyalties. I find no evidence to support the view that this process destroys a society's power to resist the establishment of authoritarian rule, or, to put it the other way round, that a social class has an exceptional, or even unique, superiority as a defender of the liberties of all against the assaults of the few. I do not believe, for example, that the recent upsurge of Welsh and Scottish nationalism on behalf of the basic liberties derives its vital force from the class structure of those two societies. What social classes are particularly good at defending is privilege.

The second argument for the vulnerability theory is the familiar one that the mass media weaken the capacity for independent thought and provide a means by which aspirants to power can establish control, not only over the acts, but also over the minds of the people. This is coercion without the use of force, and would, I suppose, be classed by Etzioni as an exercise of 'symbolic power'. Abraham Kaplan expresses it rather more bluntly when he says that 'virtue is lost to seduction much more often than to rape, and anyone who is concerned with the preservation of virtue must pay particular attention to the devices of securing consent. . . .

Thus the powerlessness of the Negroes is not due simply to lack of rights, but to much deeper causes – to a status in the total society which makes rights of small account. While this status persists, few Negroes can make effective use of such rights as they have, and those who succeed in doing so are drawn inevitably out of the negro community and assimilated to white society; they lose their identity as Negroes and therefore gain no measure of power. They are, in Charles Silberman's words, 'co-opted into inactivity', like William Dawson, the black Congressman from Chicago. Their basic status remains unchanged, as one can see, writes James Baldwin, from 'the unfortunate tone of warm congratulation with which so many liberals address their Negro equals'. The sterotype remains unshaken. For, to quote Baldwin again at his most subtle, 'one had the choice of either "acting just like a nigger" or of *not* acting just like a nigger, and only those who have tried it know how impossible it is to tell the difference'. Take two brief examples of the way in which the possession of *powers* by Negroes does not give them *power*. In one County where 81 per cent of the population was black, the negroes wanted to link their political organisation with the national Democratic Party. They could not, since the Party could not have a Negro body as its official branch. But when they tried to form a separate party of their own, they were accused of playing 'third party politics'. Efforts have been made to enable Negroes in some of the Black Ghettoes to be the real managers of their own local affairs – to have, not merely nominal rights, but real power. In one area a group of religious leaders recently proposed to raise a fund of $10 million 'to help Black Americans develop political and economic power' over their own local affairs. But that is not so easily achieved. For in another place those trying to help the Negroes to self-government in the field of welfare were caught in a dilemma. If Negroes were put in charge of the agencies, they found it very difficult to raise money; if whites are put in charge, it was said, this 'reinforces the pattern of colonialism'. In other words, the status of Negroes being what it is, neither rights nor 'powers' can enable them to achieve power. They must, they feel, go straight out for power. (Marshall, 1969:141–3, 151–2).

3 The debate in *Sociology* B) Wants and interests

Power does not emerge again until the debate surrounding Steven Luke's *Power: A Radical View* (Lukes, 1974). Contributions to the discussion of power in the journal over the next eight years were to all intents and purposes a debate with Lukes, and when that finally ran into the epistemological sands, discussion of the concept disappeared from the pages of *Sociology*. The central problem was whether power should be identified when it was people's wishes, or their interests, which were frustrated, and, if it were their interests, was power being exercised even if people appeared not to resist or complain? What meaning, in other words, could be given to the notion of an interest that could be identified by a social scientist even if it was not apparently articulated by the person who was alleged to hold it? Alternatively, if those who were the objects of power concurred in the exercise of power, either because they regarded it as legitimate or for some othe reason, was it appropriate to talk about power at all? The debate between Steven Lukes and Alan Bradshaw in 1976, which begins the argument, centres on the question of intention and decision in the exercise of power, on the possibility of identifying the interests of the objects of power, and on the relation between group or collective power and individual action (Lukes, 1976; Bradshaw, 1976). In attempting to straddle some of these obstacles, Lukes argues that decision is not necessary for the exercise of power, but that responsibility is a rather delicately balanced position to occupy. It was an aim of those such as Lukes to use the concept of power to get beyond the simple observation of individual success or advantage. But the shift from individual agency to collective cultivation, which was frequently made when the circumstances of social power were examined, often involved losing in the transition the notion of moral responsibility, for this could be attached more readily to individuals than to institutions or structures. The maintenance of the attribution of responsibility was an important aim of the renewed debate:

Steven Lukes' assertion that 'real interests' are empirically identifiable in the manner that he describes is surprising in view of the author's support for Marx's observation that, 'Men make their own history but they do not make it just as they please; they do not make it under circumstances chosen by themselves, but under circumstances directly encountered, given and transmitted from the past'. We should recall that in all the American case studies cited by Lukes liberal democracy *is* the circumstance directly encountered, given and transmitted from the past, and that Lukes agrees with Crenson that pluralism is 'no guarantee of political openness or popular sovereignty. It is therefore a nonsense for him to suggest that democratic participation constitutes 'relative autonomy' and independence of A's power since the whole tenor of his argument is that the reverse can well be true. In short, Lukes' refutation of pluralism on the theoretical basis of discrepancies between false consciousness and real interests re-espouses pluralism to 'empirically' demonstrate this divergence.

Thus, it is difficult to believe that Steven Lukes' basis for the identification of 'real interests' *is* operational (on his own action approach definition of the term). And, Lukes' tendency is, in fact, to accept an *observer's* assessment of real interests – e.g. his support for what he sees as Crenson's assumption that people would rather not have their air poisoned by steel companies. This assumption is unsatisfactory as it stands because it involves Lukes in introducing a *ceteris paribus* condition ('assuming, in particular, that pollution control does not necessarily mean unemployment'). The assumption simply tosses away the action approach, earlier advocated by Lukes, to the identification of real interests by the power object himself.

To summarize these points, the empirical basis for Lukes' 'three-dimensional view' falls down *theoretically* because it vaunts, for the purpose of identifying real interests, that 'democratic participation' which elsewhere it implies may serve to stifle the emergence of real interests. And this theoretical failure is revealed in *practice* by Lukes' abandonment of the action approach when the 'real interests' of the citizens of Gary (one of the towns in Crenson's study) are to be discovered. There is no evidence that Lukes' appreciation of the situation was shared by the actors (many, on the contrary, may have imagined that pollution control *would* bring on unemployment). In short, by *assuming* the real interests of the population of Gary, Lukes is, even if correct in his assessment, breaking the rules of his own method.

In view of the author's claim that all treatments of power rest on a conception of interests and that his approach is 'essentially contested', 'ineradicably evaluative' *and* 'empiricably applicable', a more general discussion of Lukes' concept of 'real interests' may be useful here. Lukes' argument suffers from employing a Marxian notion in a very non-Marxist way. Whereas Marxists are able to justify the terms '*real* interest' and '*true* consciousness' of individuals as objectively 'real' and 'true' by their appropriateness to what Marxism considers to be the inevitable, transcedent course of history, Lukes' usage lacks the Marxian dimension of objective social inevitability, retaining instead the merely subjective aspect of personal preference. Whereas Marxists are able to measure 'true' and 'false' consciousness alongside (future) historical events, Lukes lacks such a measure. Marxists can guarantee, at least to themselve, that their 'true' and 'false' will be vindicated by (the end of) history. Lukes' scenario lacks such security for there is no explanation or reassurance from the author that his 'conditions of relative autonomy' can ever be obtained. Indeed, it can be alleged that the hypotheses derivable from Lukes' definition of 'real interests' are only falsifiable in the impossible event of our being able to manipulate society as a huge laboratory, removing the effects of A's power over B without altering any other components of the system. Lukes' concept of 'interest' certainly may be 'essentially contested', but, because of the unorthodox way in which it is used, it is so at the expense of the 'three-dimensional view' being credibly operational. At least between the sheets that Steven Lukes provides, 'empirical' and 'value-laden' do not make harmonious bedfellows. (Bradshaw, 1976:122–3).

Bradshaw is critical of the claim that B's real interests may be revealed by observing B exercising choice under conditions of relative autonomy and, in particular, independently of A's power – e.g. through democratic participation. He argues that such a procedure will lead to the crystallization of different preferences but '*not necessarily* [my emphasis] to the revolution of real interests', since it is likely that B will continue to be subject to other sources of power inimical to B. But, far from refuting my three-dimensional view of power, this argument actually *employs* it, since it postulates that other sources of (three-dimensional) power, than A may shape B's preferences, in a manner inimical to B.

Bradshaw then goes on to argue that, since 'we cannot envisage a scenario in which any actor is somehow liberated from all structural conditions', we cannot construct the hypothesis necessary for the correct identification of his [sic] real interests. But this does not follow. I nowhere speak of absolute autonomy; and I agree with Bradshaw that the problem is 'that of coming to some agreement about what constitutes "relative autonomy" '. The basic idea here is that A may exercise power over B, within given structural conditions, by precluding the options that B *would* take up but for the power of A. Of course, other sources of power . . . may intervene, but, unless Bradshaw seriously maintains that *all* our preferences are heteronomous, and the products of some exercise of power, then he must allow that some of A's (actual or hypothetical) preferences and choices are authentically A's.

As for my claim that his relative autonomy is best revealed in conditions of democratic participation, I have in mind one central strand of democratic theory since Rousseau and Mill, which has always criticized existing political systems in the light of an ideal to which the universal practice of such participation is central, precisely because it *is* an authentic assertion of autonomy. It is no argument against my claim that I also criticize the political processes celebrated by pluralists on the ground that they perpetuate the mobilization of bias: indeed, they do so in part by disturbuting and limiting such participation along highly unequal, and unequally effective, lines.

I deny that my account of real interests is an 'observer's assessment'. My assumption that Gary's citizens would rather not be poisoned, had they (uncoerced) choice and adequate information, is a hypothetical prediction: if, implausibly, under such acknowledged conditions, they actually preferred continued pollution, I would abandon the claim that air pollution was against their real interests. The fact that in reality 'many . . . may have imagined that pollution control *would* bring on unemployment' does not show my claim to be mistaken. Suppose they were right. That merely shows that U.S. steel would be prepared to reduce its production schedule and increase unemployment in Gary if pollution control is introduced, thereby coercing Gary's citizens and civic leaders to accept pollution. Whether right or wrong (and indeed the very uncertainty about this was important), the continued maintenance of this widespread belief was certainly a most potent element in U.S. Steel's power. (Lukes, 1976:129–30).

With Peter Abell's (1977) contribution, a discussion which was already in danger of becoming baroque teeters on the verge of the rococo. But the point at issue is important. If power is detected where people's interests, rather than their expressed wishes, are being frustrated, then by what criteria other than the whims of the observer are those interests to be defined? In approaching this point, Abell argues that there is an important distinction between persuasion, which he calls influence and treats as distinct from oppressive power, and manipulation. The difficulty with Lukes' position, Abell argues, is that it depends on an identification of real interests in order to distinguish between the two, whereas the use of a notion of autonomy would avoid that. Lukes might well argue that autonomy, or relative autonomy, is not only what he is talking about, but the very phrase which he uses.

In recent years, both within the framework of general sociological theory and in the more restrictive context of organization theory, we have witnessed a resurgence of interest in the concept of 'power' and its many close relatives like influence, persuasion, manipulation, inducement, and so on. This is in part, I suspect, a reaction to functionalism which, at least in the hands of its most distinguished proponent, largely relegated issues of conflict resolution – and thus at least one conception of power – to a special case of the consensus-model of social systems. Despite, however, the increased attention the concepts have attracted, many of the old conceptual hazards remain, and the seemingly intractable problems of locating operational definitions which capture the concepts in anything like their full complexity, have not been solved. Furthermore, with one or two notable exceptions, most attempts, both conceptual and operational, to use the concept are afflicted with the endemic sociological disease, namely a failure to situate the concepts in models which reflect actual social process. It is relatively easy to detail fine conceptual distinctions, but unless we can project these into models of social process which generate reasonably general explanations of social phenomena they are only of marginal interest to the sociologist. . . .

The Marxian/Lukesian view is disarmingly straightforward; it implies that in deciding when a shift in B's preferences, induced by A, is to be regarded as a case of A's manipulation, or influence, we merely have to ask whether the shift takes B nearer or further from his latent interests. Thus, when neither of the preferences reveal B's interests per se then we have to impose some external criterion. It cannot, by definition, be available to B, for if it were, he [sic] would clearly adopt it. The possible authoritarian implications of this viewpoint are well known and the implied justifications in over-riding preferences of those suffering from 'false consciousness' have disturbed many of a liberal frame of mind.

It seems to me that in adopting the base line 'individual autonomy' one begins to overcome these difficulties for in describing B as manipulated we do not have to take recourse in an external criterion involving his *objective interests*. Is this correct – can we specify the conditions for B's autonomy indpendently of B's *latent* interests? I think we can, but to make this evident would involve a much deeper analysis of autonomy than I have space for here. (Abell, 1977:3, 20–1)

Keith Thomas's 1978 footnote to Abell points out the difficulties of studying intentions with the precision necessary to distinguish between an increase and a decrease in autonomy without relying once again on a notion of real interests. He argues that psychological evidence suggests a very complex continuum from behaviour to belief, and that the two cannot be easiy distinguished in the manner that Abell proposes:

There is a great deal of evidence in the psychological literature that the notion of dichotomous categories such as the presence or absence of sanctions, and compliance (behaviour change only) versus internalization (change in 'state of mind') are grossly over simplified. Whether applied directly to power and influence process, or more generally to questions of persuasion and attitude change, neither of these processes can be conceived as strictly dichotomous and the picture is further complicated by evidence of interactions between these two 'continua'. In the familiar cognitive dissonance experiments which examine 'forced compliance' and attitude change, it has repeatedly been shown that under some circumstances not only does a change in 'state of mind' appear to *follow* from compliant behaviour but that this effect is dependent on the individual's perceptions and interpretations of the sanctions or incentives used. Further, the literature on attitude-behaviour consistency shows that the relationship between convictions and overt behaviour is neither simple nor uni-directional. Abell's definition of influence (and manipulation) in terms of changed 'states of mind' glosses over complexities in cognitive processes which could contribute both to the differentiation between power on the one hand and influence and manipulation on the other, and also to the informational criteria which underly his conception of autonomy.

Abell defines manipulation as the process leading to a change in convictions and behaviour which occurs (in the absence of sanctions) when 'A controls B's access to *relevant* (italics added) information, such that he either (a) reduces B's understanding of his situation, or (b) reduces the perception of means open to him'. He further defines autonomy thus: '. . . by degree of autonomy I mean an actor's range of alternatives and freedom from control, or determination by agencies beyond his [sic] control'. Abell suggests that autonomy, in this sense, is evidenced by examining B's cognitions about the range of his alternatives or his degree of understanding before and after the influence or manipulation attempt. The increase or decrease in autonomy being simply a quantitative comparison of information present on the two occasions. I should like to argue that autonomy as he defines it cannot be assessed either by a synchronic examination of B's cognitions about his range of alternatives, or his degree of understanding, nor can a change in B's autonomy be demonstrated by a simple *quantitative* comparison of these cognitions before and after the influence or manipulation attempt *unless* one is prepared somehow to divorce the quantitative aspects of the information from its substantive content. Further, although it may be possible to construe 'range' in quantitative terms, the evaluative implications of each choice, the qualification of 'relevance' and the use of the concept 'understanding' all imply the need for external criteria of totality or verdicality of the information supplied. And it seems inevitable that these sorts of criteria will relate to the utility of the information with respect to means-paths and goals and hence ultimately to the 'real interest' of the individual.

It appears therefore that the criticisms of a theory of power which depend on inaccessible 'real interests' can equally be applied to a model which replaces 'real interests' by 'autonomy'. But despite the limitations of Abell's concept of autonomy his initiative in this direction and away from 'real interests' as a base line is still valuable for at least two reasons. First, the use of autonomy conceived in terms of a range of alternatives draws attention to decision freedom (the extent of choice and the process of choosing) as a potential explanatory concept in the area of power and influence. Second, this initiative is important from a political point of view. While admitting that there is no absolute sense in which either 'real interests' or autonomy are accessible or measurable, attempts in the direction of defining and measuring a multi-faceted conception of autonomy characterized by flow of information, changes in information, and the range and comparative utilities of alternatives (i.e., extent of choice) temporally remove the need for external evaluative criteria. It follows that the use of this conception of autonomy (rather than 'real interests') as a baseline for the study of power processes is more robust in the face of the criticism of authoritarianism and less open to political abuse. (Thomas, 1978:333–4).

The debate on power had begun as a criticism not only of the theoretical structures of Talcott Parsons, but also of the more empirical studies by the American pluralists of city politics. But having launched off from this solid platform and left the precise political concerns of writers like Marshall far to one side, the discussion quickly went into theoretical orbit, and did not re-enter the atmosphere of empirical social science, but rather continued to examine increasingly familiar theoretical concerns, such as the nature of 'interest' in theories of power. Here Barry Hindess's contribution of 1982 recognises the cleft stick in which thinking about power is caught, on the one hand needing to be precise about the terms in which a concept such as power is constructed, and on the other constantly needing to refer to historical or empirical evidence which qualifies the general theories in innumerable particular ways:

Now consider the conception of interests as a set of objectives that agents may be prevented from recognizing through the operation of power. This conception has at least the merit of recognizing that the objectives agents recognize are not inherent in the agents themselves but are rather subject to a variety of conditions, including the practices of political parties, unions and other organizations. But that recognition is unfortunately combined with the view that agents (or at least human individuals and possibly some collectivities) do have real interests of which they may or may not be aware. On this view different interests may be acknowledged in different situations, but some are more real than others. It is this conception of 'real' interests that underlies Lukes' three-dimensional view of power and the Gramscian notions of hegemony and of rule by consent.

There are several difficulties here. First, the attribution of 'real', but unrecognized, interests to agents is generally by virtue of their sharing some particular conditions with other members of a category, class, sex, being victims of monopoly power or of multinational companies, or whatever. Here interests are thought to inhere in agents as a direct result of their membership of a category which specifies certain of the conditions in which they find themselves. The problem is that some further explanation is required of why the conditions shared by agents in that category should be considered effective in determining real interests while other conditions which are not shared are considered ineffective. Why, for example, should conditions that are supposed to be common to those of the same gender or same class entail equally common interests that are 'real', unlike 'interests' pertaining to conditions not shared within those categories?

Secondly, to talk of 'interests' that are real but unrecognized is to suggest, at least in principle, conditions in which they would indeed be truly recognized. Lukes, for example, refers to conditions of democratic participation as allowing individuals to recognize what their interests really are. There is the obvious difficulty here that there seems no good reason why interests acknowledged in one situation should be considered any more *real* than those acknowledged in another. Different interests may indeed by acknowledged under conditions of democratic participation than under authoritarian populism, and there may be all kinds of good reasons for preferring one set of conditions to the other. But that hardly requires us to consider one lot of interests 'real' and the other not.

What is at issue in this singling out of certain 'interests' as ontologically privileged is a problematic of domination and, at least implicitly, of emancipation under the guidance of the enlightened few. The problem posed here is: why do the dominated put up with it? For example, in the case of hegemony, why are the popular masses not mobilized around their real interests (the overthrow of capitalist domination), why are they mobilized in ways which fail to pose their real interests as an object of struggle? What has to be explained here is an absence of recognition and, therefore, of action. What is missing is enlightenment, and it is said to be missing because of rule by consent, bourgeois hegemony, three-dimensional power, or what-

ever, an approach which reduces a complex variety of specific conditions, practices and struggles to yet another of the great simplicities.

Once again, this conception of interests and the related conceptions of power domination, hegemony, are at best misleading guides
to analysis. If we are concerned with arenas of struggle and the
relations between them then the problem is not so much why certain
objectives, the real interests, are not pursued but rather the determinants of those that are: what means of posing objectives are
available to agents and forces in particular arenas and how are they
deployed in the mobilization of agents; how are these forces constituted and what means of action and strategies are open to them; in
what respects are these forces, their means of action, possible strategies and means of mobilizing support, dependent on conditions set
in other arenas; and so on. These questions concern the
identification of the particular conditions involved in the constitution
of existing arenas, forces and objectives. It is a matter not of the use of
some non-existent state of affairs (in which agents do pursue their
real interests) as a measure of the present and trying to explain away
its non-existence but rather of the identification of conditions and of
what can be done to change them. (Hindess, 1982:508–9).

The limitations of the concept of power arose from the attribution of
intention and responsibility. Yet it was precisely this ability to nail responsibility to the active wielders of power that was the concept's central attraction. The problem arose as soon as the move was made from individual
action to social structure. This is because the most substantial consequences of the oppressive use of power were not in the relations between
individuals, but in social experience of whole groups, whether workers, or
women, or racial minorities. Yet whilst it might be relatively easy to
attribute direct intent to individuals, it was more difficult to do so to
organisations or institutions, and impossible to do so to social structures.
Blaming society was not only ineffectual, but strictly speaking meaningless.
The debate over the theory of power has become stuck in the gravitational
pulls between individual action and social structure, and between needs
and wants.

Ted Benton's contribution returns to the central issue when he examines what he calls 'the paradox of emancipation' as it occurs in the arguments of Lukes and the American political theorist William Connolly
(Benton, 1981). He considers at some length the conflict between interests
and wants as ways of understanding the concept of power, and proposes
resolving the difficulty by recognising the actual struggle or conflict within
existing experience. Like Thomas, therefore, he is insistent that wants,
consent, agreement, and resistance, are all aspects of complexities of

experience, and that all of them may be present to some degree in the same group or person at the same time. But the very uncertainty which characterises actual historical experience, and which has been used by critics to question the usefulness of the concept of power, is employed as evidence of how power is identified and challenged:

> The attractions of Lukes's approach, then, to radicals, including Marxists, who wish to understand the nature and distribution of political power are obvious. but what is disappointing about Lukes's approach, from the same perspective, is that it seems to generate precisely the same central problem with which Marxists have been confronted, both in theory and practice, sometimes with disastrous consequences. In its simplest form this is the problem of how to reconcile a conception of socialist practice as a form of collective self-emancipation with a critique of the established order which holds that the consciousness of those from whom collective self-emancipation is to be expected is systematically manipulated, distorted and falsified by essential features of that order. If the autonomy of subordinate groups (classes) is to be respected, then emancipation is out of the question; whereas if emancipation is to be brought about, it cannot be self-emancipation. I shall refer to this problem as the 'paradox of emancipation'. The (early) Leninist conception of the role of the revolutionary party was designed to deal with this problem under conditions of Tsarist autocracy in Russia. The Stalinist substitution of party for class in the consolidation of bureaucratic rule in the Soviet Union was yet another 'resolution' of this dilemma. Diverse anti-Stalinist currents in Marxism have repeatedly attempted, but failed to provide coherent theoretical responses to this paradox – that socialism is both identical with the most complete democracy, and yet seemingly cannot be established by democratic means. The practical counterparts to this theoretical dilemma are constitutive of our contemporary world: in the East, a failure to develop democratic socialism, in the West failure to achieve socialism by democratic means. . . .

But a further condition of possibility of the social practices and associated discourses which I have collectively labelled 'ideological struggles' is that the social production of wants, preferences and identities is an internally contradictory process. By this, I mean that it cannot be the case that the mechanisms which operate to produce a pattern of wants, etc. in conformity with the purposes of those who hold power act without confronting, or even simultaneously producing counter-tendencies. It is a condition of possibility of 'struggle' that opposition of some form persists. A woman who has been socially constituted as a member of a family and identifies with her position and role within that family may also, through contact with feminist ideas and organizations, come to acquire partially or even wholly, conflicting identifications, and so come to deploy a new conception of her interests which, under at least some circumstances, may issue in courses of action inconsistent with her identity as a member of a family. Similarly, an employee who has come to identify himself/herself and therefore his/her interests with his or her firm, and simultaneously with his or her work-mates and their union will experience a deep-rooted conflict of loyalty, and even a 'crisis of identity' when called upon by either union or employer to perform actions inconsistent with the alternate nexus of identifications.

Such patterns of actually or potentially cross-cutting, interlocking or conflicting identifications, loyalties, and locations of interests are the raw materials in everyday life which provide the essential 'purchase' for the whole range of persuasive uses of the concept of interests. To attempt to persuade someone that one course of action rather than another is in their interests is to play a part in the social constitution and/or reconstitution of their social personal identity. Ideological struggles are, in general, struggles over the constitution and incorporation of individuals into opposed patterns of social identity, loyalty and commitment, together with the interests that these carry.

Of course, such struggles are not exhaustively or exclusively 'discursive' in content. Rational persuasion, involving the use of concepts such as 'interests' is, indeed, one aspect of such struggles. But 'rational persuasion' shades off imperceptibly into more 'practical' forms of incorporation: involvement in the works sports team, going with management to receive the Queen's award for industry, getting promoted, etc., versus mass meetings, election as a shop steward, going on a trade union training course, learing to call your work-mates 'brother' and 'sister' at branch meetings, and so on. The use of language, including the language of 'interests' is involved in all these activities, but it does not achieve its effects without the practical involvements and commitments with which it is interwoven.

Now, what I have called the 'paradox of emancipation' is resolvable only if what I have just identified as the conditions of possibility, in everyday life, of ideological struggle, are really present. To be *persuasive*, oppositional uses of the concept of interests must be rooted in at least some aspect of the life-experience of those for whose identifications they are in competition. Otherwise they have no purchase, no relevance to their 'target' actors, and offer no means of active participation in the advocated shift of identity. Unless, then, the social form is one which simultaneously produces self-reproducing and self-dissolving oppositional patterns of social identification in at least some of its agents, the conditions of possibility of *persuasive* uses of the concept of interests for oppositional and emancipatory ends do not exist.

To deny, or to overlook, the counter-tendencies to the social production of consensual wants and identifications is to deny the possibility of ideological and political struggle which is simultaneously democratic and genuinely radical and emancipatory. It is to remain locked within a strategic perspective which offers only imposition of 'solutions' on an unwilling population, or acquiescence in the *status quo*. It is, complementarily, to remain within a theoretical perspective which offers criticism anchored in the shifting sand of a transcendent value-standpoint, as its only coherent alternative to the legitimation of prevailing patterns of social distribution of power. (Benton, 1981:162, 181–2).

Benton's article, by examining the problem in terms of a specific kind of power, provides the first occasion on which the position of women and the claims of feminism are brought into a discussion of power within the pages of *Sociology*. He argues that power is resisted when those subjected to it become aware of alternative identities to those which they have hitherto accepted, the worker aware of alternatives to simply being an agent of the employer, the woman aware of other possibilities than that of house and family wife. Benton's example of the conflict between a feminist identity and a housewifely one is picked up in a critical note by David Knights and Hugh Willmott (1982). Their rejection of Benton begins with the self-defeating argument that since all social science must begin from a particular point of view, any judgment within it must be value subjective. In which case, one might mischievously reply, everything goes out of the window, including their own article. But it is their response to the example of the conflict between a feminist consciousness and a housewifely role that is the more interesting. They come close to arguing that the adoption of any identity which is not already intimated in existing social relationships of power can inhibit 'the full realization and development of human powers' (Knight and Willmott, 1982:582). They go on, with a form of never letting go of nurse for fear of meeting something worse, to object to Benton's notion of conflicting identities because this extends rather than transcends the conflict inherent in the existing power relationship and ignores what is positive in them:

By concentrating on a particular form in which the contradictions and resistance to coercive power or domination may be expressed (e.g. identity conflicts), Benton subscribes to the view of power as primarily associated with control that he had previously questioned. In other words, he assumes that resistance to a subordinate position

in the family has its source in the contradiction between the new
feminist identity and the previous role-expectations. But this is to see
power and subordination in roles or identities rather than in relationships. The woman in Benton's hypothetical example may also be
seen to share these same assumptions. Her response to a sudden
realization of subordination is not to re-explore the relationships
that throughout her life she had taken as given but to reject them in
favour of some presently preferred identity.

In selecting this example to illustrate emancipation, Benton
reveals precisely the kind of individualistic conception of relationships that lead to a view of 'power as control'. Both the woman in
the example, and Benton who has authored it, see no alternative but
to resist this control by escaping from, or at least becoming attached
to, an *alternative* identity that excludes those family relationships.
This is because she has to separate herself off from the forms of
subordination that threaten or fail to reinforce her new found
feminist identity. An exact parallel is offered for the devoted
employee whose attachment to a subordinate status or identity is
threatened by the union's challenge to management rule. The conflict which the employee suffers is the product of his desire to secure
a coherent view of self in the face of competing definitions.

An alternative elaboration of these accounts can be made. So, for
instance, the scenario of the feminist could be painted as follows: Not
only did contact with the feminist movement alert her to how she had
subordinated herself to the family but also it revealed how the desire
for a secure and stable identity as a wife and mother bore at least
some responsibility for this state of affairs. Similarly, despite appear-
ances to the contrary, the devoted employee could understand how
the union's challenge to management autocracy revealed that his
desire to secure a stable identity had led him to identify with the
image offered to him by management of himself as subordinate.
Rather than merely switching identities, both the feminist and the
employee could recognize how it is precisely their desire to secure
identity that leads them to subordinate self to powerful 'others' and
stands in the way of the practical realization of relationships of
interdependence. However, nothing in Benton's use of these
examples would intimate this reading, in contrast to the earlier
account, of the feminist housewife's and the devoted employee's
problems. . . .

We have questioned whether an identification with an oppositional
cause, such as feminism or trade unionism, is necessarily emancipatory in its origins and effects. When involving an *attachment* to
securing an oppositional identity, the results in terms of liberation
can easily be counter-productive. For, disregarding the sense in
which a preoccupation with personal identity may be seen as a form of

self-repression, a strong attachment to an identity that opposes the status quo can readily generate polarized positions of an irreconcilable nature. In the example of feminism, this may result not only in the continued distortion of discourse between the sexes, but in a blindness towards *attachments* to oppositional as well as conventional gender roles as a major source of sexual conflict and harassment. Similarly, within industrial relations, the polarization of attitudes and interests between management and workers undermines the very dialogue that could lead to a radical transformation of the social organization of production. (Knights and Willmott, 1982:582–3)

Benton's argument can clearly withstand these criticisms. The solution to the wants/needs debate lies in the direction which he takes. However pervasive the structures, they are not monopolistic, and conflicts or tensions exist both within them and within the experience of individuals and groups. Power is exercised in the conflict between the alternatives thus offered, whilst 'objective' interests which dominant ideologies allegedly deny have a subjective reality in the discontents which characterise all structures.

In other words, the flaw in both the individualist and the structuralist conception of power is the assumption of single-mindedness. A patient, or a housewife, or a part-time cleaner may accept in effect reluctantly and with discontent, in circumstances where power is not visibly being exercised. This qualifies the individualist view. But it also means that it is possible to identify the interests which are opposed by the exercise of power by looking at articulated, or half-articulated, wants.

4 The debate in *Sociology* C) Foucault and the pantheistic theory of power

The re-jigging of the concept of power by Michel Foucault appeared to offer possibilities for a new start, though with Foucault power seemed to have objects but no subjects, which limited the attraction of the concept. (Foucault, 1976). Foucault's arguments, and his application of them in historical studies, provided both material and examples for those who want to examine the ways in which social identity is constructed rather than naturally determined. It also provides material for those seeking to argue and advise on the liberation of those for whom this creation means domination. It is of less use for those who wish to see power as in any sense being exercised by responsible agents.

Foucault's revival of the concept of power did so in ways wider than those which had characterised the Anglo-Saxon debate represented in the pages of *Sociology*. He extended the concept to areas such as sexuality, to which power, defined sociologically as an essentially public concept, had not previously been applied. This facilitated the employment of the concept of power in the feminist analysis of society, an analysis which had not had much use for the concept before the interest in Foucault's writing.

When Foucault's arguments were drawn on in contributions to *Sociology*, however, it was usually in order to illuminate more traditional areas of investigation. David Knights and Hugh Willmott, who had been so unhappy about Benton's discussion of power and housework, bring Foucault's theories of power to bear on their interest in industrial relations, and whilst paying attention to the theoretical possibilities offered by Foucault's work, do not pursue it into the historically specific areas such as sexuality and gender to which his own work leads (Knights and Willmott, 1989). An essay by Russell Dobash, on the other hand, provides an example of how Foucault's work could direct attention towards topics without necessarily illuminating their interpretation (Dobash, 1983). His study of prisons in England and Scotland begins with a brief resume of Foucault's writing on 'micro-systems', but then proceeds with a fairly conventional piece of narrative history. Whilst it is clearly valuable to look at intentions and functions in penal practice, the concept of power as a deliberate controlling relationship between subject and object is not one which is readily provided either by Foucault's general arguments or by the kind of topics to which his work has drawn renewed attention:

> In contrast, Foucault has emphasized the moral, social and institutional basis of confinement. Based on a more general analysis relating to the 'micro-physics' of power he identifies the prison as one of the most significant models of the new instruments of discipline in capitalist society. His general method leads to a rejection of purely economic and structural considerations as a sufficient basis for explanation of the micro-physics of power and domination. There is, he argues, no necessary or direct correspondence between global strategies of domination, economic forces, policies of the state and any specific form of coercion and punishment. Since we cannot assume that macro political and economic structures and processes automatically produce corresponding and concomitant micro technologies of power, each site or location of discipline and punishment must be investigated in its own right.
>
> It should not be assumed, however, as some have done, that Foucault rejects the significance of the economic and structural basis of society. For him the transformation in the technologies of responding to crime, disorder and mendicancy must be located

relative to the rise of capitalism. For example, he argues that pre-capitalist modes of punishment, such as public executions, should be understood primarily as forms of signification within the context of monarchical power. Constituting 'theatres of punishment and instruction', such spectacles and public rituals were intermittent, irregular, sporadic and disorderly. However, with the emergence of mercantile capitalism such responses were first supplemented and then replaced by a variety of coercions, exercises, schema of constraints, regulation, and regimentation applied continuously within an institutional context. By the mid-19th century the dramatic response was replaced by more minute technologies and forms of surveillance directed at the alteration of the minds and bodies of the labouring poor. Thus, according to Foucault, the social and material changes accompanying the rise of capitalism produced the carceral or panopticon society with the penitentiary at its centre. (Dobash, 1983:2)

When Peter Miller and Nikolas Rose (1988) attempt critically to build on the work of Foucault and others, they come close to dissolving general patterns in particular intentions in a way that would be familiar to many historians, but at the same time they come up against the problem of subjectivity. If, as Foucault argued, it is a mistake to see the subject as given, since subjectivity is itself created, then what grounds are there for the moral criteria implicit in the notion of power? The radical and the conservative response to individuality come remarkably close at this point.

We propose an alternative analysis of the rise of the regulatory expertise of subjective life. Three themes mark this perspective off from those of class analysis, ideology critique, social control and medicalisation. First, a conception of government neither as power exerted by an omniscient and calculating state, nor as the mundane activities of a bureaucratic administrative machine. Government here embraces all those programmes which seek to secure desired socio-political objectives through the regulation of the activities and relations of individuals and populations. Govenment, understood in this sense, draws our attention to the ways in which the conduct of personal life has beome a crucial mechanism in the exercise of political power, including the active promotion of social well-being and the public good through initiatives and programmes ranging from the remodelling of urban architecture and sewage systems, through the control of vagrancy and pauperism, to the ordering of family life and personal habits. But it is misleading, we suggest, to find the hand of 'the state' behind all such innovations in political thought and strategies. Instead, we need to analyse the often

sporadic, ad hoc and local emergence of detailed techniques and
systems of rule. Rather than searching for causes and determinants,
we need to try to identify the ways in which diverse arrays of events –
institutional, technical, political, moral – are articulated together to
provide a set of conditions which make changes of this type possible,
and the heterogeneous powers and capacities which have been called
into play in these new ways of thinking and acting. (Miller and Rose,
1988:173–4)

5 Wider debate

Contributions to the other two principal British sociology journals lack the
thematic coherence which concentration on the work of Lukes brought to
Sociology. In both the *Sociological Review* and the *British Journal of Sociology*,
as in *Sociology*, discussion emerged in the late 1960s and early 1970s, in part
because of the kind of dissatisfactions which Giddens had expressed with
the opportunities offered by Parsons' use of the concept of power. Attention was concentrated on trying to break out, often via exchange theory, of
the seeming impasse between conflict and consensus models of society,
and on terminological clarification, often via a return to classic arguments
such as those of Max Weber. Not that the pages of *Sociology* ignored such
discussions – but they were limited almost entirely to one piece of textual
exegesis of Weber on *Macht* (Walliman, Rosenbaum, Tatsin and Zito,
1980). Like *Sociology*, the other journals failed to break out either into
empirical application of the notion of power, apart from an interesting
discussion by Brogden in the *Sociological Review* of agenda-setting in a
police authority (Brogden, 1977) or into the field of gender. Some attention
was given to 'the microphysics of power' both in the *Sociological Review*
(Law, 1986a), and in a *Sociological Review Monograph* of 1986, where a
number of detailed studies of the techniques of power accompanied more
traditional and essentially epistemological discussions of the relations
between terms such as power and authority (Law, 1986b).

6 Feminism and the theory of power

The publication of Nancy Hartsock's (1983) *Money, Sex and Power* might
have revived the possibility of putting the concept of power to use once
again. Hartsock argued that power as conventionally conceived was
essentially masculine, and that feminism could be the source of a more
adequate understanding. But there was no significant response in any of
the British journals to the questions or possibiities which this raised, any

more than there had been to the rather more tangential possibilities offered by the work of Foucault. Indeed by the mid-1980s the study of power had come full circle. The space programme of theory had come to an end, or at least had been replaced by historical and empirical studies which, whilst deeply informed by theory, were nonetheless of the earth rather than of the sky. Yet Michael Mann's (1986) magisterial *The Sources of Social Power*, whilst it had much to say about the theoretical understanding of social relations, adopted with little alteration the existing conceptions of power as something exercised in the public realm. Gender was once again quietly left off the agenda. Yet it was the power relations of gender which Benton had picked out in 1981, and to which Foucault's pantheistic theory of power pointed, as it did to almost everything else.

What use has feminism made of power, and why has it not made more? The concept, with its combination of collective action and moral responsibility, seems well suited to an analysis of patriarchy. But though the term 'power' has certainly been used in feminist writing, the concept has not been widely put to work. Rather than speak of power, feminists have more frequently spoken of 'patriarchy', which, though often defined as a system of domination, is as frequently characterised as a system of unequal, oppressive, or exploitative division of some good. The emphasis, understandably, is on patriarchy as an aspect of the experience of women, rather than as a system of control, manipulation, or domination (see for example the discussion in Walters, 1989; Walby, 1989; Acker, 1989, and by Janet Finch in this collection).

Since power is most evident when there is coercion, and since government is the most sustained and structured form of coercion, the debate over power has concentrated on the politics of the public sphere. The discussion of domestic power has come second best, or even third best after the discussion of economic and social power in the public space between state and family. It is significant that when feminism has approached a theory of the state, it has done so through theories of law, which can be as much concerned with the objects of legal enforcement as with the procedures of law making and law application (MacKinnon, 1990).

But as Nancy Hartsock points out, there is a further reason why feminism has made relatively little use of the concept of power. Power concentrates attention on the institutions and persons who exercise it, whether state institutions or patriarchal ones. The principal emphasis within feminist social science has been not on power or domination, and hence the institutions and cultures of men and masculinity and patriarchy, but rather on inequality, exploitation, and oppression, and hence on the condition of women (Hartsock, 1983:123). The absence until relatively recently of any feminist theory of the state can be seen as an aspect of this wider choice of standpoints and targets. The recent discussion by Vicky Randall (1991) of feminism and political science both indicates and illustrates this. On the one hand, she argues, feminism is about gender power, but on the other the stages of feminist analysis which she identifies are not about power as a relationship structured on gender, but about the condition of women and the neglect of such analysis of that condition as has been carried out by female and feminist social scientists.

There is a further reason for its absence. To use the concept of power as a means of understanding social divisions is to specify an enemy. This is what is done when rape is explained as an exercise of coercive male power (Brownmiller, 1975; Stanko, 1985; Hanmer, 1978). But the tactics of feminist theory have retained a good deal of liberal rationalism. What after all is the point of reasoned argument if what you faced was conscious and deliberate oppression?

The development of a feminist theory of power may be one of the next creative steps in social science. A social theory employing the distinction of gender has, potentially, as much to say about the oppressors as about the oppressed, and enjoys the capacity to illuminate areas which feminism has so far not touched, and which other perspectives in the social sciences have only been able inadequately to illuminate.

7 Information and power

An article by Andrew M. Pettigrew in 1972 had examined a case study of the use of information as a power resource, using a systems theory approach. Pettigrew's article came at the end rather than at the beginning of a debate, but information was not to disappear from the discussion of power, but to re-emerge with the discussion of the power of large organisations, particularly governmental ones, in an age of developing information technology. The promotion, in the information technology age, of knowledge and information as the contemporary sources of power, might seem to upstage the feminist contribution. Certainly it has been conducted with little reference to it, and when a *Sociological Review Monograph* was devoted to *Power, Action, and Belief* in 1986, issues of gender were not addressed. But an analysis of information as power is entirely compatible with a feminist perspective. One of the principal deprivations which feminist analysis has identified is the deprivation of knowledge, both as an absolute and as an instrumental deprivation. One of the classic techniques of power has been the throwing of a veil of secrecy and mystification around the often quite ordinary knowledge and skills which assist the powerful to govern, manage, or in some other way retain their advantages. The formalisation of this exclusion by notions of differences in understanding or intelligence is one of the most familiar ways in which the keys of power can be retained. Their retention is justified, not because to give them up would be to give up power, but by the claim that to give them up would be to put them into hands which could not use them, under the direction of minds which could not understand them. De-skilling is in this sense one of the principal weapons of power, and one which is employed with particular effect in the control of knowledge.

Carol Huggett's (1988) study of the application of information technology in a university research department neatly illustrates how new technologies of knowledge, which might on the face of it seem to have radical implications for the distribution of power, simply 'overlay' existing power structures, and are used to sustain them. Huggett's study was carried out in a university department, which illustrates that academics can be just as readily turned into data as can anyone else. And if it suggests that there is a long way to go before the insights which can be gained from a theory of power are connected to mundane affairs, it may also indicate how much potential the conept still has.

8 The contemporary possibilities of a theory of power

Over the last fifteen years the arguments and policies of the new right have had a double effect in putting power back on the agenda. On the one hand the use of the idea of freedom by the right indicated wide support for giving effect to people's wishes, whatever their interests might be thought to be. On the other the left was brought to refurbish its own understanding of freedom and of popular power, not as the serving of a single interest or the expression of a collective will, but as the diversification of the possibilities of the individual choices of the powerless. Both left and right versions of freedom involved the stigmatisation of power used to control people, and the identification, though in different places, of those who exercised too much of it.

Since 1989 the end of the Cold War, with the abdication of communist regimes in Eastern Europe, has made possible a renewed attention to divisions of power, in place of attention to divisions over different ways of managing economies. The deluge of nationalism has compelled such attention. And as with the politics of race, the politics of nation draw attention to the double face of power. Those who complain of their powerlessness in the face of an oppressive state are at the same time, whether explicitly or implicitly, frequently making claims to exercise power over those whom they consider 'their people'. Both the demands for statehood by nationalist politicians, and the demands for recognition by the leaders of internal, domestic, religious or ethnic minorities, are both against a dominant government of society, and against those, particularly children and women, who might slip outside the fold of traditional or dominant values and practices.

The 1990s offer just as many occasions as did the 1960s for using the concept of power to unravel the secrets of political, economic, and domestic supremacies. But like other concepts, 'power' must be used with care. The choice of language in the social sciences is neither innocent nor arbitrary. The terms and concepts we use do more than simply affect the way in which we understand social relations and events. They come into play at a much earlier stage, giving shape to those events and structures and hence influencing not only how we understand social phenomena, but what social phenomena we construct, intellectually, before the process of understanding has even begun. Concepts are not just the tools with which we work, but the building bricks of the structures on which we employ those tools.

To write about power, rather than about income stratification or religious beliefs, is to make a clear choice about how the world is to be understood. So it is necessary to be very wary of assuming that a particular writer is talking about class, or ideology, or power, if thse are not in fact the terms she uses. An understanding in terms of power will give a classification which cuts right across categorisations in terms of well-being – though power is a great ally of well-being! Power is thus distinct from inequality, deprivation, or oppression. It can in theory and sometimes in practice be exercised benevolently in a way which avoids or even removes those distinctions. But both inequality and deprivation are measures of outcomes. They do not preclude, but nor do they include, judgments about the means by which those outcomes are secured. The concept of power is thus a lever for prising open the oyster of allegedly uncomplaining material contentment.

The study of power makes possible, at least in theory, an investigation of what lies below the concealing draperies of alleged consent. That means that it can illuminate not only the public world of politics, government, and paid employment, and hence divisions of both class and ethnicity, but also the private one of domestic production and familial relations. That it has not in fact been widely employed to do so is one of its great failings. One of the attractions of the idea of power, after all, is that it implies deliberate intent on the part of the powerful, and therefore allows the attribution of moral responsibility for inequality.

References

Abell, P. (1977), 'The many faces of power and liberty: revealed preference, autonomy, and teleological explanation', *Sociology*, 11, pp. 3–24.

Acker, J. (1989), 'The problem with patriarchy', *Sociology*, 23, pp. 235–40.

Benton, T. (1981), ' "Objective" interests and the sociology of power', *Sociology*, 15, pp. 161–84.

Bradshaw, A. (1976), 'A critique of Steven Lukes's, "Power: A Radical View" ', *Sociology*, 10, pp. 1–27.

Brogden, M. (1977), 'A Police Authority – The denial of conflict', *Sociological Review*, 25, pp. 325–49.

Brownmiller, S. (1975), *Against Our Will: Men, Women, and Rape*, New York, Bantam.

Dobash, R. P. (1983), 'Labour discipline in Scottish and English prisons: moral correction, punishment and useful toil', *Sociology*, 17, pp. 1–27.

Foucault, M. (1986), 'Disciplinary power and subjection' (repr. from *Power/Knowledge: Selected Interviews and Other Writings 1972–77* ed. Colin Gordon, Harvester, 1976) in Steven Lukes (ed.), *Power*, Oxford, Blackwell.

Giddens, A. (1968), ' "Power" in the recent writings of Talcott Parsons', *Sociology*, 2, pp. 257–72.

Hanmer, J. (1978), 'Violence and the social control of women', in G. Littlejohn, B. Smart, J. Wakeford, & N. Yuval–Davies (eds.), *Power and the State*, London, Croom Helm.

Hartsock, N. C. M. (1983), *Money, Sex and Power: Towards a Feminist Historical Materialism*, London, Longman.

Hindess, B. (1982), 'Power, interests and the outcome of struggles', *Sociology*, 16, pp. 498–511.

Huggett, C. (1988), *Participation in Practice: A Case Study of the Introduction of New Technology*, Watford, Engineering Industry Training Board.

Knights, D. and Willmott, H. (1982), 'Power, values and relations: A comment on Benton', *Sociology*, 16, pp. 578–85.

Knights, D. and Willmott, H. (1989), 'Power and subjectivity at work: from degradation to subjugation in social relations', *Sociology*, 23, pp. 535–58.

Law, J. (1986a), 'On power and its tactics', *Sociological Review*, 34, pp. 1–38.

Law, J. (ed.) (1986b), *Power, Action and Belief. A New Sociology of Knowledge?*, London, Routledge.

Lukes, S. (ed.) (1986), *Power*, Oxford, Blackwell.

Lukes, S. (1976), 'A reply to Bradshaw', *Sociology*, 10, pp. 129–32.

Lukes, S. (1974), *Power: A Radical View*, London, Macmillan.

MacKinnon, C. A. (1990), *Towards a Feminist Theory of the State*, Cambridge, Mass., Harvard University Press.

Mann, M. (1986), *The Sources of Social Power: A History of Power from the Beginning to AD 1760*, Cambridge, Cambridge University Press.

Marshall, T. H. (1969), 'Reflections on power, *Sociology*, 3, pp. 141–55.

Miller, P. & Rose, N. (1988), 'The Tavistock programme: the government of subjectivity and social life', Sociology, 22, pp. 171–92.

Mills, C. W. (1956), *The Power Elite*, New York, Oxford University Press.

Parsons, T. (1960a), 'The distribution of power in American society', in T. Parsons, *Structure and Process in Industrial Societies*, New York, Glencoe Free Press.

Parsons, T. (1960b), 'Authority, legitimation and political action', in *Structure and Process in Industrial Societies*, New York, Glencoe Free Press.

Parsons, T. (1963a), 'On the concept of political power', *Proceedings of the American Philosophical Society*, 107, pp. 232–62.

Parsons, T. (1963b), 'On the concept of influence', *Public Opinion Quarterly*, 27, pp. 37–62.

Parsons, T. (1964), 'Some reflections on the place of force in social process', in H. Eckstein (ed.), *Internal War*, New York, Glencoe Free Press.

Parsons, T. (1966), 'The political aspect of social structure and process', in D. Easton (ed.), *Varieties of Political Theory*, Englewood Cliffs, Prentice-Hall.

Randall, V. (1991), 'Feminism and political analysis', *Political Studies*, 39, pp. 513–32.

Stanko, E. A. (1985), *Intimate Intrusions: Women's Experience of Male Violence*, London, Routledge & Kegan Paul.

Thomas, K. (1978), 'II. Power and autonomy: further comments on the many faces of power', *Sociology*, 12, pp. 332–5.

Walby, S. (1989), 'Theorising Patriarchy', *Sociology*, 23, pp. 213–34.

Walliman, I., Rosenbaum, H., Tatsin, N., and Zito, G. (1980), 'Misreading Weber: The concept of "Macht" ', *Sociology*, 14, pp. 261–75.

Walters, M. (1989), 'Patriarchy and viriarchy: An exploration and reconstruction of concepts of masculine domination', *Sociology*, 23, pp. 193–211.

Further reading

Barnes, B. (1986), 'On authority and its relationship to power', in J. Law (ed.), *Power, Action and Belief: A New Sociology of Knowledge*, London, Routledge and Kegan Paul.

Barry, B. (1989), *Democracy, Power, and Justice*, Oxford, Clarendon Press.

Davis, K., Leijenaar, M. and Oldersma, J. (eds.), (1991), *The Gender of Power*, London, Sage.

Dowding, K. (1991), *Rational Choice and Political Power*, Cheltenham, Edward Elgar.

Lane, R. E. (1988), 'Experiencing money and experiencing power', in I. Shapiro and G. Reeher (eds.), *Power, Inequality, and Democratic Politics: Essays in Honour of Robert A. Dahl*, Boulder and London, Westview Press.

Patton, P. (1989), 'Taylor and Foucault on power and freedom', *Political Studies*, 37, pp. 260–76.

Taylor, C. (1989), 'Taylor and Foucault on power and freedom: a reply', *Political Studies*, 37, pp. 227–81.

Ward, H. (1987), 'Structural power – a contradiction in terms?' in *Political Studies*, 35, pp. 593–610.

Conceptualising gender

Introduction

The theme of 'conceptualising gender' emerges in a series of articles which appear in *Sociology* between 1979 and 1991, most of them since 1985. Their relatively recent origin reflects the developing debates about the concept of gender within the discipline of sociology as a whole during the same period. A sense of tackling new issues pervades these articles. They capture quite accurately the flavour of the debates as they emerged, changed emphasis and moved on.

Alongside the sense of newness, there is also a clear sense that the writers of these articles see the area of gender relations as something of fundamental importance to sociology. The fact that its importance was not acknowledged in the past makes its development the more urgent and the more necessary. Bob Connell's comments about the study of gender relations, in one of the articles reviewed here, express this point forcibly:

> We are in the middle of the most important change in the social sciences, and in Western social thought generally, since the impact of class analysis in the mid-nineteenth century . . . [The structure of gender relations] is a social structure not a biological one. It is, among other things, a structure of power, inequality and oppression; a structure of great scope, complexity, and consequence in our affairs. (Connell, 1985:260).

Precisely *what* a study gender relations consists of is itself a matter of debate. The writers of the twelve articles reviewed here would probably agree on two fundamentals: the concept of gender refers to relationships between women and men; and these relationships have to be analysed in ways which make visible particular forms of inequality, subordination and oppression (the choice of terms here would depend somewhat on other intellectual positions). Beyond that, there would be definite differences of emphasis in these articles on questions such as: Does an analysis of gender divisions also have to incorporate race and class divisions? Should an analysis of gender relations go beyond the simple men–women distinction, and explain the processes whereby some men dominate other men (and possibly also relations of domination between women)? Can an effective conceptualisation of gender relations only be produced by someone who is also a politically commited feminist?

As a convenient starting-point for discussion of these articles, they can be categorised in the following four groups:

1. One article by Mary Maynard (1990), which is a survey of the field of the society of gender, covering both empirical and theoretical work.

2. Five articles which are specifically about conceptualising and theorising gender, partriarchy and related ideas, by Malcolm Waters (1989), Sylvia Walby (1989), Joan Acker (1989), Bob Connell (1985) and David Bouchier (1979). The first three were published as a set of articles on 'Theorising Patriarchy', with the Acker article discussing issues raised by Waters and Walby.

3. Four articles which take substantive topic areas in sociology and discuss gender issues in that context, by Diana Kay (1988), Sylvia Walby (1988), Caroline Ramazanoglu (1989) and Hilary Graham (1991).

4. Two articles which are about the professional discipline of sociology, and gender issues in professional relations between sociologists and the society in which we work, by Margaret Stacey (1982), BSA Equality of the Sexes Committee (1986).

This is a rather disparate collection of articles, though their variety reflects the developing field of which they form part. They span both intellectual questions – sometimes of a very abstract kind – and also convey a strong sense that working on gender as a sociologist in the 1980s meant engaging with issues which were very practical and (in the broadest sense) political. In this area – perhaps more than any other discussed in this volume – there is a real sense that the intellectual and the political are inextricably interwoven. I have tried to reflect both dimensions in this review though – since the topic is 'conceptualising' gender – the specifically intellectual dimensions are given somewhat more space.

Feminist politics and conceptualising gender

It is impossible to consider conceptualising gender as an *intellectual* issue without acknowledging that the roots of this enterprise lie in the *political* movement which began in the late 1960s, in the United States, and which is now referred to as second wave feminism. First and foremost these were ideas developed for use: to highlight the disadvantages and oppressions suffered by women and to indicate ways of overcoming them. This political context has continued to affect intellectual debates about gender, in sociology as in other disciplines.

The most direct way in which the continuing links with feminist politics are reflected in the articles published by *Sociology* is through the two which are about the profession of sociology itself. The article co-authored by the Equality of the Sexes Committee of the British Sociological Association (1986) makes clear the link which was being forged between feminist politics and the intellectual concerns of the discipline of sociology. It is a report of a short survey of the treatment of gender in the curriculum of sociology degree courses, and the arrangements for teaching it.

> Our first aim was straightforward, in that information was lacking on how far sociology teaching in Britain had begun to take gender issues and sexism into account, and how far the establishment of feminist sociology since the 1960s had had an impact on teaching. In looking for evidence of progress, we were very conscious that this is a time of crisis for higher education in Britain, with contraction and restructuring occurring throughout the system. The transformations *within* sociology have been complex and there has been no review of how changes are affecting teaching. We are looking at one aspect of this. Lack of information motivated the committee to undertake the survey not only to fill a gap, but also because the BSA is committed to achieving the equality of the sexes in the profession. If this commitment is to have substance we need active monitoring, a sense of what has been achieved and of what remains to be done. We also need to draw attention to these achievements, even to encourage other disciplines to review their own assumptions and practices.
>
> In addition to the information that a survey could yield, our questionnaire involved a direct call to members and their departments to reflect on the quality of their teaching and to consider the extent to which they recognised and tackled inequalities of gender and sexism. (BSA Equality of the Sexes Committee, 1986:348, emphasis original)

The survey found that women were still – in the mid-1980s – in a very small minority in teaching positions on sociology degree courses and often under considerable pressure to carry a good deal of teaching – sometimes all the teaching on courses about gender issues, courses which were frequently very popular with students. On the question of *how* gender was being taught, different department in universities and polytechnics were taking different approaches to the topic: some treated it as simply a specialism, to be offered in a separate course; others appeared to be trying genuinely to incorporate gender across the curriculum; others again said that they believed that gender issues *should* be incorporated across the curriculum but the evidence that this was actually happening was less than convincing. In commenting upon the survey, the Equality of the Sexes Committee highlighted the connection between the composition of the sociology profession and the way in which gender issues are taught:

> If the incorporation of gender issues into sociology is to be effective, there is a need for the integration of gender issues into sociology courses across the board, rather than adding a section on women which leaves the rest of the course untouched. We see this as an essential prerequisite to, rather than a guarantee of, satisfactory teaching on gender issues. A major problem, exacerbated by the present crisis in education, is pressure on women to undertake the burden of course development in this area. The setting up of women's studies courses has been primarily of interest to women, but the tendency to regard all gender issues as women's issues leaves a small number of women with a major task of adapting compulsory courses to take account of gender and sexism. Although some men are involved in teaching on gender issues, this is not enough. *All male sociologists need to recognise the significance of challenge made by feminist ideas throughout sociology and to re-examine the power relations within which they themselves operate.* (BSA Equality of the Sexes Committee, 1986:360, emphasis original).

A similar sense that it is important for gender issues to permeate the discipline – both in terms of its intellectual concerns and the way in which it is organised professionally – comes through in different ways in the article by Margaret Stacey, which is a written version of her Presidential Address to the British Sociological Association in 1982. She addresses the political pressures which were apparent at that time, and which affected higher education in general and sociology in particular: public expenditure cuts plus a form of anti-intellectualism which many believed to be inspired by right-wing politics. Linking these with questions of gender divisions in the profession, she argues that women sociologists are well placed to fight the battle to 'preserve and improve the social sciences and institutions of learning' (1982:420), having learned in the previous decade the importance of establishing the right to work creatively against the background of oppression. Like the Equality of the Sexes Committee, she links an argument about the *content* of the discipline of sociology with the political *context* in which sociologists operate both individually and collectively, as is evident in the following extracts:

> Change may be inevitable, but the form that change takes is not . . . There are alternative ways of approaching change: the restrtictive and the imaginative. And it is here that I think we women probably have something important to offer. We have not been involved in these last years in accepting the society in which we find ourselves. We have been engaged in finding ways to recreate society so that it shall become more human. For example . . . women have had to work their imaginations hard to think of ways in which, whether we want to have children or not, we can live without male domination and without oppressing other women . . .
> Women academics have fought hard for the places we have got; some of us have had to deny ourselves children for them; many carry the double burden, but we want our paid work. Women's jobs may be more at risk even than those of men but women know what we have to fight for and why it is worth it . . . If the struggle for academic freedom and the social sciences is predicted on liberation and imagination, then it may well be possible to recruit the anger that women have learned from oppression, and the creativity that they have developed in aiming to emerge from it. Women will not be supine. (Stacey, 1982:418, 419).

I have begun this discussion of conceptualising gender, not with intellectual questions but with a consideration of the ways in which gender politics are intertwined with the introduction of the concept of gender into the professional work of sociologists. Perhaps this is putting the cart before the horse. But to begin at this point underlines the importance of not divorcing the intellectual from the political in the field of gender – the intellectual issues cannot themselves be understood without a feel for the political context. Furthermore, the issues which have been raised in this section all are of central importance as *intellectual* issues in conceptualising gender, as I hope to show in the remainder of this chapter.

To most writers this link is a positive strength, ensuring that theory is grounded in empirical reality and lived experience. However a cautionary note is struck in two articles in particular, pointing out some of the limitations of this dual use of theory. Malcolm Waters suggests that the key concept of patriarchy, derived from feminist politics, looks too vague and amorphous when translated into social science:

> . . . while 'patriarchy' is of first rank importance in feminist political struggles, the diversity of meanings which it receives generally in

social scientific thought deprives the concept of theoretical and explanatory power. 'Patriarchy' becomes ... an orienting term, which directs attention to an area of discourse – it is a redescription rather than an explanatory account. (Waters, 1989:201)

For his part David Bouchier – in an article which attracted some critical responses when it was published – argues that the problem lies more in compromising the radical political potential of feminism. In the process of broadening the scope of both feminist politics and feminist analysis during the 1970s, he argues, a critical edge was lost – that critical edge which was provided in the late 1960s by radical feminism, a form which he calls 'radical idealism' or utopianism. By 1975, he argues:

The deradicalisation process was complete. The radicals had failed to maintain their voice or develop their theory in the face of reformist and professionalising forces, and the early radical history of the movement was being progressively devalued and forgotten by the women who were now its public leaders ...
The radical groups failed to maintain their voice in the communication/interaction process, either within or outside the whole women's movement, while the women's rights liberals were highly successful at both levels.
My central argument is not that the radicals were 'right' and their liberal opponents 'wrong' – clearly a nonsensical proposition – but that the exclusion of the radical line had serious consequences for the movement as a whole, by eliminating one of its best resources for the development of feminist theory. Theory is *essential* to the survival and growth of any movement which seeks radical social change. (Bouchier, 1979:395–7, emphasis original)

In rather different ways, Bouchier and Waters are both pointing out that, in the development of theories of gender, the intertwining of feminist politics with intellectual analysis may make the pursuit of both more difficult. However, for the most part the writers of other articles reviewed here regard this as a challenge rather than a constraint.

What is being explained?

My starting-point for treating 'conceptualising gender' as an intellectual issue is to ask: what exactly is being explained? The process of defining and redefining the nature of the phenomenon has been an integral part of the debate. Nonetheless key questions of definition can be summed up like this: Is the concern principally with women, or with men, or with the relationships between the two?

Since the intellectual task of conceptualising gender has its roots in the feminist movement, it is not surprising that the main focus has been upon women and their social position. That continues to be important, though in more recent work it is often made clear that the context is an analysis of gender relations, rather than simply upon research which is 'about women'. This distinction is made very clear in Caroline Ramazanoglu's (1989) article, which is focused on women, but with gender relations providing a strong theme in her analysis. The distinction is drawn out through the author's advocating sociological work that takes 'a feminist standpoint', which she explains thus:

> Nancy Hartsock put forward a conception of feminist standpoint (as opposed to an interested position of female bias) which was rooted in the marxist distinction between essence and appearance. By taking a feminist standpoint women can discover the 'real' relationships between people, such as the nature of marriage, which are mystified by patriarchal ideology. A feminist standpoint is 'interested in the sense of being engaged'. Women's political engagement enables them to produce knowledge of social life which is not otherwise discoverable.
>
> A standpoint, however, carries with it the contention that there are some perspectives on society from which, however well-intentioned one may be, the real relations of humans with each other and with the natural world are not visible . . .
>
> The notion of a feminist standpoint from which to produce knowledge is a response to the need to connect feminist understanding of social life with feminist political practices. Feminism constitutes attempts to transform the bases of current social, economic and political relationships between women and men. A feminist standpoint on social life does enable us to make connections which otherwise are not made, but also raises a number of problems. (Ramazanoglu, 1989:428).

Ramazanoglu uses the concept of feminist standpoint to reanalyse some research which she herself did in the 1960s, on married women employed in shiftwork. She would, she says, now 'see a number of features of the lives of shiftworking women' which she did not see when the definition of her task was shaped by the (then) completely dominant sociological paradigm, which took it for granted that 'men were the centre of the social world; women were defined in relation to men'. Within this paradigm, one was obliged to adopt 'a male-centred scientific standpoint . . . which constructed married women shiftworkers as 'abnormal'. Shiftworking cut across women's 'normal' obligations to husband and children'

(Ramazanoglu, 1989:429). As a consequence she now sees the work which she produced as of limited value, focused as it was on the conflicts which women experience in their roles as mothers and employed workers, and concluding that 'shiftwork could suit women well, but only for certain periods of their lives' (p.430). By taking a feminist standpoint she would now, she says, be able to do a much better piece of research on women who work shifts. She would be able to do it in a way which makes visible that which was previously unseen, including 'the persistent but never-mentioned problem of being female in a male world', in a world where 'women were very openly treated as sexual objects, belittled and patronised.' (p.430).

Ramazanoglu's article documents an important change in the way in which work 'on' women has been conceptualised within the discipline of sociology. Women's lives do remain a central focus of much work on gender, though frequently analysed in a more sophisticated way than in the past. However, more recently there has been a growing body of literature on men, much of it written by male authors. The starting-point for this has been the argument that previous work on gender had tended to treat 'men' as an unproblematic category. Though there were one or two earlier exceptions (Morgan, 1981), it is really only since about 1987 that a substantial literature has begun to grow which subjects men's lives and experiences to critical scrutiny, using the concept of gender relations as an organising framework (see for example: Brod, 1987; Kimmel, 1987; Hearn, 1987; Hearn and Morgan, 1990). None of this work has appeared as articles in *Sociology*, though several of the more recent articles reviewed here do refer to this body of writing and Maynard's review article discusses it directly. The following extracts from that review serve to illustrate the general case for studying men, in order the better to conceptualise and understand gender relations:

> [In the past] it was men in a genderless sense who were being given attention. . . . There was little direct focus on the social construction of 'men'. The significance of being male, of having masculine characteristics and behaviour, was rarely confronted in the literature. It was as if the nature of manhood and the qualities associated with it were irrelevant in analysing how the social world was structured and organised . . .
>
> It is, of course, self-evident that the characteristics of masculinity need to be explored in any discussion of gender relationships. But it is also the case that women and femininity cannot be understood without reference to men and masculinity also. In fact literature written about women which has the most analytical depth is precisely

that which has also included an analysis of male privilege and power. (Maynard, 1990:282, 283).

A good concrete illustration of the general theoretical points being made by Maynard is offered by another of the articles being reviewed here, Sylvia Walby's (1988) discussion of gender in the specific context of the sociology of political action. She argues that, in order to grasp fully the significance of gender relations in the political context, men as well as women must be studied. In developing this point she offers the case of the women's suffrage movement as an illustration:

> [Most] studies omit men as actors in gender politics. Yet the patriarchal political practices are of vital significance to gender politics. It is as if the existing studies take men as gender-neutral and only women as gendered subjects. This turns the study of women's politics into the study of a deviant minority . . . One, perhaps obvious, instance is that of the opposition to women gaining the vote in Britain. Women (and a very few men) did not struggle for the vote against a vague, non-gendered object. Rather men (and a very few women) struggled against these feminist demands. Those opposing the demand for the vote for women were not passive, but rather active participants in a battle which raged for decades. They banned women from political meetings . . . and forcibly ejected women from these meetings. (Male) police arrested protesters; (male) magistrates convicted protesters; (male) Members of parliament passed Acts which regulated the imprisonment and temporary release of women suffragettes . . . male bystanders beat up women attempting to present petitions to the Prime Minister . . . We cannot understand the suffrage struggle unless we understand the nature and extent of the opposition to feminist demands by patriarchal forces. (Walby, 1988:223)

The dominant view emerging through these articles – and, I think, in the wider debate about these issues – is that a renewed focus upon men *is* appropriate provided it is informed by theoretical questions which direct us towards seeing men's position and experience in the overall system of gender relations rather than taken out of that context. The reasons for this interweave the intellectual and the political. In terms of intellectual analysis, men's position and experience cannot be grasped fully outside the context which shapes it. But also at a political level, continuing to focus on this context should counter any tendencies for this renewed interest in men's lives to modify the way in which women's lives are viewed – to defuse the sense that men continue to be the socially dominant group, and women the subordinate. As Maynard puts it:

A case can be made for the further study of men and the social construction of masculinity. Both male and female researchers have a contribution to make to this endeavour. What is rather worrying, however, is the possibility that this may become a discrete topic area. Rather it seems appropriate that the new found interest in masculinity be set within the context of understanding gender relations overall. This implies that the focus should be men's power over women and the relationship of masculinity to structures of privilege and subordination. (Maynard, 1990:285).

The emerging consensus (reflected to a limited extent in articles published in *Sociology*) is that there should be a renewed emphasis on men and masculinity, and upon the context of studying gender *relations*, rather than men *per se*.

However, to complicate the matter further, there is another strand of argument which questions whether an analysis of 'gender' can use the categories 'women' and 'men' in a unproblematic way. This issue does appear in the pages of *Sociology*, mainly in Bob Connell's article where he proposes a more complex way of looking at 'gender', principally through introducing sexuality into the frame:

The scope of a social theory of gender is not easily defined. There are a number of speculative abstractions which appear to define it, such as the 'dialectic of sex', 'relations of reproduction' and the astonishing new science 'dimorphics'. But these are more slogans for a particular way of theorising than specifications of what is being theorised. It is better to accept that the social theory of gender is not a tightly-knit logical system. It is, rather, a network of insights and arguments about connections. For instance, one argument connects the dynamics of industrial capitalism and its sexual division of labour to the structure of the family, while another connects the structure of the family to the production of femininity. The scope of the theory of gender at any given time is defined by the reach of this network of arguments.

We may reasonably say that at present the network firmly connects the following issues: the social subordination of women, and the cultural practices that sustain it; the politics of sexual object-choice, and particularly the oppression of homosexual people; the sexual division of labour; the formation of character and motive, so far as they are organised as femininity and masculinity; the role of the body in social relations, especially the politics of childbirth; and the nature and strategies of sexual liberation movements. The field defined by this network has no name in common use, though terms like 'patriarchy' and 'sexual politics' are useful to pointing to sizeable parts of it. Young *et al.* speak of the 'social relations of gender', a precise but somewhat awkward term. 'Gender relations' is perhaps the most practical name for the whole network. (Connell, 1985:261)

Some commentators might see this as an illustration of how recent intellectual developments take the force out of arguments about women's oppression. Others would acknowledge that there is a genuine intellectual issue here, which gets more complex as we ask more sophisticated questions about how 'gender' is to be conceptualised.

The scope of the task and the concept of patriarchy

In conceptualising and theorising gender relations, much of the focus has been upon one idea: patriarchy. Whether 'patriarchy' is a concept adequate or appropriate to this task has been a central question which continues to engage scholars, including in a set of papers by Waters, Walby and Acker, published together by *Sociology* in 1989. The debate about patriarchy is both a debate about *how* to explain the forms which gender relations take, but also about *what* is being explained. Thus the question of defining the phenomenon of study remains contentious even when we look at explanatory concepts.

The main issue can be put like this. In understanding gender relations, is it necessary or desirable to work towards a theory which will explain the subordination of women everywhere, living under different social and economic systems, and across human history? Or is it sufficient to explain why men dominate women under specific historical circumstances and specific socio-economic conditions?

This has been the central intellectual problem in this field which has engaged both social science and feminist politics. In my view it remains a matter of debate. On the one hand it seems an impossibly ambitious task to produce a theory which will apply equally across all human societies and all human history, and probably naive to believe that such a theory is possible. On the other hand we are faced with empirical evidence that – almost without exception in human history everywhere – men do in fact dominate women. They do it in different ways, and possibly to a different extent, in different times and places. But they do it – and it is very difficult to find genuine examples where they do not. Faced with that kind of evidence, it seems obvious to look for explanations in something fundamental to the human condition. The alternative seems even more naive: to produce explanations which imply that it just happens by chance that men dominate women in all human societies, but there is no common thread running between these experiences.

The concept of patriarchy has become an important – though not the exclusive – focus for this dilemma since its early use in the feminist movement, which implied that it encapsulated a general theory of women's oppression which would apply cross all human societies. As Joan Acker explains:

> In the 1960s and 1970s patriarchy provided the essential focus and identification of the theoretical object for rapidly developing innovative thinking about the subordination of women. Feminists criticised social theory as inadequate for explaining this widespread phenomenon . . . Theorising patriarchy was the first step to reconceptualising the subordination of women and to correcting flawed social theory, even to achieving a paradigm revolution. Patriarchy also identified, at least for important sections of the women's movement in industrial societies, a political goal: the whole structure of male domination would have to be dismantled if women's liberation were to be achieved. . . . However serious difficulties with the concept became evident. Patriarchy, in radical feminist versions, was seen as a universal, trans-historical, trans-cultural phenomenon; women everywhere were oppressed by men in more or less the same ways. Such notions of patriarchy tended towards a biological essentialism that provided no basis for theorising the vast historical and contemporary variations in women's situations. (Acker, 1989:235).

Since these early debates a great deal has been written on the concept of patriarchy both by feminists and by other social scientists. In many ways it became the focus for the central intellectual disagreement between the two dominant strands in feminist thought. The radical feminist strand argued that oppression of women by men is the overriding structure of power relations in any society. Meanwhile Marxist feminists took the view that men's oppression of women flows from a particular organisation of social and economic production, principally capitalism. Protagonists from both sides claimed the concept of patriarchy for their very different theories, whilst other commentators called into question the utility of the concept of patriarchy itself (see, for example: Delphy, 1984; Burton, 1985; Walby, 1986; Barrett, 1989).

None of the articles published in *Sociology* forms a direct contribution to these debates, but several – especially the most overtly theoretical – deal with some of the issues which they raise, in particular the three articles published by *Sociology* under the heading of 'Theorising Patriarchy'. Each takes a rather different view about the definition and the utility of the concept. Broadly, Walby wants to reassert the explanatory value of the concept of patriarchy, provided it is defined in particular ways. Waters wants to retain 'patriarchy' but to restrict its use. Acker is inclined to reject the term patriarchy altogether. The following extracts serve to convey something of the flavour of their different positions:

The concept of patriarchy is an essential tool in the analysis of gender relations. However some of the existing accounts using it have shortcomings. Critics of the approach have suggested that the flaws are irredeemable. This paper is designed to show that this is not the case; that, while existing accounts have weaknesses, they are not intrinsic to the concept of patriarchy . . .

Patriarchy needs to be conceptualised at different levels of abstraction. At its most abstract level it exists as a system of social relations. In contemporary Britain, this articulates with capitalism and with racism. However I do not wish to imply that it is homologous in internal structure with capitalism. At the next level down, patriarchy is composed of six structures: the patriarchal mode of production, patriarchal relations in paid work, patriarchal relations in the state, male violence, patriarchal relations in sexuality, and patriarchal relations in cultural institutions such as religion, the media and education . . .

Patriarchy can take different forms; it is not a universalistic notion, despite the arguments of critics. The different forms are dependent upon the interaction of the patriarchal structures set out earlier. In different times and places some of the structures are more important than others. The elimination of any one patriarchal structure does not lead to the demise of the system as a whole. (Walby, 1989:213,214,227)

[My major concern in] this analysis is masculine gender systems. Masculine gender systems are theorised in terms of the confinement of women to the domestic sphere, and their exploitation within it, and of the virtual monopolization of the public sphere by men. This description of the structure of masculine gender systems may be employed as a way of distinguishing between different types of MGS . . .

[In some societies] there are no separate structures of economics and politics, but a single fused structure of kinship. Masculine gender systems operating under these structural arrangements are hereafter restrictively described as *patriarchal*. That is, they are structured in terms of economic and political roles by kinship practices . . . [In other societies] there are differentiated structures of government, economic production and family relations. To describe masculine gender systems which occur in these differentiated contexts I propose a new term *viriarchal*, which is derived from the Latin word for adult male . . . plus the suffix meaning rule. In a patriarchal MGS the senior male members of extended kinship systems have control; in a viriarchal MGS all adult males have control but not necessarily by virtue of their location in kinship systems. (Waters, 1989:202,203, emphasis original)

[The theoretical and empirical work of the last fifteen years has involved] a shift in the theoretical object from patriarchy to gender, which we can define briefly as structural, relational and symbolic differences between women and men. From asking how the subordination of women is produced, maintained and changed we move to questions about how gender is involved in processes and structures that previously have been conceived as having nothing to do with gender . . . Walby's structures of patriarchy approach such comprehensiveness but, in the interest of maintaining system boundaries between patriarchy, capitalism and racism, she seems to argue that certain relations are 'gender relations' while others are something else. Of course some processes are more directly focused on relations between women and men than others; but both the tenaciousness of the subordination of women and feminist scholarship indicate that gender is implicated in the fundamental constitution of all social life. Analytical strategies that set boundaries and put certain areas off limits seem to me to constrict the possibilities of understanding fully the deeply embedded character of the subordination of women and the pervasive influence of gender . . . The focus on gender in the full range of social life and institutions promises to lead to the transformation of social theory to account for much that has been previously hidden. Patriarchy conceived as a structure, or a series of structures, does not contain that potential. (Acker, 1989:38)

Though these articles represent a wide range of views on the utility of the concept of patriarchy, there are also common themes. All three writers acknowledge that it is important to move beyond a single explanatory principle, and that it is important to ground explanations of gender relations in empiracal knowledge about the different social circumstances in which women and men live their lives. In this kind of sociological writing 'patriarchy' is far removed from being simply a political slogan. At the same time it is clearly not a concept whose meaning and value is widely understood and accepted amongst practising sociologists.

Patriarchy therefore remains a contested concept at every level. The question of scope is key here, in two senses. First there is the question – to which I referred above – of whether an adequate theory of gender relations must necessarily be applicable in all times and places. The articles reviewed take slightly different views here, by implication if not directly. Waters is the most overtly concerned with being cross-cultural and trans-historical. His proposal is to confine the concept of patriarchy to societies where social dominance is organised through the kinship system. He then creates the term viriarchy to apply to other societies, where the dominance of men over women is not tied to kinship. His aim is to create a cross-cultural classification of different types of 'masculine gender systems'. Walby, whilst making passing references to cross-cultural explanations, is really concerned with something very much more specific, namely the forms which patriarchy has taken, and the structures which support it, in Britain over the last hundred years.

The question of scope of theories of gender also emerges in a second way from these articles, particularly from Acker's. The question here is: can theories of gender relations be 'bracketed off' as just one dimension of social life? Acker puts the point very sharply when she suggests that theories of patriarchy which treat gender relations as a 'system', especially those such as Walby's which postulate other 'systems' of capitalism and racism with which patriarchy interacts, run the risk of seeing 'certain relations as gender relations, while others are something else'. This denies, she believes, the advances of recent years in conceptualising gender, where it has been increasingly recognised that the subordination of women is 'deeply embedded' in social structures and processes and that gender has a 'pervasive influence' in areas of social life where previously it had been treated as irrelevant.

If we put together these two issues of scope, we have a project of exceedingly ambitious proportions: to produce a theory of gender relations which applies across time and place and which spans the whole of social life. At the same time, all the writers represented here accept the current common wisdom that theories of gender relations must move beyond the highly abstract and engage with the specific forms which such relations take in different social circumstances.

Conceptualising gender and sociological orientations

So far I have emphasised that the intellectual work of conceptualising gender owes a good deal to feminist politics and is not the exclusive property of one academic discipline. How does this relate to the discipline of sociology specifically? I shall tackle this question in two ways. In this section I shall argue that the discipline of sociology does have its own intellectual boundaries and priorities, and that these are reflected in sociological writings about conceptualising gender. In the next section I shall consider the specific contributions which sociologists have made to the broader enterprise of conceptualising gender in an interdisciplinary context.

The articles reviewed here are all, in different ways, written in a recognisably sociological tone. They emphasise certain facets of the task of conceptualising gender which reflect perspectives and debates of current importance within sociology. In so doing, they de-emphasise certain other issues which are of more significance within the wider interdisciplinary debate about gender.

One obvious example concerns biology. How far is the subordination of women based upon natural, biological differences between women and men? Arguments that biology is part of the explanation of gender relations – if considered at all – get short shrift in these articles. The point is put most directly by Connell:

> How can a social theory of gender relations . . . deal with the question of the biological 'bases', the natural differences of sex? There must be, first, a really thorough rejection of the notion that there *is* a 'basis' of gender, that social patterns are somehow an *elaboration* of natural difference . . . Natural-difference doctrines result in an untenable view of the nature of human life and the relation between the social and the non-social. Natural difference is a passively suffered condition, like being subject to gravity. If human life were (in its basic structures) so conditioned, human history would be unthinkable . . . Social gender relations do not *express* natural patterns. They *negate* the biological statute . . . The social is radically unnatural and its structure can never be deduced from natural structures. (Connell, 1985:268–9, emphasis original)

Connell takes it as read that explanations of gender must be social *rather than* biological. This would be common ground between all the writers of these articles, I think. It reflects not simply a particular sociological approach to gender, but also the way in which the discipline of sociology deals in general with the biological dimensions of the human condition. Save for the 'school' of socio-biology, which in any event has had little impact in the UK, sociologists look for social explanations of social phenomena, not biological ones. As a consequence when sociologists talk about gender they are likely to have very little to say about biology, which is quite important when the issue is debated in some other contexts (Burke, 1986).

This lack of interest in biological differences is one obvious – and perhaps very predictable – way in which sociological writing on gender displays particular emphases which reflect the discipline of sociology itself. Other aspects of this are perhaps more subtle. I shall summarise the most important of these – as they emerge in the articles being reviewed – as an emphasis on social structure rather than upon individuality.

The emphasis on 'structures' comes through strongly in several of the articles which I have already discussed. For example, the two articles on patriarchy by Waters and Walby both (in different ways) are concerned with identifying the different institutional forms within which the domination of women by men is located, and specifying the analytical connections between them. In most of the other articles, the analysis also is pitched at the structural rather than the individual level, though the authors are not necessarily discussing 'structures' in the same formal way as Waters and Walby. Approaches which focus on social structures can carry the danger of being to deterministic, but that is not an inevitable consequence. One way of countering this danger is, in the common sociological wisdom, to ensure that your account gives some space for 'human agency'. Work on gender also reflects this current priority in sociological theorising. As Maynard puts it, there are moves to:

> reinstate human 'agency' in the understanding of domination. So it is not patriarchy, the 'system', which oppresses women . . . (This approach) stresses the existence of active agents who 'do' the oppressing. In addition there has been a change of position from that where women were portrayed as passive victims of a mechanistic and deterministic system in which they were completely controlled. Instead, the possibility of struggle, resistance and active defiance is now admitted. (Maynard, 1990:274)

In emphasising social structures, these articles are following dominant modes of thought within sociology. This means that they have relatively little to say about, for example, the formation of men's and women's experiences at an individual or more properly individualist level, including such matters as socialisation, stereotyping, the construction of identity, femininity and masculinity. Where these issues do appear, they tend to be criticised as inadequate ways of understanding gender relations, as for example in Connell's discussion of sex role theory:

> The analysis of gender relations along the lines intitially proposed by Mead and Parsons, as a social script which people learn and enact, is attractive in several ways. It gives, on the face of it, full weight to the social character of gender, emphasising the stereotyped expectations ('role norms' etc.) for women's and men's behaviour. It appeals to familiar facts: the colour of a baby's bonnet, the pitch of a Marlboro advertisement, the script of John Wayne westerns, the aunt murmuring do's and dont's in a schoolgirl's ear. It connects social structure with the formation of personality, via the idea of role

learning or internalisation: thus women become feminine by learning
the 'female role'. It can be specific about what 'agencies of
socialisation' are responsible for this learning, pointing the finger at
parents in the family, teachers in the school, scriptwriters and direc-
tors in television and film etc. and the approach leads
straighforwardly to a particular kind of political practice . . .
[However] sex role research highlights the attitudes which create
artificially rigid distinctions between women and men and plays down
the economic, domestic and political *power* men exercise over
women. The project of feminism becomes a programme of role
reform, of loosening social conventions, not of contesting power and
overthrowing injustice. (Connell, 1985:262–4, emphasis original).

Maynard's discussion of the developing sociological interest in theories of
men and masculinity also reflects disapproval of analyses focusing solely at
the level of individual experience. She finds them lacking because: 'the
emphasis seems to be more on uncovering the social characteristics of what
men *are* rather than what men *do*'. (Maynard, 1990:283, emphasis original).

In emphasising the social and the structural rather than the biological
and the individual, the articles published in *Sociology* reflect the priorities
for conceptualising gender within this particular discipline. In so doing,
there are facets of the interdisciplinary debate which are given less attention. But the issues which are addressed nonetheless are of central concern
to all who think and write about this topic, as I indicated in the previous
section.

The contribution of sociologists to conceptualising gender

What, if anything, does sociological work on gender have to offer to the
wider sociological debate? The articles published in *Sociology* show a
reasonably representative selection of the work being undertaken by
sociologists. They include articles which contribute to building theories at
the most general level, and in ways which would be readily recognised as
important within the wider interdisciplinary debate.

But there is another way in which sociological work can make an
important and distinctive contribution. I shall call this building theory from
the bottom upwards. This approach is vital if theories of gender relations
are to move beyond a very general and abstract level, as most commentators
now believe they should. Such a project is bound to run into difficulties
unless it seeks specific empirical evidence about how gender relations
actually work . Such evidence can, of course, come in many forms. But
empirical evidence represents the essential building-blocks through which

concepts can be developed and refined. Sociologists have skills not only in 'doing theory' but also in collecting empirical data in a way which is theoretically informed and which enables such theoretical developments – working from the bottom upwards – to be stimulated.

This approach is sometimes described as 'middle-range theory' and it is, as Maynard says, one area in which British sociologists in particular have made significant contributions to developing theories of gender in recent years:

> Not all feminist theorising has focussed upon overarching systems of power, dominance and control. In recent years particularly, there has been a trend to developing theorising which is pitched at a less abstract level. This focusses on more discrete, substantive areas of analysis, rather than on the properties of over-arching systems. This 'middle-range theorising' conceptualises and explores issues raised by women's role and position in particular institutional areas. (Maynard, 1990:273)

Maynard goes on to cite a number of examples of different institutional areas in which sociological work has made an important contribution: forms of employment which are gendered (part-time work, home working, unemployment); segregation at work and the mechanisms through which it occurs; studies of family dynamics; the constitution of gender relations and identities through the social organisation of schools and classrooms (for references to this work, see Maynard, 1990). In elaborating the point about middle-range theories I shall refer here mainly to two articles published in *Sociology* which I have not yet mentioned, by Diana Kay and by Hilary Graham. Each of these provides a good illustration of how focusing upon an institutional area, and working at the level of middle-range theorising, can help to develop broader insights into conceptualising gender.

Kay's article is essentially the report of a small-scale and in-depth empirical study of gender relations amongst women and men who had come to the UK as exiles from Chile, after the overthrow of the Allende government in 1973. At first sight this may seem of very specialised interest, and to have little potential for developing theories of gender relations in a global context. However the main point which I want to take from Kay's article is that it shows how a very specific (and sometimes a very unusual) situation can provide what we might call a 'critical case' through which theories of general relevance can be tested and refined. In particular, it enables us to test two, somewhat opposing, theories which have been central to debates about gender: first, the argument that men's role as breadwinners enables them to dominate women in the domestic sphere;

second, the idea that women and men are socialised into different sex roles from a very early age, and subsequently are trapped by that socialisation.

What the example of Chilean exiles offers is an unusual case in which men's breadwinning role was removed very suddenly from people for whom it had previously been secure, to be replaced, in many cases, by reliance on the state benefits system once they were in the UK. This, argues Kay, had the effect of loosening men's control over women by undermining the basis of their domestic authority. At the same time, women felt more able to re-negotiate the terms of the gender order with their husbands:

> In the struggle to renegotiate the terms of the gender order, the women played an active role in setting some of the ground rules and laying down some of the limits. In this way they exercised power and influence by re-drawing the map of male–female relations. By speaking up and making claims on men, some . . . women underwent a change in self image from the 'women who put up with their lot' or the 'little birds' which they described themselves as having been before the coup . . .
> There are a number of factors which account for the women's abandonment of their resignation. Some of these relate to the removal of mechanisms of control over the womens lives . . . Many men spent long periods unemployed in exile. The loss of men's breadwinning role had implications for their authority over women in the family. Living off social security was not regarded by the men or the women as giving the man the same claims over his wife and her labour as if he had earned the money directly himself. Furthermore the fact that in cases of marital breakdown the women could support themselves economically through the social security system loosened the economic dimension to women's resignation. (Kay, 1988:11–12)

My second illustration of how articles published in *Sociology* have helped to develop middle-range theory comes from Hilary Graham's (1991) article on the concept of caring. Graham addresses herself more centrally to theoretical issues than does Kay, but these issues are pursued through the analysis of a specific dimension of women's lives, namely work performed in households to service the personal and practical needs of children, the elderly and the sick. The concept of 'caring' has been used in recent writing as a focus for the development of theories of gender relations in this field.

The central point of Graham's discussion is to submit to scrutiny the research done by feminists on the concept of caring and the analyses which underpin it. In particular, she argues that this work urgently needs to take on board the issue of racial divisions. Graham sets out her argument in the following terms, drawing on analyses published by black women writers in the US and the UK:

[There are] tendencies in feminist research which obscure dimensions which should be central to its analysis. I would identify two particular areas of weakness.

Firstly, caring is seen as all about the unpaid work of those who are related to each other through birth or marriage. As a result, it is difficult to identify and conceptualise forms of home-based care which are not determined through marriage and kinship obligations. Secondly, caring is seen as all about gender. Because of the way in which caring is defined, feminist research has constructed a one-dimensional perspective on social divisions. These two problems are closely related. With care defined as the unpaid work of families, it is gender divisions that emerge – alone – as central to understanding everyday reproduction within the home . . . [The effect is to] side-step the complex issues that arise when we try to integrate different forms of care and different social divisions into an analysis of women's experiences of looking after people at home.

While these issues have been marginal to British research on caring, they have figured centrally in feminist analyses which have sought to build the divisions of 'race' and social class into their analysis of social reproduction . . .

Glenn suggests that, while the notion of 'the family' as a 'private domain' may be particularly useful in understanding white women's experiences, it is less useful when black women's experiences are included in the analysis. She notes that black women's lives have been shaped historically by a 'colonial labour system' in which black women's work outside their own families took precedence over the needs of their own families. For black women, she suggests, it is the absence rather than the presence of a clearly defined private sphere which has structured their experiences. The struggle was, and is, to care for one's kin and to keep one's family together. Thus, rather than experienced in oppressive ways, caring for partners, children and older relatives can be experienced as a way of resisting racial and class oppression. (Graham, 1991:68–69).

The problem with previous concepts of caring discussed by feminists, Graham is arguing, is that their analysis has derived solely from the experience of white women. Not only does this overlook the experience of black women, but also it produces inadequate theory. In developing her argument, Graham then takes the example of domestic service as her 'critical case', which enables her to elaborate the kind of conceptual and theoretical developments which need to flow from introducing the issue of 'race' into this particular aspect of conceptualising gender.

Though on one level both Graham's and Kay's work seem to be focused on very narrow topics – the history of racial divisions in domestic service, the experience of Chilean exiles – both are in fact dealing with big questions in the context of conceptualising gender. This kind of work provides the essential building blocks through which gender can be conceptualised in a way which is intellectually rigorous. Though addressed principally to a sociological audience, it has clear application to the wider debate about gender relations, and to feminist politics. It is one of the very important ways in which sociologists can and do make a significant contribution to that broader enterprise.

Conclusion

In this article I have not attempted to set out a 'position' on how gender *should* be conceptualised. Rather I have tried to assess the current state of this art, drawing on twelve articles published in *Sociology* which to a large extent reflect the broader debate within other disciplines and within feminist politics. In making this assessment I would emphasis two final points.

First, this area of intellectual endeavour has been and continues to be closely bound to the politics of feminism, and seems likely to remain so. This does not mean that it operates at the level of political slogans rather than rigorous intellectual analysis – far from it. The articles reviewed here for the most part are very sophisticated in their understanding of how theories get constructed and tested, and the status of the knowledge about the social world which is generated in different contexts. But there is a strong sense of being *engaged* by and in this area, in more than an intellectual sense. This is so in articles by both female and male authors. In so far as work on gender is a specifically sociological enterprise (and it does, as I have argued, stretch wider than that), this is sociology with its historic orientation as a discipline which not only attempts to understand social change but also to identify ways in which further changes can occur.

Second, there is also a strong sense of unfinished business in work reviewed here. I have emphasised the considerable differences between the authors of these articles on a number of dimensions, all pointing to the fact that conceptualising gender is an area of sociological endeavour where there are few matters of consensus. Given the relative newness of this area, this is not surprising. It also is an indication of the continuing intellectual liveliness of work in this field and the challenges still to be met.

References

Acker, J. (1989), 'The problem with patriarchy', *Sociology*, 23, pp. 235–40.

Barrett, M. (1988, 2nd edn.), *Women's Oppression Today*, London, Verso.

Bouchier, D. (1979), 'The deradicalisation of feminism: ideology and utopia in action', *Sociology*, 13, pp. 387–402.

BSA Standing Committee on the Equality of the Sexes (1986), 'Teaching gender – struggle and change in sociology', *Sociology*, 20, pp. 347–61.

Brod, H. (ed.), (1987), *The Making of Masculinities*, London, Allen and Unwin.

Burke, L. (1986), *Women, Feminism and Biology: The Feminist Challenge*, Brighton, Wheatsheaf.

Burton, C. (1985), *Subordination: Feminism and Social Theory*, Sydney, Allen and Unwin.

Connell, R. W. (1985), 'Theorising gender', *Sociology*, 19, pp. 260–72.

Delphy, C. (1984), *Close to Home: A Materialist Analysis of Women's Oppression*, London, Hutchinson.

Graham, H. (1991), 'The concept of caring in feminist research: the case of domestic service', *Sociology*, 25, pp. 61–78.

Hearn, J. (1987), *The Gender of Oppression: Men, Masculinity and the Critique of Marxism*, Brighton, Harvester.

Hearn, J. and Morgan, D. H. J. (eds.), (1990), *Men, Masculinities and Social Theory*, London, Unwin Hyman.

Kay, D. (1988), 'The politics of gender in exile', *Sociology*, 22, pp. 1–21.

Kimmel, M. (ed.), (1987), *Changing Men: New Directions in Research on Men and Masculinity*, London, Sage.

Maynard, M. (1990), 'The re-shaping of sociology? Trends in the study of gender', *Sociology*, 24, pp. 269–90.

Morgan, D. H. J. (1981), 'Men, masculinity and the process of sociological enquiry' in H. Roberts (ed.), *Doing Feminist Research*, London, Routledge and Kegan Paul.

Ramazanoglu, C. (1989), 'Improving on sociology: the problems of taking a feminist standpoint', *Sociology*, 23, pp. 427–42.

Stacey, M. (1982), 'Social sciences and the state: fighting like a woman', *Sociology*, 16, pp. 406–21.

Walby, S. (1986), *Patriarchy at Work*, Cambridge, Polity Press.

Walby, S. (1988), 'Gender politics and social theory', *Sociology*, 22, pp. 215–32.

Walby, S. (1989), 'Theorising patriarchy', *Sociology*, 23, pp. 213–34.

Waters, M. (1989), 'Patriarchy and viriarchy: an exploration and reconstruction of concepts of masculine domination', *Sociology*, 23, pp. 193–211.

Further reading

Barrett, M. (1989, 2nd edn.), *Women's Oppression Today*, London, Verso.

Brittan, A. and Maynard, M. (1984), *Sexism, Racism and Oppression*, Oxford, Blackwell.

Connell, R. W. (1987), *Gender and Power*, Cambridge, Polity Press.

Crompton, R. and Mann, M. (eds.) (1986), *Gender and Stratification*, Cambridge, Polity Press.

Eichler, M. (1980), *The Double Standard: A Feminist Critique of Feminist Social Science*, London, Croom Helm.

Hearn, J. and Morgan, D. H. J. (eds.), (1990), *Men, Masculinities and Social Theory*, London, Unwin Hyman.

Ramazanoglu, C. (1989), *Feminism and the Contradictions of Oppression*, London, Routledge.

Smith, D. (1987), *The Everyday World as Problematic: A Feminist Sociology*, Boston, Mass., Northeastern University Press.

Subject index

Author index